Routledge Guides to Practice in Libraries, Archives and Information Science

Guidance for Librarians Transitioning to a New Environment
Sara Duff and Tina Herman Buck

Recordkeeping in International Organizations
Archives in Transition in Digital, Networked Environments
Edited by Jens Boel and Eng Sengsavang

Trust and Records in an Open Digital Environment
Edited by Hrvoje Stančić

For more information about this series, please visit: www.routledge.com/
Routledge-Guides-to-Practice-in-Libraries-Archives-and-Information-
Science/book-series/RGPLAIS

Trust and Records in an Open Digital Environment

Edited by Hrvoje Stančić

Routledge
Taylor & Francis Group

LONDON AND NEW YORK

First published 2021
by Routledge
2 Park Square, Milton Park, Abingdon, Oxon OX14 4RN

and by Routledge
52 Vanderbilt Avenue, New York, NY 10017

Routledge is an imprint of the Taylor & Francis Group, an informa business

British Library Cataloguing-in-Publication Data
A catalogue record for this book is available from the British Library

Library of Congress Cataloging-in-Publication Data
A catalog record for this book has been requested

ISBN: 978-0-367-43200-3 (hbk)
ISBN: 978-0-367-43699-5 (pbk)
ISBN: 978-1-003-00511-7 (ebk)

Typeset in Sabon
by Apex CoVantage, LLC

Contents

Figures

Tables

Contributors

Stefano Allegrezza is Associate Professor in the Department of Cultural Heritage at the University of Bologna Italy, where he teaches archival science and digital archival science. Formerly, he was Assistant Professor at the University of Udine, Italy (2011–2017), and Associate Professor at the same University (2017). He was involved in the InterPARES 3 project as a member of the Italian Team (2011–2012) and in the InterPARES Trust project as member of the Team Europe (2013–2019). Since 2015, he has been a member of the steering committee of AIDUSA (Italian Association of University Professors in Archival Science) and since 2016 a member of ANAI (National Association of Italian Archivists). His research activities focus on the theoretical and methodological principles related to the creation, management, and preservation of digital archives, and in particular those related to personal digital archives, including issues related to the preservation of electronic correspondence (e-mail), preservation of social media, and web preservation.

Sandrine Anderfuhren is Data Governance Manager for a renowned architect's office in Switzerland. She holds both bachelor's and master's degrees in Information Sciences, and a Certificate of Advanced Study (CAS) in Information Governance of Organizations – Data Protection, Security and Conformity of Information. She is involved in several national organizations (AVA, VSA-AAS, ASDPO, and CLUSIS). She is active as coordinator and community manager for Swiss Research Data Days and as a researcher for AVA in the management of digital documents. She participated in the InterPARES Trust study *Information Governance Maturity in EU Public Administration* (EU29) during phase 1 *Case of Geneva Administration*. For the last four years, she has been a guest lecturer in archival science classes of both the bachelor's and master's degree programmes in Information Sciences, and research methodology classes of the Master of Information Sciences at the Information Sciences Department, Geneva School of Business Administration, University of Applied Sciences and Arts, Western Switzerland. Her research, lectures, and publications focus on data governance norms, information systems appraisal, data protection, and other issues related to the lack of information governance. She is also interested in information systems security and compliance of information systems.

Jenny Bunn is Head of Archives Research at The National Archives (TNA), UK. Having worked as an archivist in a variety of institutions including the Royal Bank of Scotland and the V&A Museum, she taught on the MA in Archives and Records Management at University College London, UK, from 2010–2020. She is a past Editor of *Archives and Records* and the current Chair of the Archives and Records Association's Section for Archives and Technology.

Tolga Çakmak is Assistant Professor at the Department of Information Management, Hacettepe University, Turkey. He received his doctoral degree in 2016 with a dissertation entitled *Digitization and Digital Preservation Policies in Turkey: A Proposed Model*. He previously worked as an assistant librarian in various libraries. He was also Vice President of the University and Research Librarians' Association in Turkey and is a member of the European RDA Interest Group (EURIG). He graduated from the Department of Information Management in 2008 and studied information technologies at the Middle East Technical University. His main research interests are information organisation, information technologies, enterprise content management, museum informatics, digital libraries, and digitisation.

Lluís-Esteve Casellas is Head of the Department of Records Management and also the Data Protection Officer of the City Council of Girona, Catalonia, Spain. He is a member of the Expert Group on Appraisal of the International Council on Archives (ICA) and of the Ad Honorem Committee of RADI (Network of Ibero-American Diplomatic Archives). He has been a member of the National Commission of Catalonia on Records Access and Appraisal (CNAATD, 2001–2015), and of CTN50/SC1 of the Spanish Agency for Standardisation (AENOR, 2006–2010). He has participated in university training, mainly at the ESAGED (High School of Archives and Records Management, of Autonomous University of Barcelona) and International University of Andalucía, meetings, in working groups and projects, such as InterPARES Trust (Team Europe) and InterPARES 3 (Catalan Team), and the Latin American Forum of Appraisal Records (FIED-ICA) among others. He has published over 100 works on archival science, archaeology and history, the latest ones about functional analysis, appraisal, open data, and transparency.

Sue Childs was Senior Research Fellow in the iSchool, Department of Computer and Information Sciences, Northumbria University, UK, from 2000–2016. She conducted externally funded research projects in a range of subject areas within the domain of information and communication studies. Her particular research interests are health information, records management, electronic provision of information, and use of new technologies, and evidence-based practice. She worked on projects including: *DATUM: Research Data Management* (https://www.northumbria.ac.uk/datum); *AC+erm: Accelerating Positive Change in Electronic Records Management* (https://www.northumbria.ac.uk/acerm); and an investigation into the use of Microsoft SharePoint in UK higher education institutions (HEIs).

Luciana Duranti is Professor at the University of British Columbia, Vancouver, Canada, where she teaches courses on diplomatics, records appraisal for selection and acquisition, preservation of digital records, and advanced archival theory. Her research aims to find solutions to digital record issues that can be universally applied. She was the Project Director of the four consecutive InterPARES projects for the last 20 years (1999–2019). She has been the lead investigator for a number of SSHRC-funded research projects, such as *Records in the Clouds* and *Digital Records Forensics*, all accessible from the Center for the International Study of Contemporary Records and Archives (CISCRA). She has published extensively in the areas of archival diplomatics and archival theory, and presented at conferences around the globe. She serves on the Association of Canadian Archivists (President 2017–2018), co-chairs the Steering Committee on Canada's Archives, and has helped develop educational guidelines for the education of Canadian archivists.

Tove Engvall is Research Fellow in Information Systems at the University of Agder, Norway, and has been a lecturer in archives and information science at Mid Sweden University. Previously, she worked as a municipality archivist and e-archivist, and has been involved in national projects around e-archives. Her research interest revolves around the role and meaning of recordkeeping in a transforming and technologically complex world, and what our domain can contribute to sustainable development.

Şahika Eroğlu is currently a faculty member of the Department of Information Management at Hacettepe University, Turkey. She previously worked as an e-government expert at the Republic of Turkey Ministry of Interior. She received her bachelor's and master's degrees at the same department. She holds a PhD on the topic of public sector information management and open government in Turkey. Her main research interests are electronic records management, enterprise information systems, e-government, open government, intellectual property rights, and information law.

Liudmila Fionova is Professor and Head of the Department of Information Support for Management and Production at Penza State University, Russia. She has a PhD in management of social and economic systems. She has conducted externally funded research projects in a range of subject areas within the domain of information and management documentation.

Currently she is head of the master's programme in Documentation Support of e-Government Administration. She is the author of two monographs, two textbooks, and more than 200 scientific papers. She gives classes at undergraduate and graduate levels in information systems and records management and leads postgraduate research. She was member of the Team Europe of InterPARES Trust.

Andrew Flinn is Reader in Archival Studies and Oral History in the Department of Information Studies, University College London (UCL), UK. He holds a PhD from the University of Manchester, UK (1999). Between 2006 and 2015, he was Director of the Archives and Records Management Masters programme at UCL and chair of the UK and Ireland Forum for Archives and Records Management Education and Research (FARMER) between 2008 and 2011. He is currently a Work Package Leader of the EU Marie Sklodowska-Curie project CHEUROPE, the Vice Chair of the UK Community Archives and Heritage Group, a member of the steering committee of the International Council on Archives' Section on Archival Education, a member of the Team Europe of the InterPARES Trust research project, and one of the leadership committee in the joint University of Gothenburg/UCL Centre for Critical Heritage Studies. Prior to joining UCL, he held a number of academic and research positions including Freedom of Information Officer at the British Museum. His research interests include access to information rights, the use of records and heritage materials for the purposes of justice and citizens' rights, and the application of participatory and community-based approaches to cultural heritage and information resources (https://www.ucl.ac.uk/dis/people/andrewflinn).

Maria Guercio was State Archivist at the National Archives in Italy (1979–1998), Professor of Archival Science and Electronic Records Management at the University of Urbino, Italy (1998–2011), and at the University of Rome La Sapienza, Italy. She has contributed to relevant national and international initiatives on electronic recordkeeping and digital preservation (e.g. InterPARES, MoReq) and EU-funded collaborative projects (e.g. ERPANET, CASPAR, APARSEN). She has contributed to the definition of the Italian legislation for building electronic recordkeeping systems and digital preservation repositories. Since 2011, she has been a member of the ICA Programme Committee. In 2009, she was awarded the Emmett Leahy Award for outstanding contribution to information and records management. She was President of the National Association of Italian Archivists (ANAI) (2015–2019). She is co-director of the journal *JLis*, and the author of many articles and manuals on archival science, electronic records management, and digital preservation.

Tomislav Ivanjko is Assistant Professor and Chair of Knowledge Organisation at the Department of Information and Communication Sciences,

Faculty of Humanities and Social Sciences, University of Zagreb, Croatia. He has published more than 30 scientific and professional papers and has presented at numerous conferences (full bibliography available at: http://bib.irb.hr/lista-radova?autor=314670&lang=EN). His research interests relate to the organization and description of digital records, as well as the use of social software and crowdsourcing in the heritage domain.

Sevgi Koyuncu Tunç is a computer engineer and is working as a programme manager at Comodo Cyber Security in Turkey. She saw the need for improvement in human-computer interaction concepts in Turkey because of usability problems in e-government systems during her professional career. After she completed her master's degree in the Department of Computer Engineering at the Middle East Technical University, Turkey, she undertook research on the *Evaluation of Electronic Records Management System in Terms of Usability and Human-Computer Interaction: The Example of Hacettepe University (Turkey)* and received her PhD degree in 2019 from the Department of Information Management. Her main research areas are usability assessment, server log analysis, path analysis through server logs, and web analytics.

Julia Kukarina has a PhD in history. She is Associate Professor and Chair of Records Management, Audio-visual, Scientific and Technical Archives at the Department of Records Management and Technical Archives of the Russian State University for the Humanities, Moscow, Russia. She was a member of the InterPARES Trust project's Team Europe. She has published more than 70 scientific and professional papers and has presented at numerous conferences (full bibliography available at: https://www.fdta.ru/struktura-fakulteta/kafedra-dokumentovedeniya/2-uncategorised/61-kukarina-yuliya-mikhajlovna.html). She is one of the authors of two textbooks *Records Management* (2016, 2018), and the author of the *Handbook of Paperwork for Practical Usage* (2018). She was the organiser of the international scientific-practical conference *Records Management: Past, Present, Future* (2013, 2015, 2017), and co-editor of the book *The Materials of the International Scientific-Practical Conference "Records Management: Past, Present, Future."*

Özgür Külcü is Professor in the Department of Information Management at Hacettepe University, Turkey. He has a master's degree and a PhD in Records Management from the Department of Information Management, Hacettepe University, Turkey. He completed three post-doctoral programmes at the University of British Columbia, Canada; University of North Carolina at Chapel Hill, USA; and University of California Berkeley iSchools, USA. He has participated in several international projects including InterPARES 3, InterPARES Trust, AccessIT, and the LoCloud Project. At undergraduate, graduate, and doctoral levels at Hacettepe University's iSchool, he teaches courses on organisational information,

information systems, and records management. His research interests are organisational information philosophy, information systems, records management, digital archiving, and social media. He has authored five books and (co)authored more than 30 research papers.

Grigory Lanskoy is Dean of the Department of Records Management and Technical Archives at the Institute of History and Archives of the Russian State University for the Humanities, Moscow, Russia. He is also Associate Professor at the Department of Regional Studies and Foreign Policy of the same university. He is the first Vice President of the Russian Society of Historians and Archivists. In 2011, he gained a PhD in historical sciences specializing in the historiography, methodology, and diplomatic practice of historical studies. He participates in the coordination and realisation of scientific and educational projects at the Russian State University for the Humanities with the Ecole Nationale des Chartes, France, AMEU University, Slovenia, Hanoi University for Human Affairs, Vietnam, and national universities in Kazakhstan and Uzbekistan. From 2015, he participated in the InterPARES Trust project, where he focused on the themes devoted to informational policy of Russian archives and the theory and practice of work with audio-visual documents in traditional and electronic forms. He has authored more than 170 published scientific works – two authored and two co-authored books, and more than 100 papers in scientific journals. They are published in Russia, France, Slovenia, and Vietnam in the language of these countries, and in English. His scientific interests are focused on audio-visual and electronic archives, theory and methodology of documentary studies, and methodology and practice of historical studies.

Elena Latysheva is full Professor and Head of the Department of Documentation and Archival Sciences at the Faculty of History, V. I. Vernadsky Crimean Federal University. She laid the foundation for the training of specialists in documentation and archival sciences in Crimea, organising and heading the Department in 2015 as the only establishment in the Republic of Crimea that prepares professionals in this sphere. She successfully participated in grant programmes of the Russian Fund of Fundamental Research. She is an organiser of the Interregional Scientific and Practical Conference *Document in Modern Society* for students of secondary, higher, and professional schools, which she chaired for the fifth time in 2018. She is also in charge of organizing the International Scientific and Practical Conference *Topical Issues of Documentation and Archival Science: Challenges of the Time*, which takes place annually in Gurzuf, the Republic of Crimea. She has published more than 100 scientific articles. She is the author of the monograph *Formation and Development of System of State and Cooperative Property Insurance in Ukrainian SSR in 1920–1930 (Historic Aspect)* (2014) and four study guides. Her research interests are history and organisation and functioning of the

state institutions in Russia and Crimea. She is a member of the Methodological Council at State Committee for Matters Concerning Archives in
the Republic of Crimea, and of several scientific councils. She was member of the InterPARES Trust project's Team Europe.

Elizabeth Lomas is Associate Professor in Information Governance at University College London, UK, and an experienced practitioner having worked
in information management policy and practice across private and public
sector contexts. Her work has included developing information rights
law guidance including Data Protection and Freedom of Information in
the UK. In 2019, she chaired work on the archival derogations under the
GDPR, and has previously served as a member of the Department of Digital, Culture, Media and Sport's Advisory Council on National Records
and Archives, including deputizing for the Master of the Rolls as Chair
of the Forum on Historical Manuscripts and Research. She is Co-Editor
of the *Records Management Journal*. Her recent research has included
designing an information governance toolkit for the EU public sector,
reviewing information and communication technology sector needs in
the light of the Brexit decision, and developing an international research
network focused on the research needs for the digital evidence base. See
https://www.ucl.ac.uk/information-studies/dr-elizabeth-lomas.

James Lowry is Assistant Professor at the Graduate School of Library and
Information Studies, Queens College, City University of New York, USA.
Previously, he was Co-Director of the Liverpool University Centre for
Archive Studies, UK. He holds a PhD from University College London,
UK. His research is concerned with information and governance, particularly in colonial, post-colonial, and diasporic contexts. His current projects include *Displacements and Diasporas*, exploring the technical and
theoretical problems connected with disputes and claims over displaced
records. He is also collaborating on the *Refugee Rights in Records* project based at the University of California, Los Angeles, USA. That project
seeks solutions to the informational problems experienced by displaced
people. His recent publications include the edited collection *Displaced
Archives* (2017). James is Editor of the *Studies in Archives* book series
published by Routledge.

Basma Makhlouf Shabou is Professor in the Information Sciences Department at Geneva School of Business Administration, University of Applied
Sciences and Arts, Western Switzerland. She holds a master's degree in
Social Studies, a postgraduate degree in records management PhD for
research she conducted at the University of Montreal (EBSI-UdeM). She
is involved in several international organisations, such as PIAF (https://
www.piaf-archives.org/) and the ICA (PCOM and Africa programme).
She is an active researcher, reviewer, editor, co-editor in several international projects and research groups (InterPARES *Trust*, https://

interparestrust.org/; RIC, http://recordsinthecloud.org/; GREGI, http:// gregi.ebsi.umontreal.ca/; GIRA, http://gira-archives.org/ etc.). She leads several consulting mandates and has more than 20 years of professional and academic experience in the field of records and information management. Her research, lectures and publications focus on archival appraisal, information quality measurement, access and accessibility to public data, and other issues related to information governance. She is also interested in research data management and is responsible for the training, consulting, and teaching for the *Data Life-Cycle Management (DLCM)* (https:// www.dlcm.ch/) project.

Maria Mata Caravaca has been the Archivist of ICCROM (The International Centre for the Study of the Preservation and Restoration of Cultural Property) in Italy since 2002. She graduated in fine arts at the University of Granada, Spain, and trained in conservation and restoration in Florence. She received her professional archival degree from the Paleography, Diplomatics and Archives School of the Vatican City (2000) and specialized in archives and library science at the University Roma La Sapienza, Italy (2012), where she also obtained her PhD in Archival Science (2017). At ICCROM, she has attended international courses on *Scientific Principles of Conservation*, Rome, 1996, and *Conservation of Archives and Library Collections*, Santiago de Chile, 2001. She has lectured on preservation planning in the CollAsia course on *Conserving Photographic and Archival Collections*, Vietnam, 2018. She participated in InterPARES 3 (International Research on Permanent Authentic Records in Electronic Systems) (2008–2012). Her most recent articles relate to policies for recordkeeping and digital preservation, records classification and filing, and audio-visual preservation planning.

Julie McLeod is Professor in Records Management at the iSchool, Department of Computer and Information Sciences, Northumbria University, UK. She has lead research in digital records management (e.g. *RecordDNA*, https://recorddna.wordpress.com; *AC+erm: Accelerating Positive Change in Electronic Records Management*, https://www. northumbria.ac.uk/acerm; *DATUM: Research Data Management*, https:// www.northumbria.ac.uk/datum) and teaches information governance and records management. She has published more than 50 academic and professional articles and books, and has presented at many conferences internationally. She is Consulting Editor of the *Records Management Journal* and, in 2014, received the Emmett Leahy Award for outstanding contribution to the field of information and records management. See https://www.northumbria.ac.uk/about-us/our-staff/m/julie-mcleod/.

Göran Samuelsson is an information specialist at the Swedish Transport Administration and works with BIM (building information modelling) and asset management. He is also a part-time Senior Lecturer in Archives and Information Science at Mid Sweden University and a project leader. Previously he worked as an archive strategist and coordinator at the National Land Survey of Sweden dealing with organisational and strategic questions. His research focus includes information architecture, storage, and long term preservation of records in the digital environment, recordkeeping systems dealing with geospatial information, and education and professional development for the archives and records management community. He is a board member of the Swedish Association for records and information management (https://www.fai.nu). He is also a Certified Business Architect.

Silvia Schenkolewski-Kroll is Senior Lecturer at the Department of Information Science, Bar-Ilan University, Israel. She has published articles about archival science and archival education in *Archival Science* and other journals. Between 1989–1999 and in 2018, she was Chair of the Editorial Committee of *Arkhiyyon* published by the Israel Archives Association. She was a member of the steering committees of ICA/SAE and ICA/SBL (1996–2004). She has taught courses in the Escuela de Archivologia (University of Cordoba, Argentina) (2007, 2011, 2014) and, in the same years, delivered lectures at the VII, IX CAM, Viña del Mar, and Asunción del Paraguay, the University of British Columbia, Vancouver, and the Universidad Nacional de Chile. From 2013–2019, she was a member of the InterPARES Trust project's Team Europe, where she was responsible for the study *Retention and Disposition Processes in an Internet Website of the Government of Israel: The Ministry of Foreign Affairs as Case Study*. Since 2015, she has been a member of the Council on Archives of the State of Israel. At the XII CAM (2017), University of Cordoba, she delivered the keynote address on *Archives and Archivists in Contemporary Society: Realities and Challenges* and spoke at the XXIV Jornadas CAU-ICA/SUV Conference (2018) at Salamanca University, Spain. She supervises PhD and master's students on archival science. Her complete list of publications is at https://is.biu.ac.il/en/node/1163.

Anna Sexton is Lecturer in the Department of Information Studies at University College London (UCL), UK, on the Masters in Archives and Records Management. She has held several practice-based roles in the recordkeeping field, most recently as Head of Research at The National Archives (TNA), UK. Her research experience includes developing participatory and community focused approaches to archives and records, documenting lived experience of mental health from a survivor perspective, using recordkeeping perspectives to examine the secondary re-use of government administrative data, examining the intersection between open data initiatives and the protection of personal information, and exploring the technical integration of XML encoding standards to develop platforms for users to view archives. She has a varied portfolio of public engagement projects including pilot work, funded by UCL's policy unit, to bring together care-experienced members of the public with social workers and information professionals to co-develop a recordkeeping framework for social care records. Her current research interests include participatory and trauma informed approaches to archives and recordkeeping, as well as data equity and ethics, particularly in relation to personal health data.

Elizabeth Shepherd is Professor of Archives and Records Management in the Department of Information Studies at University College London (UCL), UK. Her research interests are in rights in records (including for care-experienced people @*mirraproject*), records management and information policy compliance, and government administrative data in UK Research Council-funded projects. She is researching the life and work of pioneering women archivists in England as part of her scholarly output on the development of the archive profession in 20th century England. She serves on the editorial boards of *Archival Science*, *Archives & Records*, and the *Records Management Journal*, and was a member of the Lord Chancellor's Advisory Council on National Records and Archives from 2000–2006, the AHRC Peer Review College, and the UK national research excellence framework RAE2008 Panel 37, REF2014 Sub-Panel 36 and REF2021 Sub-Panel 34. She has published numerous articles, (with Geoffrey Yeo) the best-selling book *Managing Records: A Handbook of Principles and Practice* (2003) and is author of the monograph *Archives and Archivists in 20th Century England* (2009). See https://www.ucl.ac.uk/information-studies/elizabeth-shepherd.

Hrvoje Stančić is full Professor and Chair of Archival and Documentation Sciences at the Department of Information and Communication Sciences, Faculty of Humanities and Social Sciences, University of Zagreb. He was Director of the InterPARES Trust project's Team Europe. He has published more than 80 scientific and professional papers, and has presented at numerous conferences (full bibliography available at: http://bib.irb.hr/lista-radova?autor=244003&lang=EN). He published the book *Digitisation* (2009), a co-authored dictionary *Archival Science Dictionary: English-Croatian, Croatian-English* (2015). He co-edited the book *Heritage Live: IT Tools-based Heritage Management* (2012) and six proceedings of the biennial international conference *The Future of Information Sciences*, which he was in charge of organising (2007, 2009, 2011, 2013, 2015, 2017; all available at: http://infoz.ffzg.hr/infuture/conference-proceedings). At the Croatian Standards Institute, he is President of the mirror technical committee for development of ISO/TC 307 Blockchain and distributed ledger technologies.

Assaf Tractinsky is Director of Knowledge Planning and Management (R&D) at the Israel State Archives (ISA). He participated in the development of methodology and requirements for the management and preservation of electronic records systems for government departments, and in planning and implementing the Israel Archives Portal. He was a member of the ISAD(G) translation team responsible for its translation into Hebrew. He received his PhD from Bar-Ilan University with a thesis entitled *The Construction of a Bilingual Hebrew-English Thesaurus for Archives in Israel Based on Information and Knowledge Presentation Technology* (2012), under the supervision of Dr Silvia Schenkolwski-Kroll. He and Dr Schenkolwski-Kroll co-edited the article "Archival Description, Information Retrieval, and the Creation of Thesauri in Israeli" (2006). From 2013 to 2019, he was member of the Team Europe of the InterPARES Trust project.

Liudmila Varlamova has a PhD in History and is Adjunct Professor of the Records Management and Technical Archives Department of the Russian State University for the Humanities (RSUH), and a senior expert of both the Russian Federal Agency of the Technical Regulation and Metrology (ROSSTANDART) and the International Organization for Standardization (ISO). She was Vice-Director and Scientific Secretary of the All-Russian Scientific and Research Institute for Records and Archives Management (VNIIDAD) (2018–2020). Until 2018, she held the position of Deputy Dean for academic work in RSUH. She was Head of the Russian team, part of the Team Europe, of the InterPARES Trust project. She has published more than 100 scientific articles in Russian and international journals, three textbooks (2016, 2017, 2018) and co-authored the dictionaries: *Records Management: English-Russian Annotated Dictionary of Standardized Terminology* (2017) and *Records and Archives Management: English-Russian Dictionary of Standardized Terminology* (2019). She has participated in numerous national and international conferences. More details at: http://rsuh.ru.

Acknowledgements

First and foremost, I would like to thank Luciana Duranti for inviting me to be part of the InterPARES Trust research project and for her visionary project leadership. I would also like to thank Karen Anderson for choosing me to continue her great work as the Team Europe Director. It was not an easy task, but it was one that I took with great respect. I hope to have proved to be up your expectations.

I would like to acknowledge the passionate work of the Team Europe members, for their dedication to the research, believing in us as a team, and for making this book possible. It would not have been possible without them and the numerous graduate research assistants who were involved.

I would also like to thank Julie McLeod and Corinne Rogers for taking the time to proofread the book after my editing. They have spotted many significant details and helped in making this book consistent.

Finally, I would also like to thank my wife Irina for her continuous support of my work, and for being there for me all the way!

Hrvoje Stančić
Editor

Acronyms

4C	Collaboration to Clarify the Costs of Curation
ACM	Anatolian Civilization Museum, Turkey
AdES	Advanced Electronic Signature
AgID	Agency for Digital Italy
AGRkMS	Australian Government Recordkeeping Metadata Standard
ALTO	Analyzed Layout and Text Object
ANAC	National Authority for Transparency and Accountability, Italy
AOC	Consortium of Open Administration of Catalonia (Cat. Consorci Administració Oberta de Catalunya)
APARSEN	Alliance Permanent Access to the Record of Science in Europe Network
ARK	Archival Resource Key
ARMA	Association of Records Managers and Administrators
AWS	Amazon Web Services
BnF	National Library of France (Fra. Bibliothèque Nationale de France)
CA	Certificate Authority
CARARE	Connecting Archaeology and Architecture in Europeana
CASPAR	Cultural, Artistic and Scientific knowledge for Preservation, Access and Retrieval
CEF	Connecting Europe Facility
CIDOC	International Committee for Documentation
CIS	Commonwealth of Independent States
CISCRA	Center for the International Study of Contemporary Records and Archives, Canada
COP	Chain of Preservation
CR	Certificate Repository
CRL	Certificate Revocation List
CRM	Conceptual Reference Model
CSP	Cloud Service Provider
CQC	Care Quality Commission, UK
DC	Dublin Core

DCC	Digital Curation Centre, UK
DCF	Discounted Cash Flow
DDoS	Distributed Denial of Service
DELOS	Developing a European e-Learning Observation System
DLM	Document Life Cycle Management
DLT	Distributed Ledger Technology
DNPV	Differential Net Present Value
DoD	Department of Defence, USA
DoS	Denial of Service
DPE	DigitalPreservationEurope
DTR	Draft Technical Report
E-ARK	European Archival Records and Knowledge Preservation
EAD	Encoded Archival Description
EAG	European Archives Group
eARD	E-archive or e-Diary (Swe. e-Arkiv och e-Diarium)
ECAI	Electronic Cultural Atlas Initiatives
EDMS	Electronic Document Management System
EDRMS	Electronic Document and Records Management System
EGAD	Experts Group on Archival Description
EHR	Electronic Health Records
ENSURE	Enabling knowledge Sustainability Usability and Recovery for Economic value
ERMS	Electronic Records Management System
ERPANET	Electronic Resource Preservation and Access Network
ESI	Electronic Signatures and Infrastructures
FAQ	Frequently Asked Questions
FCA	Full Cost Accounting
FOIA	Freedom of Information Act
FRBR	Functional Requirements for Bibliographic Records
FRBRoo	Functional Requirements for Bibliographic Records – Object Oriented
G2B	Government to Business
G2C	Government to Citizens
G2G	Government to Government
GA	Google Analytics
GDPR	General Data Protection Regulation
GOST	State Standard (Rus. Gosudarstvennyy Standart)
GP	General Practitioner
HAM	Hatay Archeology Museum, Turkey
HCI	Human-Computer Interaction
HE	Heuristic Evaluation
HECTOR	Hybrid Electronic Curation, Transformation & Organization of Records
HEFCE	Higher Education Funding Council for England
HEI	Higher Education Institution

HES	Hospital Episode Statistics
HESA	Higher Education Statistics Agency, UK
HR	Human Resources
HSCIC	Health and Social Care Information Centre (now NHS Digital), UK
IaaS	Infrastructure-as-a-Service
ICA	International Council on Archives
ICA-CER	International Council on Archives – Committee on Electronic and Other Records
ICCROM	International Centre for the Study of Preservation and Restoration of Cultural Property
ICT	Information and Communication Technologies
ICOM	International Council of Museums
ID	Identification (card)
IDABC	Interoperable Delivery of European e-Government Services to public Administrations, Business and Citizens
IFLA	International Federation of Library Associations
IG	Information Governance
InSIDE	Infrastructure and Electronic Documentation Systems (Spa. Infraestructura y Sistemas de Documentación Electrónica)
InterPARES	International Research on Permanent Authentic Records in Electronic Systems
IoT	Internet of Things
IPS	Intrusion Prevention System
IRR	Internal Rate of Return
IS	Information System
ISA	Interoperability Solutions for European Public Administrations
ISAD(G)	General International Standard Archival Description
ISAAR(CPF)	International Standard Archival Authority Record for Corporate Bodies, Persons and Families
ISDF	International Standard for Describing Functions
ISDIAH	International Standard for Describing Institutions with Archival Holdings
ISO	International Organization for Standardization
IT	Information Technology
ITrust	InterPARES Trust project
KPMG	Klynveld Peat Marwick Goerdeler
LC	Library of Congress
LIDO	Lightweight Information Describing Objects
LOCKSS	Lots Of Copies Keep Stuff Safe
NESTOR	Network of Expertise in Long-term Storage of Digital Resources in Germany
NHS	National Health Service, UK
NIST	National Institute of Standards and Technology, USA

NPfIT	National Programme for IT, UK (cancelled)
NPV	Net Present Value
NSC	National Service Centre, Sweden
NSS	National Student Survey, UK
MASHAV	Israel's Agency for International Development Cooperation (Hebrew acronym)
METS	Metadata Encoding and Transmission Standard
MIRRA	Memory-Identity-Rights in Records-Access
MLA	Museums, Libraries, and Archives
MODS	Metadata Object Description Schema
MoReq	Model Requirements for Records Systems
MSEG	Member States Expert Group, EU
NPV	Net Present Value
OAC	Online Archive of California
OAI-PMH	Open Archives Initiative Protocol for Metadata Harvesting
OAIS RM	Open Archival Information System Reference Model
OCLC	Online Computer Library Center, USA
OCSP	Online Certificate Status Protocol
ODI	Open Data Institute, UK
OGD	Open Government Data
OGP	Open Government Partnership, UK
ORG	Open Rights Group, UK
OSF	Open Society Foundations
PA	Public Administration
PaaS	Platform-as-a-Service
PERCILES	Promoting and Enhancing Reuse of Information throughout the Content Lifecycle taking account of Evolving Semantics
PI	Privacy International, UK
PII	Personally Identifiable Information
PKI	Public Key Infrastructure
PLANETS	Preservation and Long-term Access through Networked Services
PPI	Public-Private Initiative
PREMIS	Preservation Metadata: Implementation Strategies
PSI	Public Sector Information
RA	Registration Authority
RDA	Resource Description and Access
SaaS	Software-as-a-Service
SALAR	Swedish Association of Local Authorities and Regions
SAML	Security Assertion Markup Language
SAP	System Applications and Products in Data Processing
SAT	State Archives of Turkey
SC	Subcommittee
SCAPE	Scalable Preservation Environments
SCM	Structured Capital Markets

SFS	Standard Filing System
SLA	Service Level Agreement
SSHRC	Social Sciences and Humanities Research Council, Canada
SSL	Secure Sockets Layer
SSN	Social Security Number
SSO	Single Sign-On
STORK	Secure Identity Across Borders Linked
TAS	Trusted Archival Service
TDR	Trusted Digital Repository
TC	Technical Committee
TCO	Total Cost of Ownership
TIMBUS	Timeless Business Processes and Services
TLS	Transport Layer Security
TNA	The National Archives, UK
TRAC	Trustworthy Repositories Audit & Certification: Criteria & Checklist
TRT	The Real Thing
TRUSTER	Model for Preservation of Trustworthiness of the Digitally Signed, Timestamped and/or Sealed Digital Records
TSA	Timestamping Authority
UCL	University College London, UK
UI	User Interface
URL	Uniform Resource Locator
VIP	Validity Information Preservation
VNIIDAD	All-Russian Scientific and Research Institute for Records and Archives Management
WCMS	Web Content Management System
WG	Working Group
WIPO	World Intellectual Property Organization
WS-S	Web Service Security
XAdES	XML Advanced Electronic Signature
XHTML	eXtensible HyperText Markup Language
XML	eXtensible Markup Language

Introduction

Luciana Duranti and Hrvoje Stančić

The book *Trust and Records in an Open Digital Environment* brings together results from the interdisciplinary research studies accomplished by Team Europe of the InterPARES Trust project.

InterPARES (International Research on Permanent Authentic Records in Electronic Systems, also Latin *inter pares* – among peers) is a series of projects funded by the Social Sciences and Humanities Research Council of Canada (SSHRC) since 1999, which built a global, multidisciplinary research network unmatched by any other in the field of archival science. Its focus has been the preservation of the authenticity of digital records throughout their lifecycle across changing technologies and in different cultural and legal contexts. The knowledge built in the course of the first three projects (1999–2012) served as the foundation of the fourth one, InterPARES Trust, which is discussed in this book. InterPARES Trust – hereinafter ITrust (2013–2019); https://interparestrust.org/ – is aimed at the development of integrated and consistent local, national, and international networks of policies, procedures, regulations, standards, and legislation capable of ensuring public trust in digital records created and/or stored in a cloud environment.

The ITrust's theoretical framework, its methodology, and its internationally applicable findings are presented in detail in a volume edited by Luciana Duranti and Corinne Rogers, respectively the Director of InterPARES and the ITrust Coordinator, entitled *Trusting Records in the Cloud* (Duranti & Rogers, 2019). This book complements it by presenting the research work conducted by ITrust's Team Europe.[1] In fact, while the research conducted in the course of the three InterPARES projects preceding ITrust was organised according to the issues driving the investigation (i.e. archival theory and methods in the first, types of records creators in the second, and amount and types of resources in the third), the ITrust research team believed that the answers to the research questions to be addressed in the fourth project were directly linked to the cultural and legal contexts of cloud users. Those questions related to the protection of human and legal persons' confidentiality and privacy; organisations' forensic readiness and compliance with the law; verifiable records accuracy, reliability, and authenticity; and enforcement of organizations' records and information security; as well as maintenance of information governance on records entrusted to cloud providers, and the authentic preservation and continuing accessibility of records of permanent value. The questions were addressed within domains of inquiry (i.e. infrastructure, security, control, access, and law), as well as cross-domains (i.e. policy, social issues, resources, education, and terminology).[2] Each ITrust cultural team worked on the same questions. However, within each question, the areas of interest were different. For example, while Team Europe was very much concerned with public records and technological authenticity, the Transnational Team was concerned with security classification, Team North America with providers' contracts, Team Latin America with freedom of information, Team Asia with digital government processes, Team Australasia with Indigenous records, and Team Africa with auditing.

Regardless of contextual differences among the teams, all ITrust researchers agreed at the outset on the fundamental concepts that would drive the entire research – among them, the key ones were those of record, preservation, and trust.

With regard to the concepts of record and preservation, the researchers maintained the ones used in the previous three projects. A record – or archival document – is any document made or received in the course of activity and kept for further action or reference. Being a document (i.e. information affixed to a medium), a record has stable content and fixed form. Because of the circumstances of its creation, a record is natural (a by-product of activity), interrelated (linked by an archival bond to all records that participate in the same activity), impartial (not created to answer questions researchers may ask of it in the future), and authentic (with respect to the creator, when used as an instrument of its activity). To preserve a record means to ensure its physical and/or technological stabilization for the purpose of extending its life indefinitely, and the protection of its intellectual content and relationships. Thus, digital preservation is the process of maintaining digital materials authentic and accessible during and across different generations of technology over time, regardless of where they are stored.

Trust was a harder concept to pin down and it involved the writing of a position paper at the outset of the research, with the mutual understanding that, by the end of our investigations, we might have developed different views of what is involved in trust in records. The position paper found that, in legal theory, trust involves a relationship of voluntary vulnerability, dependence, and reliance. In business, it involves confidence of one party in another, based on alignment of value systems with respect to specific benefits. In everyday life, trust involves acting without the knowledge needed to act, by substituting the information that one does not have with other information. In general, trust is linked to perception and is often rooted in old mechanisms, which may lead to trusting untrustworthy entities. The views of trust considered by the research team, as well as all concepts either developed or used in the course of the research, are included in the terminology database, which is available in English, Spanish, and Portuguese.[3]

There was no doubt, however, on what trustworthy records are. This was established in the second InterPARES project and has guided the research ever since. Trustworthiness, when referring to records, includes reliability (i.e. trustworthy as a statement of fact, based on the competence of the author and the controls on its creation), accuracy (i.e. trustworthy as data, based on the competence of the author and on controls on creation, transmission, and access), and authenticity (i.e. trustworthy as a record that is what it purports to be, untampered and uncorrupted, based on its identity and integrity). Of course, integrity is a major concept in digital authentication, and Team Europe has focused on what it involves in an online environment, especially with regards to public records.

The ITrust Teams also used the same methodology. As ITrust is at its core an archival project, the fundamental methodology was archival and diplomatic; that is, it was focused on the records, their form and process of creation, and their contexts. However, in order to understand the cloud environment, its benefits, and its issues, the teams chose a very interdisciplinary approach. Because the key reason why records creators and preservers use the cloud environment is economic in nature, we used resource-based analysis, which studies the technologic, managerial, and relational means of maximizing competitive advantage; because entrusting records to a third party involves risk, we used risk management to study vulnerabilities and ways to mitigate them; because our purpose was to develop policies for environments that are similar to black boxes, we used design theory, which studies policy in situations with unknown variables; and because it studies the authenticity of digital materials that do not reside in the systems in which they were produced and kept, we used digital forensics. In addition, we looked for relevant knowledge in human-computer interaction, aero-spatial, cybercrime, and telecommunication laws, and organizational theory.

One of the reasons the ITrust team broadened its area of inquiry to so many fields of study is that, at the time ITrust began, there was virtually no literature on the subject of its research other than that produced by the same researchers who started ITrust, in the context of projects such as *Records in the Cloud*[4] and *The Law of Evidence in the Digital Environment*.[5] Since the beginning of ITrust, most scholarly writings on the matter have resulted from its research, with a few notable exceptions, such as Yoo and Blanchette (2016). If one considers that the project has involved over its life 42 countries and more than 400 researchers, it is easy to imagine that, if one excludes the writing of standards, business forecasts and assessment, and white papers for specific business endeavours, all publications on the trustworthiness of records in the cloud environment are linked to this project. They are accessible on the ITrust website, on the Dissemination page.[6]

This book has a European perspective, as the challenges addressed in it draw from the research of ITrust's Team Europe and concern issues important for the European Union (e.g. legal issues related to EU regulations, such as those concerning privacy and digital signatures). However, the topics investigated and discussed have global relevance, as they involve general matters: economic models for cloud storage, metadata interoperability, establishing trust in online records, etc., which are relevant to everyone anywhere who is entrusting cloud providers with public or private records.

The book focuses on the need to understand the fragility and yet persistence of digital materials, and on the fact that public records should ensure public trust, grounded in evidence of good governance. To create new value and offer new services, trust in the records that are openly provided by governments is a prerequisite for citizens and businesses. However, building such trust calls for specific actions aimed at reviewing and amending current established practices for the management and preservation of digital records in order to embed into them consideration of the networked nature of the records created and stored in cloud environments, establish the role of new players – the cloud service providers (CSP) – and estimate the consequences of implementing new, disruptive technologies, such as blockchain. Therefore, this book presents the findings of research into the relationship of three interconnected areas of investigation – the *state*, *citizens*, and digital records' *documentary form* – forming a circle around the all-permeating topic – the *cloud*, the environment where digital materials are being created, managed, used, and preserved. The discussion of the relationship between *state* and *citizens* focuses on issues around open government using cloud services, whereas that of the relationship between *citizens* and *documentary form* places emphasis on ideas around open access in the networked environment. Finally, the discussion of the relationship between *state* and *documentary form* examines issues around recordkeeping and digital preservation in the cloud. Figure 0.1 illustrates this perspective.

The structure of the book reflects the interrelationship of these three areas of focus and comprises three parts – I. State, II. Citizens, and III. Documentary form – each consisting of a number of chapters. The individual chapters present the results of one or more Team Europe studies.

Part I focuses on the state. It examines the role of records managers and archivists in open government, the role and quality of policies and standards for recordkeeping and digital preservation, and the impact of the legal framework for cloud computing on electronic recordkeeping and digital preservation systems. Further, it discusses topics of information governance and interoperability of governmental e-services within and between the EU member states, as well as the benefits of inter-organisational collaboration on e-government. This part closes with an investigation of economic models-based selection of digital information storage services in the cloud.

Part II focuses on citizens. First, it investigates the topics of open data, privacy, and public trust in online, openly accessible records. Then, it examines the role of records managers in ensuring the release by governments of data, information, and records which are authentic, reliable, and usable, but at the same time not contravening data protection or privacy legislation. Further, it examines the usability of electronic records management systems (ERMS)

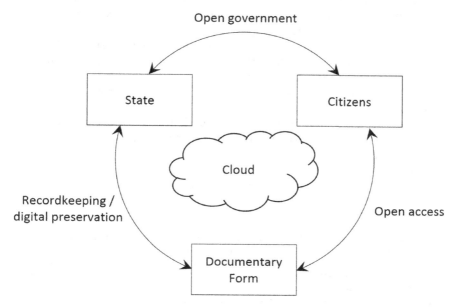

Figure 0.1 Relationship among book parts

by the application of heuristic evaluation methods. This part closes with an evidence-based discussion of the knowledge needed by citizens, records managers, and archivists for dealing with open data and open records, and of the university and lifelong educational opportunities they should have.

Part III focuses on digital records' documentary form. It explores topics at the intersection of digital preservation and open access. It proposes a system of appraisal methodologies and procedures for the long term preservation of websites, a model for the interoperability of digital cultural heritage objects, a model for establishing the legal deposit system for digital print masters that aims to ensure permanent open access, and a blockchain-based approach to the preservation of digitally signed and/or sealed records.

Altogether, the book integrates issues presented by managing records in the cloud with aspects of trust at the interconnections of the three key focal areas (state, citizens, and documentary form) to demonstrate the problem of managing networked records as evidence of activities and transactions. The intent of this book is to show what is needed for the establishment of an open digital environment, which incorporates open government, open access, transparency, and accountability, and is based on trust in digital records.

The book targets data, information, document and records management professionals, archivists, government representatives, regulators, information and communication technology (ICT) systems managers, lawyers, librarians, and academics and students in the ICT and social-humanities disciplines, as well as the wider public sector. It will help professionals, decision-makers, and stakeholders to make informed choices in the context of the digital economy, setting up electronic document and records management systems, choosing cloud-based services, and implementing emerging technologies to support good governance, accountability, and trust.

Trustworthy resources, which are openly accessible from government agencies, e-services, archival institutions, digital repositories, cloud-based digital archives, etc., are the key to an open digital environment that fosters trust in democracy. The ITrust team believes this book will help in getting us closer to that goal!

Vancouver/Zagreb, July 2020

Notes

1 In addition to Team Europe, the ITrust Team included Team North America, Team Latin America, Team Asia, Team Australasia, Team Africa, and a Transnational Team (comprising organization that are not subject to a national juridical system).
2 Research domains. InterPARES Trust. See: https://interparestrust.org/trust/about_research/domains.
3 Terminology database. InterPARES Trust. See: https://interparestrust.org/terminology.
4 Records in the Cloud. See: https://www.recordsinthecloud.org/.
5 The Law of Evidence in the Digital Environment: Finding Solutions to Present and Future Challenges. See: https://www.lawofevidence.org/.
6 Research dissemination. InterPARES Trust. See: https://interparestrust.org/trust/research_dissemination.

References

Duranti, L., & Rogers, C. (Eds.). (2019). *Trusting records in the cloud*. London: Facet Publishing.
Yoo, C. S., & Blanchette, J.-F. (Eds.). (2016). *Regulating the cloud: Policy for computing infrastructure (information policy)*. Cambridge, MA: The MIT Press.

Part I
State

1 Introduction to Part I

Part I of the book takes the state perspective on the challenges related to entrusting records to the cloud. It starts by examining the relationship between established records management practice and reliable open government data. The key question to ask is what it takes for open data to be considered as verifiable sources of evidence so that citizens can trust the information provided by government. Major barriers to releasing more open government data are identified. The policies and legislation regulating digital preservation in the cloud, specifically the aspects of integrity, location of the data, its portability and ownership, can remove many ambiguities and business insecurity if developed by teaming up records managers and archivists with IT professionals. Assessment of legislation regulating cloud services show that the risks of entrusting records to the cloud are not in focus. Additional insight into this is given through the four case studies on the cloud contracts signed between public administrations and private cloud service providers. However, even if the legal regulations and policies are well formulated and in place, for information governance to manage information as assets this would not be enough – it requires a multidimensional approach additionally involving strategic management, records management, information security, ICT, and ethics. Therefore, this part discusses how information governance is defined and implemented in public administrations and how it could be used efficiently to improve e-services. Governmental e-services come in great variety – for citizens, businesses, and for other public administration e-services. Their development, aligned with the *once-only* principle, can positively influence efficiency of the developed e-services and communication between public administration, citizens, and businesses. It will be argued that not only should the process of their development take both a cooperative and collaborative approach, but that the mode of inter-organisational collaboration on e-government plays an important part. This is especially important in the context of e-services interconnection, interoperability, development of single sign-on (SSO) systems, trusted exchange of identification and authentication credentials, and transborder data (information, records) flow. If this path is taken, significant benefits can be realized. The financial ones, in the context of using cloud storage services, are neither easy nor straightforward to estimate. Therefore, models for digital storage costs are analyzed and their use among the records professionals is explored. Finally, this part discusses the level of trust that public administration, citizens, and businesses can have in a cloud service provider or, consequently, in the implemented and interconnected cloud-based e-services.

This part brings together research results based on the investigation of the relevant body of literature, policies and legal regulations, interviews, assessments using checklists, and case studies from Croatia, Italy, Russia, Spain, Sweden, Switzerland, and the United Kingdom (UK), portraying the current situation in information governance, records management, storage, and archiving in the cloud from the perspective of public administration, i.e. the state.

2 The role of records managers and archivists in open government

Elizabeth Shepherd with Tove Engvall and Andrew Flinn

Introduction

This chapter builds on work published in the book produced by the international research project ITrust, *Trusting Records in the Cloud*, in particular Chapter 11, "The Role of the Records Professional" (Anderson et al., 2019). This chapter takes the framework established in that earlier work and populates it with more detail from case studies carried out by several researchers in the ITrust Team Europe. It aims to illustrate the general issues identified in that framework by reference to European-focused research to show how the broad themes come into action in a specifically European context. The cases we draw on are those carried out at University College London for the UK and those conducted at Mid Sweden University over the period 2014–2018, in which we interviewed professionals in records management, archives, information governance, digital services, information security, IT departments, and senior executives, to understand their lived experience of the practical and legislative issues which are brought out in the new open data environment. We hope that by presenting their experiences, we can identify good practice and see areas where further work is needed. Some analysis of critical information issues raised through the case studies were published in Shepherd et al. (2018).

In this chapter, we adopt the ITrust definition of a profession

> A field of work that requires advanced education and training, adherence to a code of ethics, and the ability to apply specialized knowledge and judgement in a variety of situations.
>
> (InterPARES Trust, 2018)

And of a records professional

> An individual who is trained in all aspects of managing records and information, including their creation, use, retention, disposition, and preservation, and is familiar with the legal, ethical, fiscal, administrative, and governance contexts of recordkeeping.
>
> (InterPARES Trust, 2018)

As Anderson et al. (2019) say

> The identity of the records professional has to a large degree been con-
> structed as one of a trusted custodian responsible for ensuring trustwor-
> thy records and the trustworthy management of records. The context in
> which records professionals act has always been complex, operating as
> they do within evolving legislative (e.g. Freedom of Information, Data
> Protection) and policy (e.g. Open Access) frameworks which sometimes
> contradict each other. For example, the good of open access to informa-
> tion and data can sometimes conflict with the good of protecting the
> privacy of individuals; and records professionals have to be proficient
> in balancing such conflicting interests and public goods. As the context
> in which they operate becomes increasingly networked and digital, the
> complexities faced by records professionals increase in parallel.

The inter-relationships between the key areas of information legislation
and the effects this has on records and information professionals is further
examined by Shepherd (2015).

Anderson et al.'s chapter (2019) presents an ontology developed by
Michetti and Gänser of functions and activities carried out by records professionals from records creation to long term preservation. The ontology recognizes that established roles and labels associated with records professionals
are being reshaped and repositioned in broader fields such as information
governance, information security, and digital preservation. As records professionals increasingly work in more open information environments and
with a much greater focus on digital information and records, issues around
trust in records are very significant. Understanding how records professionals operate in an open digital environment in their day-to-day practices and
approaches helps to identify good practice and standards which might be
more widely adopted. This chapter aims to share the learning from the European case studies by drawing on the practical experience of records managers and archivists in different sectors and showing how those experiences
might be adopted or provide the foundation for new and improved services
delivered by records professionals.

The ontology outlined in Anderson et al. (2019) comprises an overview
map, with nine high-level functions, and 105 submaps representing 105
functions and subfunctions. The nine high-level functions are: records management, archival appraisal, preservation, archival management, information security management, monitoring and auditing, training, governance,
and design and implementation of a records system. These nine functions are
used as the underlying structure for the rest of this chapter. Since the nine
functions are not represented evenly in the existing case studies, some will
be addressed in more detail than others here. However, these case studies
had virtually nothing to say on some topics and so they are not addressed
directly in the rest of the chapter: archival appraisal, archival management,

and design and implementation of a records system. Full information about the case studies is available on the ITrust website (https://interparestrust. org/). The case studies drawn on here are: in the United Kingdom, both at national level in the National Health Service (NHS) England (Harrison, Shepherd, & Flinn, 2015) and at a local and more practical NHS hospital trust level (Chorley, Flinn, & Shepherd, 2016; Chorley, 2017), local government (Page, Flinn, and Shepherd, 2014), and higher education (Brimble, Flinn, & Shepherd, 2016); and in Sweden, at the Stockholm City Archives (Engvall, Liang, & Anderson, 2015).

Records management

The hospital trust (Chorley et al., 2016; Chorley, 2017) provided an example of the great opportunities that open data presents to information professionals for increased collaboration and the sharing of ideas and expertise across communities which have not usually or traditionally worked together, such as system designers, data creators, technology experts, data management experts, and information security experts, alongside records and archives management professionals. Records professionals were able to draw on skills in policy and governance, digital and analogue records, data management, and information security when delivering core records management services. Records managers were able to respond more confidently to widespread and complex challenges around open data, such as trying to work out what can be published, but also the processes of how data can best be opened, by whom, and how it is going to be resourced, given organisational pressures. Proactive publication of data is still an exceptional activity and requires new capacity and capabilities before it can become a routine business function, even though the records managers in our study believed that trusted open data led to increased accountability and transparency. In the Stockholm City study, it was emphasized that organisations should know from the beginning when information is created if it can be published as open data. This is also part of strategic and political decisions (Engvall et al., 2015).

Practices of information governance, records management, and access to information in the case study hospital (Chorley et al., 2016) present significant challenges to a trusted data environment, where data might need to be shared between different health providers. The case study highlighted the need for the creation and capture of suitable and sufficient metadata for records to ensure that datasets can be interpreted, retrieved, and used, and to ensure the safeguarding of records and data by all staff to prevent security or sensitivity breaches. The size and complexity of this task is increased with the need to manage a large volume of complex records, including many that contain sensitive and confidential information, and in the absence of standardized metadata processes. Metadata for digital health and corporate records was limited to that captured automatically by computer software programmes, in the absence of a corporate electronic document and records management system (EDRMS), and for paper records, contextual information provided on the transfer forms that accompany records from the creator to the records centre was the main source. Many other organisations also lack reliable systems for capturing metadata: records professionals play a critical role in ensuring that data can be identified and linked, but at present systems to enable this are generally lacking. In the Stockholm City case study (Engvall et al., 2015), the role of metadata was also emphasized to contextualize data when it is published, in order for users to fully understand its meaning and to be useful.

The concern about the lack of reliable metadata was also expressed in the case study with NHS England (Harrison et al., 2015). As Lowry (2014) noted, a lack of metadata can result in data being "unconnected to the context of its creation, left without the essential information needed for its interpretation, and irretrievable" (p. 163). In the case study, it seemed that little was known about the metadata processes in place for the release of data for re-use in the health sector, although this problem is not unique to the health sector. While there are official and strict processes in place for applying metadata to national and official health statistics, guidance around metadata creation and collection for other health data seemed less consistent and reliable. Lowry (2014) argued for the importance of traceability using metadata, writing, "Open data is predicated on citizens trusting the information provided by government. In order for data to be trusted, it must be possible to trace the data back to verifiable sources of evidence" (p. 162). This concern was reflected by our interviewees, who said "in a lot of circumstances, it will not be possible to go back to individual level data." In a fully electronic healthcare system, planned in many jurisdictions, metadata issues are critical to trust in the record.

The local public authority case study in England (Page et al., 2014) also uncovered concerns about the lack of reliable metadata systems and standards, and the need to collect metadata systematically and transparently to support open data and for internal use purposes. The council's records retention schedules reflected the broad range of records held by local government including raw data sources, and some classes of records, such as insurance policies, education properties, public transport, and waste management recycling, reflected the categories of data that were being requested as open data and which the business intelligence team identified as being significant data sources for the council. In this case, the records management, data and statistics, information management, information technology, and communications teams all worked closely together to produce a more holistic view of the council's data needs and its ability to provide access to data.

As seems quite common, records management documentation and responsibilities at the council did not at that time extend to datasets (Page et al., 2014). The relationship between well-established records management and reliable open government data was examined: respondents believed that the first step was to focus on the general improvement of the whole information and records management corporate framework, whose quality is essential for the appropriate identification, treatment, and access to data, and agreed that the role and contribution of records management, alongside information management and governance, becomes vital in an open government data environment. The records manager did have a specific role in helping to manage the location and risk assessment for data captured in the information asset register to ensure personal data was not published. The information asset register acted as an inventory, linking physical records with the internal systems, to enable searching and locating data for open government data initiatives. The records manager was responsible for guaranteeing protective marking of records, which helped to establish data that cannot be published because it is confidential or contains personal data. They also supported the development of an internal audit process to check the reliability, accuracy, and integrity of data to be published. However, the difficulty of ensuring data accuracy across the whole of the council and implementing data checking procedures was recognised as time consuming and complex. In the Stockholm City case study (Engvall et al., 2015), one of the interviewees emphasized, though, that making information openly available should not be fully automatized, but rather humans have to make decisions regarding what is published because of the risks.

The council case study (Page et al., 2014) concluded that, overall, records management had an important part to play in the implementation of open government data initiatives in local government, including choosing which data to publish, to ensure the security of personal data, and to ensure the council met it obligations under the legislation. The lack of time and resources appeared to be a major barrier to releasing more open government data, suggesting that the re-use value of open government data needed to be promoted to create greater demand and awareness.

Preservation

The UK university case study records management service (Brimble et al., 2016) was originally set up to consolidate records across the various campuses, but quickly took on additional functions including information security and the archive. Separately, a research data management service included two data storage systems – one for published material owned by the university and the other for research data. Interviewees recognized the skills and functional overlaps and discussed how "ethical issues, sensitive data issues and . . . archiving and preserving research data requires a lot of archive skills." They sought to build on the fact that research data management was a more obvious organisational priority than harder-to-sell records management to bring together archival management and preservation functions.

In the NHS England (Harrison et al., 2015) and hospital (Chorley et al., 2016) case studies, interviewees noted that open data assumes that data can be retrieved and accessed over time, but there seemed little active consideration for digital fragility and the need to actively migrate information before it was lost, and debates concerning continued accessibility were "in general at an early stage." This might be attributed to the fact that, despite the fully electronic records system target date (2018), the NHS was still very much operating with a paper, or at best hybrid, system. Some believed that debates regarding the migration of data would occur only in reaction to a critical situation, such as a catastrophic loss of health data (although in fact these have occurred in other hospitals), and that until such time the issue of digital preservation was largely being overlooked. If greater public interest in and re-use of open data could be shown to bring significant public benefits that might also provide sufficient political leverage nationally to release the resources needed to ensure digital preservation. Interviewees suggested that anticipated benefits, such as the ability to maintain accountability through standardized retention schedules and the permanent preservation of archives in public places of deposit, alongside building public confidence, reducing corruption, creating efficiency, and creating an informed public who can scrutinize bad practice and support good practice, thereby improving transparency and trust, would in the long run result in system improvements being made.

The local council case study (Page et al., 2014) discussed the issue of digital preservation including open data. Records and information governance experts collaborated on ensuring future access and retention of digital data; for example, the *Information Management Manual* encouraged staff to consider file format to ensure data can still be accessed when systems migrate or update, and advised on regular accessibility checks of data on hard drives every six months. A digital continuity policy set out the requirements to meet the need for records retention over seven years for specific record classes.

Information security management

The UK university case study (Brimble et al., 2016) established an Information Governance Group bringing together planning and delivery of business strategy, responsibility for data assurance for statutory returns (to the Higher Education Statistics Agency [HESA], the National Student Survey [NSS], and the Higher Education Funding Council for England [HEFCE]), freedom of information, data protection, open access compliance, research data management, and a new records management role which included advising on records and information assets, information security, and information assurance. In order to deliver these multiple roles, the post holders had (between them) qualifications in law, information security, records management, library and information science, IT, and information policy. In the Stockholm City case (Engvall et al., 2015) similar concerns for the archive and information security were recognized, such as proper classification of information to know what can be open and what is confidential, and good controls as a foundation for information security as well as for records and archival management. Security was also one of the concerns that was raised about open data, and balancing openness and security is a challenge.

In the case study of Stockholm City (Engvall et al., 2015), guidance was requested by interviewees regarding appraisal and risk assessment when making decisions on what to make openly available. Ethical issues and possible consequences of the use of data also have to be considered.

Monitoring and auditing

The case study of NHS England (Harrison et al., 2015) illustrated some excellent practice around national policy and standard setting and national guidance for the whole health sector, against which progress could be monitored and audited. A central national data policy unit covered three main areas of policy work: information standards, open data, and patient care data. It sought to act as an internal consultancy or "think-tank" for NHS England, actively learning from the best across the UK and internationally and translating that into national policy. Many records professionals find themselves limited by the local practices or organisational priorities, so this was an unusual example of a really international outlook and a recognition that open and digital data was a universal issue which required multinational and multi-institutional solutions and learning.

One piece of overarching guidance was the NHS Records Management Code (UK Department of Health, 2006), (now UK Department of Health's Records Management Code of Practice for Health and Social Care 2016 [UK Department of Health, 2016]) designed as "a guide to the required standards of practice in the management of records for those who work within or under contract to NHS organisations in England" (UK Department of Health, 2006, p. 1), which covered both medical and administrative records, held on all media. While the code had many strengths, it was limited by treating records management (an inconvenient and resource-intensive aspect of everyday business "synonymous with filing") separately from open government data (seen as an innovative area of work) and information governance, which was a well understood and well embedded "necessity." This was explained by one interviewee as "the idea of patient confidentiality is one that has been at the heart of doctor patient relationship since time immemorial" (Harrison et al., 2015, p. 45). The ambition was to achieve transparency in NHS England through the embedding of the openness agenda across all work streams, "building in rather than creating something separate and different," as one interviewee put it, and a recognition that what was required was "public trust in our custodianship of national data and the controls we have put in place."

Training

In the UK university study (Brimble et al., 2016), records management had significant potential for growth by developing policy and services in information and cyber security and showing how they fitted with records management priorities. A few high-profile data breach cases in the UK made university management more likely to release the necessary resources to develop awareness and best practice training programmes for staff and students in data protection and access to sensitive data, into which records good practices could be included.

There was also discussion of training in the local authority case study (Page et al., 2014). The need for training to deliver effective open government data services and the publication of examples of organisations, teams, and individual best practice were encouraged. Training for staff would help local government to understand the importance of open government data and encourage future open government data initiatives to impact and benefit society, as well as ensuring that the council's processes were compliant with the General Data Protection Regulation (2016), as the financial and reputational consequences of data breaches were very significant. There were plans to supplement the council's published policies on records management, freedom of information, and data protection which were available on the intranet and mandatory for all members of staff. Reading the guidance was to be audited, perhaps as part of staff induction online training and quizzes, and open government data training was to be added to the e-learning modules on the intranet to raise staff awareness.

In the Stockholm City case study (Engvall et al., 2015), interviewees raised the importance of improved skills; for example, regarding technical, legal, and institutional issues. Collaboration between different professions is needed at operational levels, as well as at a political level. It is not just new skills that are required, but also changing people's mindset. Being confident in the professional role as an archivist was also emphasized, especially in collaboration with other professions.

Governance

The UK university study (Brimble et al., 2016) was required to publish a lot of statutory data about its services and performance. The interviewees believed that this broadly satisfied its obligations to open data, and that other data could be requested under access to information or data protection legislation. Alongside these requirements, academic research was increasingly published in journal articles and books in open access formats and research data frequently made accessible (although these routes often have embargo periods of months or even years). Such means of opening up data were not always linked together with archival management policies, and were dealt with as separate strands of work and policy, leading to a lack of organisational oversight of open data practices, even though they were all delivered from the Information Governance Group.

The UK hospital trust study (Chorley et al., 2016) produced and reported a range of official statistics (birth rates, death rates, etc.) through the Business Intelligence Unit within the Informatics Directorate, whereas corporate records management for internal recordkeeping, including patient records, was managed by the Information Governance Department as part of the

Corporate Affairs Directorate, while information security was located in the ICT division. As a result, governance for different data and records functions was not seen holistically and was subject to different organisational priorities and resource constraints. Information governance functions included cyber security issues, data breaches, and missing files, alongside more traditional records management functions. The hospital published a range of internal policy documents including the Records Management Code of Practice, Freedom of Information Publication Scheme, Information Governance Policy, Freedom of Information Policy, Data Protection Policy, Information Security Policy, and the Hospital Trust Retention and Disposal Policy. Internal policies were updated to reflect changes in national agendas but only reviewed every few years, so in a highly bureaucratic hospital setting, there might be a considerable delay between policy making at national level and the improvement of policy and associated practice at local level. Information governance had a very high profile within the NHS more generally, with a great deal of central policy and guidance on its operations, although policy strengths were not always matched locally by the resources needed to deliver service priorities.

In the local government authority case study (Page et al., 2014), a new team was set up, the Information Resilience and Transparency Team, which brought together experts on the delivery of information access, records management, and information governance to ensure that the council met its obligations under the Data Protection Act 1998/2018, the Freedom of Information Act 2000, the Environmental Information Regulations 2004 and the Re-use of Public Sector Information Regulations 2005. They worked closely with the Business Intelligence Team, who delivered the specialist knowledge and expertise relating to the national and local policy arena of open data and data exploitation, under the umbrella of council's Open Data Working Group, which brought in digital services. This group's responsibilities included identifying standards, principles, and protocols of open data, developing a transparency strategy, determining the processes of opening data and data quality standards, and encouraging the re-use of open government data. These layers of policy and service delivery helped the council to ensure compliance with an evolving legislative landscape around information access and to ensure that resources devoted to producing and using data were targeted well. Financial data, demographic and local economic data, and data concerning highways and schools were those most requested and, as much as possible, made available openly. Having a responsive governance process around information and data was important to the council's broader functions. The interviewees in the public authority believed that there was a tension between central government policy on open data encouraging the publication of as much data as possible and local government, with limited resources, wanting to be selective in determining which data members of the public will use and which are therefore worth preparing to be released as open data.

In the Stockholm City study (Engvall et al., 2015), a challenge that was raised was division of responsibilities, both at political level and also between the IT department and the Archive. Something that was raised as a success was that the Stockholm City Archive led the work on developing a digital archival strategy for all of the Stockholm City. The strategy recognized the role of the archive in digital records management throughout the city, as well as in realizing the e-government goal of citizens' right to access public records. In the strategy, management of open data was also included.

Conclusion

As Bunn concluded in Anderson et al. (2019, pp. 240–241), records professionals'

> primary concern remains the maintenance of a persistent digital memory and evidence base that are trusted as both an accurate record of past events and transactions and a solid grounding for future decisions and action. Their primary challenge is to work out how this can be achieved in increasingly networked, yet distributed technologies, in connected but distrustful and polarized social landscapes. Neither this concern, nor this challenge are or should be of records professionals alone. They will be able to address them on their own, but, if they are to maintain their collective sense of identity, they will need to negotiate and define what their own role and contribution can and should be towards meeting this challenge.

This chapter has sought to take us one step further on that journey by sharing the practical experience of records and information professionals in England and Sweden as an inspiration for those who are seeking paths towards improved professional competency in open digital information environments across Europe. The studies identified many gaps in skills and knowledge which records professionals need to fill.

Acknowledgements

We wish to acknowledge all the case study organisations which kindly agreed to allow us to interview and visit them and to make use of their (anonymized) experiences in this work. Much of the work was supported by UCL Department of Information Studies through the academics involved in supervising postgraduate students studying on the MA in Archives and Records Management and the student researchers themselves.

References

Anderson, K., Bunn, J., Engvall, T., Flinn, A., Gänser, G., Henttonen, P., . . . Cai, Y. (2019). The role of the records professional. In L. Duranti & C. Rogers (Eds.), *Trusting records in the cloud* (pp. 223–244). London: Facet Publishing.

Brimble, S., Flinn, A., & Shepherd, E. (2016). *The role of the records manager/records management in an open government environment in the UK: Higher education* (EU32). InterPARES Trust. Retrieved from https://interparestrust.org/assets/public/dissemination/EU32InterPARESReport.pdf

Chorley, K. (2017). The challenges presented to records management by open government data in the public sector in England. *Records Management Journal, 27,* 149–158. https://doi.org/10.1108/RMJ-09-2016-0034

Chorley, K., Flinn, A., & Shepherd, E. (2016). *The role of the records manager/ records management in an open government environment in the UK: The National Health Service* (EU27). InterPARES Trust. Retrieved from https://interparestrust.org/assets/public/dissemination/InterPARESTrustResearchReportEU27.pdf

Data Protection Act, Chapter 29 (1998) and Chapter 12 (2018).

Engvall, T., Liang, V., & Anderson, K. (2015). *The role of the archivist and records manager in an open government environment in Sweden* (EU11, Final Report). Inter PARES Trust. Retrieved from https://interparestrust.org/assets/public/dissemination/EU11_20150707_RoleRMOpenGovSweden_EUWorkshop5_FinalReport_Final.pdf

Environmental Information Regulations, S.I. 3391 (2004).

Freedom of Information Act, Chapter 36 (2000).

General Data Protection Regulation (GDPR), EU 2016/679 (2016).

Harrison, E., Shepherd, E., & Flinn, A. (2015). *A research report into open government data in NHS England* (EU19, Final Report). InterPARES Trust. Retrieved from https://interparestrust.org/assets/public/dissemination/EU19_20150421_UKNationalHealthService_FinalReport.pdf

InterPARES Trust. (2018). *Terminology database.* Retrieved from https://interparestrust.org/terminology/term/reliability%20~paL~record~paR~

Lowry, J. (2014). Opening government: Open data and access to information. In J. Lowry & J. Wamukoya (Eds.), *Integrity in government through records management: Essays in honour of Anne Thurston* (pp. 161–172). Aldershot: Ashgate.

Page, J., Flinn, A., & Shepherd, E. (2014). *The role of the records manager in an open government environment in the UK* (EU03, Final Report). InterPARES Trust. Retrieved from https://interparestrust.org/assets/public/dissemination/EU03_2014 1105_RoleRMOpenGovUK_FinalReport.pdf

Re-use of Public Sector Information Regulations, S.I. 1515 (2005).

Shepherd, E. (2015). Freedom of information, right to access information, open data: Who is at the table? *RoundTable, 104,* 715–726. https://doi.org/10.1080/003585 33.2015.1112101

Shepherd, E., Bunn, J., Flinn, A., Lomas, E., Sexton, A., Brimble, S., . . . Page, J. (2018). Open government data: Critical information management perspectives. *Records Management Journal, 29,* 152–167. https://doi.org/10.1108/RMJ-08-2018-0023

UK Department of Health. (2006). *Records management: NHS code of practice. Part 1.* Retrieved from https://www.wwl.nhs.uk/Library/IGov/DH_Guidance/DHGuidance_RecordsMgtCodeofPracticePart1.pdf

UK Department of Health. (2016). *Records management code of practice for health and social care.* Retrieved from https://digital.nhs.uk/binaries/content/assets/legacy/pdf/n/b/records-management-cop-hsc-2016.pdf

3 Policies and standards for recordkeeping and digital preservation

Maria Guercio with Maria Mata Caravaca and Liudmila Varlamova

Introduction

European initiatives are characterized, both in European Union (EU) institutions and at member state level, by contradictions and ambiguities when the attention is focused on electronic recordkeeping and digital preservation in the cloud computing dimension. For many years, projects, standards, and internal rules have been discussed, approved, and adopted in Europe with the aim of providing tools and a strategic approach in the field of open government based on qualified and innovative electronic recordkeeping systems. In national jurisdictions, the main efforts have been focused on supporting public administrations and enforcing their capacity of building a strong and consistent infrastructure of services in this field. At the same time, ICT developments encouraged the implementation of cloud computing systems based on outsourcing large portions of information processing without adequate or any attention for the risks involved in the creation and preservation of digital records in cloud systems if policies, controls, and continuing monitoring of the records systems' quality were not in place.

These contradictions and ambiguity are present in EU initiatives and are even more explicit at the state level, as testified in the case studies analyzed here (Spain, Russia, Italy). Wherever the legislation approved transition to the cloud (even if based on good standards and best practices for the creation and preservation of electronic records), records creators do not urgently establish authenticity, reliability, security, usability, retrieval, confidentiality, and privacy in the cloud environment. Outside of the traditional in-house dimension, creators are not aware of the risks involved in leaving the custody of their records and information sources to private third parties and do not understand the level of controls required for limiting the risks. Captured by immediate economic advantages and convinced by technological promises based on electronic signatures and seals, public and private organisations are more and more reducing their investments in internal infrastructures and responsibilities. The price to pay is high in terms of losing information quality and the capacity to provide evidence at any level of their activity as a consequence of renouncing the direct control of their records creation, organisation, maintenance, and access. The presence of a consistent and consolidated series of rules for electronic recordkeeping which can be applied with flexibility (in the form of internal policies and manuals) by public agencies or private corporate bodies seems the most efficient (and perhaps unique) defence mechanism for supporting the archival function for transparency, accountability, and, of course, future scientific research. Rules, directives, guidelines, and manuals must be sustained by specific checklists, created at international and national levels, for assessing cloud services not only from the legal perspective, but also for supporting the effort for quality insurance of archival institutions and programmes. The ITrust checklist (ITrust, 2016) has a relevant potentiality, as testified by the case study developed to evaluate the Italian legislative framework (Allegrezza et al., 2018).

Background to the European Union actions

The EU has undertaken actions to enhance archival policies and practices in Europe through the promotion and support of numerous research projects and initiatives. Among them are the DLM Forum[1] on electronic records and archives; the production of *de facto* standards, known as MoReq (*Model Requirements for Records Systems*);[2] the creation of expert groups such as the European Archives Group (EAG), which was created in 2006 to ensure cooperation and coordination on matters relating to records and archives; and the Member States Expert Group (MSEG), set up in 2007 to monitor the implementation of the European Commission's recommendation on digitization and digital preservation (European Commission, 2011). Moreover, within the framework of EU-funded projects, continuous research activities have been carried out on digital preservation since 2001. The first projects, such as ERPANET and DELOS,[3] aimed to raise awareness and to create a scientific community addressing collaboratively this novel and interdisciplinary topic. Projects focused on the establishment of common terminology and concepts, metadata standards, system concepts, selection and appraisal policies, and format identification, and primarily addressed office documents and images in institutional settings. To consolidate the existing work in the area of digital preservation, national initiatives and different research projects on a European level were integrated. The DigitalPreservationEurope (DPE) consortium was built on the work of ERPANET and linked other collaborative partnerships, such as NESTOR, the UK's Digital Curation Centre, PLANETS, and CASPAR, under the WePreserve Initiative.[4] In the next phase, research projects targeted more technical aspects, such as tools and frameworks for digital preservation. These projects influenced international standardization initiatives with strong European presence (e.g. PREMIS, OAIS and TRAC).[5] In more recent years, research activities have focused on the preservation of interactive objects, ephemeral data, methods

for object validation, audit and certification, development of scalable preservation systems and processes, and reuse of information, through projects
such as SCAPE, ENSURE, APARSEN, TIMBUS, PERICLES, and E-ARK.[6]
Despite all these initiatives, the existing regulations on records management
and digital preservation within the EU are insufficient and fragmented, and
a systematic and strategic approach to increase coordination and develop
common policies among European countries is still missing.

Since the 1990s the EU has issued directives on ICT, e-government, and data
protection that deal, directly or indirectly, with records-related issues. These
directives have the purpose of establishing a legal framework to ensure free
movement of information society services between member states. Within the
Europe 2020 strategy (European Commission, 2010), the Commission promotes adoption of cloud computing in all sectors of economy to encourage
productivity and employment. This led in 2012 to adoption of the European
Cloud Strategy (European Commission, 2012), which included the development of model contract terms to regulate issues such as data preservation
after termination of the contract, data disclosure and integrity, data location
and transfer, ownership of the data, subcontracting, and code of conduct for
providers. The current European Cloud Initiative (European Commission,
2016) focuses on the creation of a European Open Science Cloud for storing,
sharing, and reusing of scientific data and results, and a European Data Infrastructure to securely access, move, share, and process data in Europe. These
new developments in cloud computing require further policies to address the
risks posed to digital records.

The Spanish situation

With the progressive introduction of electronic administration in the public
sector, Spain has started to incorporate digital records management within
legislation. The state law of 1992 on common administrative procedures in
the public administration promoted the use of electronic means for the internal activities of public bodies and their relations with citizens (Jefatura del
Estado, 1992). The law of 2007 on electronic access of citizens to public services further developed e-government in Spain (Jefatura del Estado, 2007).
It consolidated the right of citizens to communicate electronically with public administrations and incorporated principles related to records management and preservation, and the right of access to information.[7] The Royal
Decree of 2010 on the national interoperability scheme for e-government[8]
gave way to issue technical rules on digital records and files, digitisation of
records, authentic copies and conversion, digital signatures, and data models
for the exchange of registry entries, as well as guidelines for the elaboration
of policies on records management in hybrid environments (Jefatura del
Estado, 2010). The last rule, Resolution 28/06/2012 (Jefatura del Estado,
2012), requires public bodies to produce and implement records management procedures, train staff, and make periodic audits of the adequacy and

application of the policy. It provides indications on records management processes, which should include records capture and metadata assignation, registration, classification (including criteria for the creation of files and records aggregations), description, access and traceability of access operations, appraisal, retention, and disposal. Additionally, tools for records management (InSide) and archiving (ARCHIVE),[9] based on the OAIS model, have been made available to public administrations through cloud computing, web services, or via other means.

Laws 30/1992 and 11/2007 were repealed by Law 39/2015 (Jefatura del Estado, 2015) on a common administrative procedure for public administrations. This new law aims at definitively pushing forward e-government. It requires that all public bodies have an electronic registry of any record that is submitted or received. Each public administration must also maintain a unique digital archive, in which files are kept in a format that guarantees records authenticity, integrity, confidentiality, preservation, and access control. These new provisions were scheduled to take effect on 2 October 2020.[10]

Despite the recent changes in legislation, the application of electronic management systems in public entities has been delayed due to the limited human and economic resources, the need to create interdisciplinary teams to manage digital records (administration, records and archives, and ICT), the need for each public body to establish a records management policy and detailed procedures, the need to have adequate tools that integrate with existing ones, and the need for personnel training. In a politically decentralized state such as Spain, coordination and cooperation among institutions, provinces, regions, and the state bodies are also necessary to be able to adopt shared services and infrastructures that improve rationalisation and efficiency.

In relation to cloud computing, specific legislation regulating issues such as the preservation, integrity, location, portability, and ownership of the data stored in cloud services has not yet been developed. The only legislation that protects consumers from the cloud computing market is that on personal data protection and digital rights, cybercrime, e-commerce, and digital signatures.

The modern Russian experience

Experience of the formation of a unified state policy and comprehensive regulation of records management and archiving in Russia has a long history. In this chapter, we will focus only on the modern stage. Among the statutory enactments systematically regulating archival issues (Varlamova, 2018a) there is only federal law "On Archiving." However, the issues of documenting and certain aspects of working with electronic documents are reflected in a number of legislative acts of the Russian Federation.[11]

The Federal Archive Agency (Rosarkhiv), which regulates records management and archives in Russia, is responsible for building the state policy in this area and developing profile-oriented normative acts and methodological documents that implement them (Varlamova, 2018b). Currently, the normative and methodological regulation of records management and archiving is carried out using a number of documents developed by the All-Russian Scientific and Research Institute for Records and Archives Management (VNIIDAD) on behalf of Rosarkhiv.[12] The Institute develops national standards used in records management and archives and takes part in the development of national standards for adjacent areas of activity. National standards used within the framework of the topic under this study can be roughly divided into two groups

- national standards regulating issues of methodology of records and records management systems[13]
- national standards regulating issues of storage and preservation of records, protection of privacy, and of personally identifiable information.[14]

The national standards will not be presented in detail here, one of the reasons being their purely practical orientation in terms of resolving issues of document storage in Russia. Nevertheless, several standards playing a crucial role should be mentioned. They are

- GOST R 54989–2012, Long term preservation of electronic document-based information
- GOST R 53647.6–2012, Business continuity management. Specification for a personal information management system for data protection
- GOST R ISO/IEC 27037–2014, Information technology. Security techniques. Guidelines for identification, collection, acquisition and preservation of digital evidence
- GOST R ISO 13008–2015, Information and documentation. Digital records conversion and migration process.

It should be noted that all of the listed documents (normative acts and standards) are interconnected and form a policy of storing traditional (paper) and electronic documents. The main point of this policy is that all documents (including electronic ones) created in any organisation are divided into several categories according to

- their retention schedule (temporary: up to 5 years; long term: over 10 years, permanent)
- type of documentation system (management documentation, scientific and technical documentation, and others)
- type (order) or subtype (order for the main activity) of the document.

Each of these categories of documents is treated on the basis of the unified state policy, normative legal acts and standards, meeting both general requirements (for example, the rules for creating, recording, and using records management systems, and organizing records preservation and archival storage) and special requirements (choosing the method of signing/certification, information carrier and format, method of transfer to the archive, etc.).

Currently, the issue of creating a trusted environment between all participants in the process of creating/storing documents is under consideration. Although presently it does not seem possible to develop uniform requirements for all variations of the process, the methodology of this work should still be defined and compiled in the foreseeable future on the basis of best practices and results of the ITrust project, in which VNIIDAD was directly involved.

The Italian case

As in the other case studies examined here, the Italian legislation (well developed in the sector of electronic recordkeeping and digital preservation)[15] does not directly connect cloud services to the recordkeeping and digital preservation systems (Allegrezza et al., 2018). The rules and the general acts run on parallel lines. More specifically, the rules relevant for cloud computing services are present in the general legislation related to procurement and tenders for the public sector, while a new area for audit and control is under development, with reference to the dimension of transparency and accountability but not directly to records creation. More recently, a national plan has been approved with the aim of creating a cloud environment for public administration, homogeneous from the contractual and technological point of view, by retraining internal resources existing in public administrations or by resorting to the resources of qualified external parties, with the use of public and private cloud for *storage* and computing and the systematic adoption of the cloud paradigm. Specific attention is dedicated to the

- reorganisation of public administration data centres through rationalisation work, both to reduce management costs and to adapt and increase the quality of services offered to public administrations
- implementation of cloud for public administration, enabling virtualisation of the existing hardware, with significant maintenance and cost management benefits
- rationalisation of public administration connectivity costs and increase in the spread of connectivity in public places for the benefit of citizens.

At the time of writing (2019), these proposals are at a starting point and do not influence the complex situation of public administrations. The analysis conducted as a contribution to the ITrust project on a group of Italian institutions has pointed out many critical aspects, including

- very limited attention given to the risks of records, of authenticity, and of integrity of the information involved in the new services based in the cloud environment

- low level of standard contracts focused only on contractual/commercial aspects and legal restrictions (such as pricing and payment, renewal, agreement term, termination and suspension, warranties, claims, limitations of liability, and obligations)
- limited attention given to preservation and only dedicated to controls of technical storage such as data location, security, confidentiality, and privacy.

Application of the ITrust (2016) checklist to national legislation, detailed in the next chapter, illustrated where the weaknesses are more dangerous but also which components of the rules could be further developed for reducing the risks involved in a cloud-based approach.

Notes

1 DLM stands for Document Life Cycle Management. The first forum was held in 1996.
2 The original MoReq specification was conceived in the late 1990s and was intended to serve the same function as US DoD 5015.2 (US Department of Defense), namely to describe a good electronic records management system. The first version of MoReq was published by the DLM Forum and European Commission in 2001. MoReq2 was published in 2008 and MoReq2010 in 2011.
3 The first project was ERPANET (Electronic Resource Preservation and Access, 2001–2005, https://www.erpanet.org/) and it was followed by DELOS (Developing a European e-Learning Observation System, 2004–2008).
4 Digital Preservation Europe (DPE) was a consortium of European academic and cultural institutions dedicated to sharing their collective digital preservation expertise and resources, https://www.digitalpreservation.gov/series/edge/dpe.html. Other collaborative partnerships were NESTOR (Network of Expertise in Long-term Storage of Digital Resources in Germany, launched in 2003, https://www.langzeitarchivierung.de/Webs/nestor/DE/Home/home_node.html), the UK's DCC (Digital Curation Centre, launched in 2004, https://www.dcc.ac.uk/), PLANETS (Preservation and Long-term Access through Networked Services, 2006–2010, https://www.planets-project.eu/), CASPAR (Cultural, Artistic and Scientific knowledge for Preservation, Access and Retrieval, 2006–2010, http://casparpreserves.digitalpreserve.info/), under the shared brand of WePreserve Initiative https://www.youtube.com/user/wepreserve/videos).
5 PREMIS (Preservation Metadata: Implementation Strategies, http://www.loc.gov/standards/premis/), OAIS (Open Archival Information System, http://public.ccsds.org/publications/archive/650x0m2.pdf), TRAC (Trustworthy Repositories Audit & Certification: Criteria & Checklist, https://www.crl.edu/sites/default/files/d6/attachments/pages/trac_0.pdf).
6 SCAPE (Scalable Preservation Environments, 2011–2014, https://scape-project.eu/), ENSURE (Enabling knowledge Sustainability Usability and Recovery for Economic value, 2011–2014), APARSEN (Alliance Permanent Access to the Record of Science in Europe Network, 2011–2014, http://www.alliancepermanentaccess.org/index.php/aparsen/), TIMBUS (Timeless Business Processes and Services, 2011–2014, http://timbusproject.net/), PERICLES (Promoting and Enhancing Reuse of Information throughout the Content Lifecycle Taking Account of Evolving Semantics, 2013–2017), and E-ARK (European Archival Records and Knowledge Preservation, 2014–2017, http://www.eark-project.com/).

7 This law responded to the European Union initiatives e-Europe (launched in 2000) and i2010 (launched in 2005), which aimed to activate the economy and improve accessibility of services for all European citizens. These initiatives were followed by the Digital Agenda for Europe, which forms one of the seven pillars of the Europe 2020 Strategy.

8 The Spanish legislation on interoperability embraces the European Interoperability Framework of the IDABC programme (Interoperable Delivery of European e-Government Services to public Administrations, Business and Citizens), and Decision 922/2009/EC on Interoperability Solutions for European Public Administrations (ISA).

9 InSIDE (Infraestructura y Sistemas de Documentación Electrónica), https://administracionelectronica.gob.es/ctt/inside#.XccoDetKios. ARCHIVE, https://administracionelectronica.gob.es/ctt/archive#.XcccY-tKios.

10 A compendium of the Spanish legislation on electronic administration at the State level is: *Código de Administración Electrónica*, Ministerio de Hacienda y Administraciones Públicas, Agencia Estatal Boletín Oficial del Estado, 2019. https://www.boe.es/legislacion/codigos/codigo.php?id=029_Codigo_de_Administracion_Electronica&modo=1.

11 For example, in the federal laws "On Electronic Signature," "On Information, Information Technologies and Information Protection," in several codes of the Russian Federation.

12 Among them are "The rules of recordkeeping in the federal executive bodies" (2009); "Methodological recommendations on the development by federal government bodies of approximate nomenclatures of cases for territorial bodies and subordinate organisations" (2018); "Rules for organizing the preservation, acquisition, recording and use of documents of the Archival Fond of the Russian Federation and other archival documents in government bodies, local authorities and organisations" (2015); and "The list of standard administrative archival documents generated in the process of activity of state bodies, local self-government bodies and organisations, specifying the time of their storage" (2010) (retrieved from http://www.archives.ru).

13 The main national standards regulating the issues of methodology of records and documentation systems management are: GOST R ISO 15489-1–2007, "Records management. General requirements" (until 2020 r.); GOST R ISO 23081-1–2008, "Records management processes. Metadata for records. Part 1. Principles"; GOST R 7.8.0–2013, "Recordkeeping and archiving. Terms and Definitions"; GOST R 55681–2013, "Information and documentation. Work process analysis for records"; GOST R ISO 30300–2015, "Management systems for records. Fundamentals and vocabulary"; GOST R 7.0.79–2016 (2018), "Organisational and administrative documentation. Requirements for paperwork /documents processing"; GOST R 101–2017 ISO 30301–2011, "Management systems for records. Requirements"; GOST R ISO 15489-1–2019, "Records management. Concepts and principles" (since 2020).

14 National standards regulating the issues of protection of privacy and of personally identifiable information: GOST R 54471–2011, "Document management. Information stored electronically. Recommendations for trustworthiness and reliability"; GOST R 53647.6–2012, "Business continuity management. Specification for a personal information management system for data protection."

15 The rules in question include the legislation on recordkeeping systems (decree of the President of Republic 445/2000 and related regulations approved with a decree of the Prime Minister 3 December 2013); the legislation on digital preservation (Code of Digital Administration approved with a legislative decree 82/2005 and continuously updated) and its regulation approved with another decree of the Prime Minister 3 December 2013); guidelines adopted by the Agency for

Digital Information in the Public Sector – AGID – with specific reference to audit and certification of digital repositories (circolare 65/2014, *Accreditamento dei soggetti pubblici e privati che svolgono attività di conservazione dei documenti informatici per conto* terzi, *Requisiti di qualità e sicurezza per l'accreditamento e la vigilanza*, Retrieved from https://www.agid.gov.it/sites/default/files/repository_files/documentazione/requisiti_di_qualita_e_sicurezza_v.1.1.pdf).

References

Allegrezza, S., Bezzi, G., Guercio, Mata Caravaca, M., Pescini, I., & Tommasi, B. (2018). *The impact of the Italian legal framework for cloud computing on electronic record-keeping and digital preservation system.* Retrieved from https://interparestrust.org/assets/public/dissemination/EU35_FinalReport2017.pdf

European Commission. (2010, March 3). Europe 2020: A European strategy for smart, sustainable and inclusive growth. *COM 2010.* Retrieved from https://ec.europa.eu/eu2020/pdf/COMPLET%20EN%20BARROSO%20%20%20007%20-%20Europe%202020%20-%20EN%20version.pdf

European Commission. (2011). Recommendation of 27 October 2011 on the digitisation and online accessibility of cultural material and digital preservation (2011/711/EU). *Journal of the European Union L 283/3.* Retrieved from https://eur-lex.europa.eu/LexUriServ/LexUriServ.do?uri=OJ:L:2011:283:0039:0045:EN:PDF

European Commission. (2012, September 27). Unleashing the potential of cloud computing in Europe. *COM 529.* Retrieved from http://eur-lex.europa.eu/LexUriServ/LexUriServ.do?uri=COM:2012:0529:FIN:EN:PDF

European Commission. (2016). European cloud initiative – Building a competitive data and knowledge economy in Europe. *COM 2016.* Retrieved from https://eur-lex.europa.eu/legal-content/EN/TXT/PDF/?uri=CELEX:52016DC0178&from=EN

ITrust. (2016). *Checklist for cloud service contracts.* Retrieved from https://interpares trust.org/assets/public/dissemination/NA14_20160226_CloudServiceProvider Contracts_Checklist_Final.pdf

Jefatura del Estado. (1992, November 27). Ley 30/1992, de 26 de noviembre, de Régimen Jurídico de las Administraciones Públicas y del Procedimiento Administrativo Común. *BOE 26318* [Law 30/1992, Legal regime of public administrations and the common administrative procedure]. Retrieved from https://www.boe.es/buscar/pdf/1992/BOE-A-1992-26318-consolidado.pdf

Jefatura del Estado. (2007, June 24). Ley 11/2007, de 22 de junio, de acceso electrónico de los ciudadanos a los Servicios Públicos. *BOE-A-2007-12352* [Law 11/2007, of 22 June, on electronic access of citizens to public services]. Retrieved from https://www.boe.es/buscar/pdf/2007/BOE-A-2007-12352-consolidado.pdf

Jefatura del Estado. (2010, January 29). Real Decreto 4/2010, de 8 de enero, por el que se regula el Esquema Nacional de Interoperabilidad (ENI) en el ámbito de la Administración Electrónica. *BOE 25*, A-2010–1331 [Royal Decree 4/2010, of January 8, which regulates the national interoperability scheme (ENI) in the field of electronic administration]. Retrieved from https://www.boe.es/boe/dias/2010/01/29/pdfs/BOE-A-2010-1331.pdf

Jefatura del Estado. (2012, July 26). Resolución 28 de junio de 2012, de la Secretaría de Estado de Administraciones Públicas, por la que se aprueba la Norma Técnica de Interoperabilidad de Política de gestión de documentos electrónicos. *BOE 178*: A-2012–10048 [Resolution 2012, of the Secretary of State for Public

Administration, which approves the technical standard for interoperability of the electronic document management policy. BOE 178: A-2012-10048]. Retrieved from https://www.boe.es/boe/dias/2012/07/26/pdfs/BOE-A-2012-10048.pdf

Jefatura del Estado. (2015). Ley 39/2015, de 1 de octubre, del Procedimiento Administrativo Común de las Administraciones Públicas. *BOE 236*: A-2015–10565 [Law 39/2015, of October 1, on the Common administrative procedure of public admini stration]. Retrieved from https://www.boe.es/buscar/pdf/2015/BOE-A-2015-10565-consolidado.pdf

Varlamova, L. (2018a). Aspects of compatibility of Russian and international standardized terminology used in records management and archives. *Archives in the Service of People. People in the Service of Archives*. Maribor, 52–56.

Varlamova, L. (2018b). International records management and archives terminology systems standardized by ISO and IEC. *Atlanti*, 2, 99–110.

4 The impact of a legal framework for cloud computing on electronic recordkeeping and digital preservation

Stefano Allegrezza

Introduction

A legislative framework plays a key role in defining cloud-based recordkeeping and digital preservation strategies, since it can impose limitations and restrictions and establish fixed rules to follow. Continuing and broadening the discussion from the previous chapter, this chapter aims to further analyze recent Italian legislation and policies for cloud computing services in the public sector and also to assess them against the fundamental requirements identified at national and international levels for effective recordkeeping and digital preservation systems. The research questions discussed in this chapter are linked to the third objective of the ITrust project (Duranti & Jansen, 2013) and tries to answer questions such as: what is the relation between the Italian legislation on cloud computing and relevant and consolidated principles in the field of recordkeeping and digital preservation systems, and is the *Checklist for Cloud Service Contracts* developed by the ITrust (Bushey, Demoulin, How, & McLelland, 2016) useful at a national level? In order to assess the Italian legal framework and common practice, four case studies are also discussed.

This chapter is based on the work of the ITrust Team Europe whose findings are collected in the Project Report EU35 *The impact of the Italian legal framework for cloud computing on electronic recordkeeping and digital preservation system* (Allegrezza et al., 2018).

State of art and legal frameworks on cloud-based recordkeeping and preservation systems in Italy

In Italy, there is no specific legislation on cloud services for public administration (Allegrezza et al., 2016), but a fragmented and not homogeneous set of regulations, laws, rules, and policies that professionals need to consider when they want to implement recordkeeping and preservation functions using cloud services. For this purpose, various categories of rules are relevant, all of them consistent with the guidelines approved in Europe by the *Cloud for Europe* project (AgID, 2014a), which uses pre-commercial procurement as an instrument for public sector innovation. Here, it is not possible to deal with all the rules and laws that regulate the matter, but the following play a crucial role and should be mentioned.

1   policies, recommendations, and guidelines focused on the use of cloud computing in the public sector but not specifically addressing record-keeping and preservation systems; among these it is worth mentioning

- "Recommendations and proposals on the use of cloud computing in the public administration" (DigitPA, 2012)
- "Characterization of cloud systems for public administration" (AgID, 2013).

Many obligations are part of the general legislation on public procurement that is contained in the Decree of the President of the Republic 207/2010 *Regulation for the implementation of the legislative decree 12 April 2006, n. 163, containing "Code of public contracts relating to works, services and supplies in implementation of Directives"* (Italian Government, 2010).

Currently, these rules imply that storage systems for digital preservation must be located in Italy to enable auditing by national authorities, such as the Agency for Digital Italy (AgID). New regulations under development seem to consider the possibility of locating the main system outside the national territory if at least "one copy" of the records/information is kept in Italy.

2   national plans, such as the *Three-Year Plan for ICT in Public Administration 2017–2019* (AgID, 2017). These define policies and strategic programmes which could be relevant for defining frameworks and requirements for cloud computing. More specifically, the Three-Year Plan will develop along three main directions

- reorganisation of public administration data centres, both to reduce management costs and to increase the quality of services offered to public administrations, including those in terms of business continuity, disaster recovery, and energy efficiency. According to the plan only a small number of national data centres will be identified at the end of the project and will support the public cloud-based services delivered by all Italian public administrations. The Central State Archive in Rome and the digital preservation centres, such as those developed by some Italian regions (i.e. Emilia Romagna, Tuscany, Marche), will be also included in this list
- implementation of the private cloud environment for public administration (the so-called PA cloud), homogeneous from the contractual and technological point of view, enabling virtualisation of all public administrations' hardware, with significant maintenance and cost management benefits. Cloud services will be offered according to the

three typical models: Infrastructure-as-a-Service (IaaS), Platform-as-a-Service (PaaS), and Software-as-a-Service (SaaS)

- rationalisation of public administration connectivity costs and increase in the spread of connectivity in public places for the benefit of citizens.

3   the main part of the legislation concerning cloud services for recordkeeping systems and digital preservation is in the form of laws, acts, regulations, and guidelines not directly related to cloud computing. More specifically, these rules are present in the general legislation related to procurement and tenders for the public sector, while a new area for audit and control is under development thanks to the initiative of the National Authority for Transparency and Accountability (ANAC). These rules include

- legislation on recordkeeping systems: the Decree of the President of the Republic n. 445, December 28, 2000, *Consolidated act of the legislative and regulatory provisions on administrative documentation* (Italian Government, 2000), and related regulations approved by the Decree of Prime Minister on December, 3 2013 *Technical rules for the electronic protocol* (Italian Government, 2014a)
- the *Digital Administration Code* approved with the Legislative Decree 7 March 2005, n. 82 (Italian Government, 2005) and continuously updated, and its regulations approved with the Decree of Prime Minister on December, 3 2013, *Technical rules on the preservation system* (Italian Government, 2014b), and with another Decree of Prime Minister on November, 13 2014 *Technical rules on creation, transmission, copying, duplication, reproduction and validation of electronic documents as well as creation and preservation of electronic documents from public administrations* (Italian Government, 2014c)
- guidelines adopted by AgID with specific reference to audit and certification of digital repositories – Circular n. 65/2014, Accreditation of public and private entities that perform electronic documents retention activities on behalf of third parties. Quality and safety requirements for accreditation and supervision and guidelines for the preservation of electronic documents (AgID, 2014b).

In conclusion, as the long and untidy list of rules and laws highlights, the Italian legislative framework is complex and very fragmented, and for those who deal with records or archives and want to start providing cloud computing services, it is difficult to understand what regulatory obligations they must comply with. This situation is not specific only to Italy but is also common to other European and international countries. According to Guercio (2019, p. 100), in Europe "despite efforts to enhance co-operation and co-ordination on records and archives policies and practices among the member countries of the European Union, the existing regulations are insufficient and fragmented." A common effort to reach a homogeneous regulatory framework specifically dedicated to these aspects is truly desirable.

Proposal of the international ISO standard "records management in the cloud"

From this point of view, the effort made by the International Organization for Standardisation (ISO) to develop an international standard on the management of records using the cloud is very positive. Although standards do not have a binding value (like laws), they have fundamental importance because they are a point of reference both for the development of legal provisions and for addressing more technical parts that cannot find a place in a law. On January 2017, a Draft Technical Report with the title *ISO/DTR 22428 Records management in the cloud: Issues and concerns* was approved as a new project (International Organization for Standardization [ISO], 2017) by the Technical Committee ISO/TC 46/SC 11 Archives/records management.

It will provide guidance on how to implement a management model for cloud-based records management that considers system, technical, social, and legal risks and issues. Regulatory and legal issues take into account good practice that would be applicable for most countries where different legislation and normative regulations will determine how to implement the model (Fernández, 2017).

According to Fernández (2017),

> the Technical Report will describe: records processes in the cloud (based on ISO 15489, ISO 30301, ISO 17068, etc.); reference architectures for digital records management; how to assess the main cloud service risk factors (from the stakeholder and provider points of view).

Its objective is to provide a practical and easy-to-understand tool for both technical and business cloud environments by introducing use cases and examples of major global schemes including "security regarding digital records; regulatory, legal and normative requirements; risk assessment in any cloud-based context for records; data backup and preservation failures to be taken into account" (Fernández, 2017).

Assessment of Italian legislation against the ITrust cloud contract checklist

Based on the previous analysis, the ITrust checklist (ITrust, 2016) was used as the framework for assessing Italian legislation on current cloud service contracts from a records management, archival, and legal perspective. The questions in the checklist are grouped into eight general areas.

1   agreement
2   data ownership and use
3   availability, retrieval, and use
4   data storage and preservation

5   data retention and disposition
6   security, confidentiality, and privacy
7   data location and cross-border data flows
8   end of service – contract termination.

To evaluate the usefulness of the checklist, the research team took into consideration the Italian national legislation. The checklist was then used as a list of essential questions to be answered by examining the national framework in each of the eight checklist areas. Since not all these questions are addressed in Italian legislation, the research team had to adapt the checklist and, in some cases, limit the number of questions. Table 4.1 lists the main findings from this assessment.

In conclusion, this assessment found that the requirements included in the first area of the checklist are usually included in the rules adopted by public administrations when they sign an agreement with private service providers. Italian policies do not focus much on merely technical issues, such as those found in some sections of the checklist, but many issues are addressed in the preservation manual that every person in charge of a digital archive is obliged to write. Detailed guidelines for building these manuals have been provided by AgID.

Assessment of four case studies against the ITrust cloud contract checklist

The ITrust checklist (ITrust, 2016) was used for assessing some specific cases studies involving four public administrations based in Italy (the Emilia Romagna region, Toscana Region, University of Udine, and the International Centre for the Study of Preservation and Restoration of Cultural Property – ICCROM). The case studies assessed

- the contract signed between Emilia Romagna region and Microsoft for the use of Office 365 in the cloud and the agreement for long term digital preservation services
- the contracts implemented for the Toscana region in relation to the use of the private cloud computing system TIX and its related ICT services
- the contract signed between the University of Udine and Microsoft in order to use Microsoft Azure Virtual Machine services to execute machine learning solutions
- the contract signed between ICCROM and Microsoft to use Azure, the Microsoft cloud service, required for supporting the proprietary financial accounting system SAP.

Due to the comprehensive nature of the checklist, not all of its questions were relevant *per se* or play a meaningful role for the specific case studies. However, analysis of the four contract assessments is particularly interesting

Table 4.1 Results of assessing Italian legislation on current cloud service contracts

General area	Findings
1 Agreement	In Italy, the Decree of Prime Minister December 3, 2013, *Technical rules on the preservation system* (Italian Government, 2014b), governs all issues involved in this area. It states the obligation of specific agreements for any services related to digital archiving, not only in the public sector but also in the case of private records. This decree rules that digital repositories must define, in their manuals, in a specific and detailed manner, all questions about responsibilities, terms of services, level of interoperability, etc. AgID has defined a prototype manual (preservation manual) that all digital repositories which intend to preserve public records and undergo the certification process can benefit from.
2 Data ownership and use	The Decree of Prime Minister December 3, 2013 (Italian Government, 2014b) covers the questions in this area as well: agreements must be in place, the general Italian legislation clearly defines ownership, and the technical issues are regulated in detail only when third parties preserve public data and records. In this case, the AgID policies and guidelines are very strict and all the fundamental aspects are considered in compliance with the OAIS reference model (International Organization for Standardization [ISO], 2012a) and ISO 16363 (International Organization for Standardization [ISO], 2012b). Metadata issues, for interoperability and also for access and privacy, are addressed by the Decree of the President of the Republic December 28, 2000, n. 445 (Italian Government, 2000) and by the Decree of Prime Minister December 3, 2013 (Italian Government, 2014b). Also, the Digital Administration Code (Italian Government, 2005) and the rules dedicated to the creation of electronic records (Italian Government, 2014c) address these issues. Furthermore, a national standard, UNI 11386 (Ente Nazionale Italiano di Unificazione [UNI], 2020). is also in place for ensuring interoperability, even if this standard has too many areas that are not well detailed.
3 Availability, retrieval, and use	The preservation manuals (of digital archives) generally address this area and there is specific obligation for all digital repositories asking for accreditation to meet the requirements included in the checklist. However, in many cases, there is no evidence of their compliance with these requirements.
4 Data storage and preservation	All digital repositories certified as trusted repositories against specific legislation must be compliant with all the relevant standards for security and preservation. Since they must be compliant with the OAIS reference model (ISO, 2012a) and ISO 16363 (ISO, 2012b), all relevant questions related to the authenticity and integrity, and their documentation and evidence, are included in the fundamental requirements the repositories have to meet.

(Continued)

Table 4.1 (Continued)

General area	Findings
5 Data retention and disposition	This area has been regulated by the National Archives with the Circulars n. 40 and n. 41 issued on 14 December 2015 (Ministry of Cultural Heritage, General Directorate of Archives, 2015). In addition, the Decree of the President of the Republic December 28, 2000, n. 445 (Italian Government, 2000) in compliance with general archival legislation, such as the Legislative Decree January 22, 2004, n. 42 *Code of cultural heritage and landscape* (Italian Government, 2002), regulate data retention and disposition issues. Controls are very strict for the public sector.
6 Security, confidentiality, and privacy	All requirements in this area are part of the general obligations of the repositories responsible for keeping public records. However, some specific rules imply the capacity of records creators to be active in controlling and assessing the quality of the service. Unfortunately, many creators (such as the municipalities and local authorities) have no technical capacity for proactive control of these requirements. Section 6.3 (Privacy) is strictly ruled according to Italian and European legislation. A special agency has the task of controlling compliance with the rules. Section 6.4 (Accreditation and auditing) is very well defined with reference to digital records created by public administration (See the circulars and the guidelines adopted by AgID previously mentioned).
7 Data location and cross-border data flows	Currently, as already mentioned, all data must be located in Italy. In the new strategic plan under development, a new rule (not yet clarified) seems to allow for an international data location with the condition that at least "one copy" must be stored in Italy.
8 End of service – contract termination	Legislation explicitly covers this topic, and therefore each specific agreement must address precisely all relevant questions.

because it allows some general conclusions to be drawn. First, the four case studies, although related to different areas and types of services, show the same kind of critical issues: very limited attention is given to the risks of records entrusted in the cloud, for their authenticity and integrity. When standard contracts are in place, the main issues are related to the contractual or commercial aspects and legal restrictions. Technical issues concerning storage systems are also considered from a very limited point of view: data location, security, confidentiality, and privacy are the basic aspects under control. The only exception has been the agreement approved by Emilia Romagna region for its digital preservation service. In that case, the public nature of the function required serious attention to the archival aspects and proved the usefulness of the ITrust checklist.

Conclusion

The research findings demonstrate the need for more focus and more specific and comprehensive effort when setting up cloud services. They also confirm the importance of a common checklist to analyze complex functions such as those necessary to implement cloud-based recordkeeping and digital preservation services. The international nature of the checklist was not a negative aspect – it could be easily applied in the national context – and it "supports the consistency and completeness of controls to be implemented by digital records creators and preservers" (Guercio, 2019, p. 102). Furthermore, the comparison was very fruitful when specifically applied to the recordkeeping and digital preservation environments. In contrast, when it is used for the analysis of contracts not specifically related to these environments or when officers did not pay attention to these aspects in the development of cloud systems and accepted standard contracts without negotiation, the checklist seems difficult to apply. However, in this case, the checklist is useful because it makes clear the risks for the recordkeeping and preservation of digital objects when record managers or archivists are not involved in the decision-making processes.

The legislative framework on cloud computing for electronic recordkeeping and digital preservation is complex and very fragmented. This applies not only to the situation in Italy, as has been explained here, but also to the European situation. A common effort to create a homogeneous regulatory framework specifically dedicated to these aspects should be truly beneficial.

Acknowledgements

A special acknowledgement goes to the members of the European Team who participated in the EU35 study (Allegrezza et al., 2018): Maria Guercio as the Lead Researcher and Gabriele Bezzi, Maria Mata Caravaca, Ilaria Pescini, and Brizio Tommasi who accompanied me as project researchers.

References

AgID (Agency for Digital Italy). (2013). *Caratterizzazione dei sistemi cloud per la pubblica amministrazione* [Characterization of cloud systems for public administration]. Retrieved from https://www.agid.gov.it/sites/default/files/repository_files/linee_guida/sistemi_cloud_pa.pdf

AgID (Agency for Digital Italy). (2014a). *Cloud for Europe Project. Realization of a research and development project (pre-commercial procurement) on "cloud for Europe"*. Retrieved from https://www.agid.gov.it/it/infrastrutture/cloud-pa/cloud-europe

AgID (Agency for Digital Italy). (2014b). *Circolare N. 65 del 10 aprile 2014. Modalità per l'accreditamento e la vigilanza sui soggetti pubblici e privati che svolgono attività di conservazione dei documenti informatici di cui all'articolo 44-bis, comma 1, del decreto legislativo 7 marzo 2005, n. 82* [Circular n. 65/2014 Accreditation of public and private entities that perform electronic documents retention activities on behalf of third parties. Quality and safety requirements for accreditation and supervision and Guidelines for the preservation of electronic documents]. Retrieved from https://www.agid.gov.it/sites/default/files/repository_files/circolari/circolare_accreditamento_conservatori_n_65_10-04-2014.pdf

AgID (Agency for Digital Italy). (2017). *Piano triennale per l'informatica nella Pubblica amministrazione 2017–2019* [Three-Year Plan for ICT in Public Administration 2017–2019]. Retrieved from https://pianotriennale-ict.readthedocs.io/en/latest

Allegrezza, S., Bezzi, G., Guercio, M., Leo, L., Mata Caravaca, M., Monte, M., . . . Tommasi, B. (2016). *Policies for recordkeeping and digital preservation. Recommendations for analysis and assessment services* (EU04). InterPARES Trust. Retrieved from https://interparestrust.org/assets/public/dissemination/EU04_20170330_PoliciesRecordkeepingDigitalPreservation_FinalReport.pdf

Allegrezza, S., Bezzi, G., Guercio, M., Mata Caravaca, M., Pescini, I., & Tommasi, B. (2018). *The impact of the Italian legal framework for cloud computing on electronic recordkeeping and digital preservation system* (EU35). InterPARES Trust. Retrieved from https://interparestrust.org/assets/public/dissemination/EU35_FinalReport2017.pdf

Bushey, J., Demoulin, M., How, E., & McLelland, R. (2016). *Checklist for cloud service contracts* (NA14). InterPARES Trust. Retrieved from https://interparestrust.org/assets/public/dissemination/NA14_20160226_CloudServiceProviderContracts_Checklist_Final.pdf

DigitPA. (2012). *Raccomandazioni e proposte sull'utilizzo del cloud computing nella pubblica amministrazione* [Recommendations and proposals on the use of cloud computing in the public administration]. Retrieved from https://www.agid.gov.it/sites/default/files/repository_files/documenti_indirizzo/raccomandazioni_cloud_e_pa_-_2.0_0.pdf

Duranti, L., & Jansen, A. (2013). The InterPARES Trust Project: Trust and digital records in an increasingly networked society. In A. Gilliland, S. McKemmish, H. Stančić, S. Seljan, & J. Lasić-Lazić (Eds.), *Information governance* (pp. 63–68). Zagreb: Department of Information Sciences, Faculty of Humanities and Social Sciences, University of Zagreb. Retrieved from https://interparestrust.org/assets/public/dissemination/2-03JansenDurantiTheInterPARESTrustProject.pdf

Ente Nazionale Italiano di Unificazione. (2020). *Supporto all'interoperabilità nella conservazione e nel recupero degli oggetti digitali (SInCRO)* (UNI 11386) [Supporting

interoperability in the preservation and retrieval of digital objects (SInCRO)].
Retrieved from http://store.uni.com/catalogo/uni-11386-2020

Fernández, C. (2017). *Records in the cloud*. Retrieved from https://committee.iso.
org/sites/tc46sc11/home/projects/ongoing/records-in-the-cloud.html

Guercio, M. (2019). Role and quality of policies for recordkeeping. In L. Duranti &
C. Rogers (Eds.), *Trusting records in the cloud* (pp. 98–102). London: Facet Publishing.

International Organization for Standardization. (2012a). *Space data and information
transfer systems – Open archival information system (OAIS) – Reference model*
(ISO 14721:2012). Retrieved from https://www.iso.org/standard/57284.html

International Organization for Standardization. (2012b). *Space data and information transfer systems – Audit and certification of trustworthy digital repositories*
(ISO 16363:2012). Retrieved from https://www.iso.org/standard/56510.html

International Organization for Standardization. (2017). *Information and documentation –
Records management in the cloud – Part 1: Issues and concerns* (ISO/CD TR 22428–
1.2). Retrieved from https://www.iso.org/standard/73173.html

Italian Government. (2000). Decreto del Presidente della Repubblica 28 dicembre
2000, n. 445 Testo unico delle disposizioni legislative e regolamentari in materia
di documentazione amministrativa. (Testo A). *GU Serie Generale n.42* del 20–02–
2001 – Suppl. Ordinario n. 30 [Decree of the President of the Republic December
28, 2000, n. 445 Consolidated act of the legislative and regulatory provisions on
administrative documentation]. Retrieved from https://www.gazzettaufficiale.it/
eli/id/2001/02/20/ 001G0049/sg

Italian Government. (2002). Decreto Legislativo 22 gennaio 2004, n. 42 Codice dei
beni culturali e del paesaggio, ai sensi dell'articolo 10 della legge 6 luglio 2002, n.
137. *GU Serie Generale n.45* del 24–02–2004 – Suppl. Ordinario n. 28 [Legislative
decree January 22, 2004, n. 42 Code of cultural heritage and landscape]. Retrieved
from https://www.gazzettaufficiale.it/eli/id/2004/02/24/004G0066/sg

Italian Government. (2005). Decreto Legislativo 7 marzo 2005, n. 82 Codice
dell'amministrazione digitale. *GU Serie Generale n.112* del 16–05–2005 – Suppl.
Ordinario n. 93 [Legislative Decree March 7, 2005, n. 82 Digital Administration
Code]. Retrieved from https://www.gazzettaufficiale.it/eli/id/2005/05/16/005G0
104/sg

Italian Government. (2010). Decreto del Presidente della Repubblica 5 ottobre 2010,
n. 207 Regolamento di esecuzione ed attuazione del decreto legislativo 12 aprile
2006, n. 163, recante "Codice dei contratti pubblici relativi a lavori, servizi e for-
niture in attuazione delle direttive 2004/17/CE e 2004/18/CE". (10G0226). *GU
Serie Generale n.288* del 10–12–2010 – Suppl. Ordinario n. 270 [Decree of the
President of Republic October 5, 2010, n. 207 Regulation for the implementation of the legislative decree 12 April 2006, n. 163, containing 'Code of public
contracts relating to works, services and supplies in implementation of Directives
2004/17/CE and 2004/18/CE']. Retrieved from https://www.gazzettaufficiale.it/
eli/id/2010/12/10/010G0226/sg

Italian Government. (2014a). Decreto del Presidente del Consiglio dei Ministri 3
dicembre 2013 Regole tecniche per il protocollo informatico ai sensi degli articoli 40-bis, 41, 47, 57-bis e 71, del Codice dell'amministrazione digitale di cui
al decreto legislativo n. 82 del 2005. (14A02099). *GU Serie Generale n.59* del
12–03–2014 – Suppl. Ordinario n. 20 [Decree of Prime Minister December 3,
2013 Technical rules for the electronic protocol]. Retrieved from https://www.
gazzettaufficiale.it/eli/id/2014/03/12/14A02099/sg

Italian Government. (2014b). Decreto del Presidente del Consiglio dei Ministri 3 dicembre 2013 Regole tecniche in materia di sistema di conservazione ai sensi degli articoli 20, commi 3 e 5-bis, 23-ter, comma 4, 43, commi 1 e 3, 44, 44-bis e 71, comma 1, del Codice dell'amministrazione digitale di cui al decreto legislativo n. 82 del 2005. (14A02098). *GU Serie Generale n.59* del 12–03–2014 – Suppl. Ordinario n. 20) [Decree of the President of the Council of Ministers 3 December 2013 Technical rules on the preservation system pursuant to articles 20, paragraphs 3 and 5-bis, 23-ter, paragraph 4, 43, paragraphs 1 and 3, 44, 44-bis and 71, paragraph 1, of the Digital Administration Code pursuant to Legislative Decree no. 82 of 2005]. Retrieved from https://www.gazzettaufficiale.it/eli/id/2014/03/12/14A02099/sg

Italian Government. (2014c). Decreto del Presidente del Consiglio dei Ministri 13 novembre 2014 Regole tecniche in materia di formazione, trasmissione, copia, duplicazione, riproduzione e validazione temporale dei documenti informatici nonche' di formazione e conservazione dei documenti informatici delle pubbliche amministrazioni ai sensi degli articoli 20, 22, 23-bis, 23-ter, 40, comma 1, 41, e 71, comma 1, del Codice dell'amministrazione digitale di cui al decreto legislativo n. 82 del 2005. (15A00107). *GU Serie Generale n.8* del 12–01–2015 [Decree of Prime Minister November 13, 2014 Technical rules on creation, transmission, copying, duplication, reproduction and validation of electronic documents as well as creation and preservation of electronic documents from public administrations]. Retrieved from https://www.gazzettaufficiale.it/eli/id/2015/01/12/15A00107/sg

ITrust. (2016). Checklist for cloud service contracts. Retrieved from https://interpares trust.org/assets/public/dissemination/NA14_20160226_CloudServiceProvider Contracts_Checklist_Final.pdf

Ministry of Cultural Heritage, General Directorate of Archives. (2015). Circulars n. 40 and n. 41 on the "destruction of original analogue documents reproduced and preserved according to the technical rules". Retrieved from http://media.regesta. com/dm_0/ANAI/anaiCMS//ANAI/000/1186/ANAI.000.1186.0012.pdf and http:// www.sa-fvg.archivi.beniculturali.it/fileadmin/normativa/circolare_DGA_n._41_ del_2015__distruzione_docc._analogici_.pdf

5 Information governance

Nature and maturity practices in EU public administrations

Basma Makhlouf Shabou with Sandrine Anderfuhren and Elizabeth Lomas

Introduction

Information governance (IG) is defined in a range of ways often dependent upon discipline perspectives (Lomas, 2010; Makhlouf Shabou, 2019). Recognized as an alternative to simple document management, IG is sometimes defined as a subset of corporate governance.

However, there is essentially agreement that it represents a multidimensional approach that draws together strategic management, information and records management, compliance (regulations, standards, e-discovery, etc.), information security, ICT, and ethics (Lomas, Makhlouf Shabou, & Grazhenskaya, 2019). It includes other functions such as content management, information asset valuation, data protection, risk management, litigation preparation, long term digital preservation, and even business intelligence (Franks, 2012; Gartner Inc., n.d.; National Archives of Australia, 2017; Smallwood, 2014). IG is dependent upon a number of dimensions covering management, archival, juridical, ethical, economic, technical, and technological facets related to different data, information, records, and archives processing during the various phases of their life. In addition, information assets must be optimized to ensure realization of strategic and operational corporate goals including delivery across society. This chapter seeks to

1   identify the main dimensions that compose and distinguish IG as described in academic studies and professional practice
2   explore IG practices and best practices in a French public administration context
3   profile the development of IG practices in UK public administration
4   profile the IG practices and best practices in European public administration; specifically, Geneva's public administration.

The chapter offers conclusions for consideration when developing IG frameworks and assessing maturity levels for public entities.

IG: dimensions and nature in the context of public entities

Particularities of public entities

Within the EU context, national setups for public administration differ somewhat in their structures. Broadly speaking, there are national and regional administrative structures with some semi-public structures. Across Europe, rights to access the documents of public administrations have been developing over several decades. Access involves a number of challenges and costs for public administrations. They need to guarantee the findability, availability, and sustainability of data, in conjunction with ensuring that trusted information is then delivered. Citizens' expectations around transparency have grown, with open data movements pushing towards open government.

Access rights must be weighed in conjunction with other considerations such as security and privacy. These concerns dominate global debates. The latter has significantly evolved in the EU context, with the 2016 EU General Data Protection Regulation (2016) mandating high standards of personal data management and security. In addition, the need to establish an effective accountability chain underpins this public need. Citizens' trust is a key information deliverable for a public administration, both in terms of protecting citizen data and providing trusted information content. In a social media context, this is contested ground. For example, Twitter and Facebook have taken different stances on engagement with political advertising, which is under scrutiny because of hostile influence on democratic processes.

An overview of previous studies and frameworks

At the academic level, several universities have developed IG courses (University of Applied Sciences and Arts Western Switzerland, Geneva School of Business, Switzerland; Northumbria University, UK; University of British Colombia, Canada; University College London, UK, etc.) to address a need for explicit IG competencies in professional and continuing education opportunities. These initiatives are delivering education which reunite professional domains including archivists, cyber security specialists, data analysts, digital curators, forensic scientists, IT specialists, librarians, and records managers. IG requires that there be a wide set of skills underpinning information delivery and security. In addition to providing education, various IG research initiatives have been conducted to better develop an understanding of this field and its needs.

Illustrative European IG initiatives

At the national level, Swedish researchers studied the articulation of how to develop an IG operational model. In a recent study, they examine the integrated IG model including records management principles, enterprise architecture (EA) with an agile-based method and the user experience design (Sundqvist, Sahlén, & Andreasen, 2019).

In the Belgian context, the interdisciplinary project HECTOR aimed to model the organisation, transformation, and preservation of hybrid documents and files (paper and digital) in the Belgian federal administrations (Maroye et al., 2016; State Archives of Belgium, n.d.; Trends Public Sector, 2018).

Wider than national perimeters, the European project E-ARK was conducted through collaboration between several public European stakeholders. Its overall goal was to harmonize archival processes at the pan-European level to keep digital records authentic and usable (E-ARK Project, 2017).

IG practices and best practices in the French public administrations context

In France, the IG domain is growing. Serda Group initiated an annual study to profile the IG practices maturity in public and private entities. The *8th Annual Report* (Serda, 2019) reveals relevant findings on major developments in information practices in this regard. Conducted among 410 organizations in France, this survey confirms that interest in IG is growing and that the main issue of digital information management is access to information resources and knowledge of the organization. A significant 85% of participants from the public sector prioritized data access and knowledge sharing control as key concerns. In contrast, the main obstacle was the lack of commitment of the public entities in this respect. The lack of knowledge of this domain was further mentioned. Around 55% of participants stated that managers are not sensitized to IG issues, around 50% think they lack knowledge on methodologies, and around 47% claim the managers under-estimate potential risks that could arise in the absence of an established corporate IG approach.

Other initiatives have been proposed in French public administration. More specifically, three relevant tools were proposed to help public administrations systematically and securely manage their data (Naud, 2019)

- *Octave*, which allows the archivist, after import, to process and manually modify file tree structures (deduplication, selection, deletion, merging, classification, renaming) (France Archives, 2020)
- *Archifiltre*, a tool for appraising structured data on the basis of a visualized file plan (Digital Factory of Social Ministries, 2020)
- *Vitam*, which allows building and manipulation of archival tree structures and editing of metadata, has import (SIP) and export capabilities (as disk hierarchy or in CSV form for file plans), and can process office files or mail containers (Programme Vitam, 2020).

However, in the French context, the multidimensional IG vision is still missing. The policy is not articulated clearly to make sure that all services, such as the tools mentioned previously, are well synchronised. The public admin-istrations are, however, more sensitized to invest in such approaches.

IG practices and best practice in UK public administration

In 1984, the UK enacted data protection legislation to protect and provide personal information rights for digital data. In 1995, KPMG, working from London, published a report which fore-fronted the place of information as an asset thus changing corporate and public sector perceptions on the place of information in strategic planning (KPMG, 1995). Recognition of infor-mation as an asset assisted in raising the responsibility for its protection to the board level. In the same year, the EU's Data Protection Directive required the EU member states to implement national legislation to protect personal data (Directive 95/46/EC, 1995). Thus, the UK developed and refined the legal requirements for managing personal data. In addition, the British Stan-dard on information security (BS7799), now ISO/IEC 27000 (International Organization for Standardization [ISO], 2018), was published.

Compared to many nations, the UK was slow to provide legislation to enable access to public sector information. The Public Records Act (1958) did provide for the protection of public documentation, but access was nor-mally delayed for 30 years. In 2000, new access legislation was enacted (the Freedom of Information Act 2000), and this changed the balance of power between citizen and state in terms of information management. The legislation required public sector organisations to have publication schemes showing their structures in terms of creation of information to establish records management programmes, under a Records Management Code of Practice (Lord Chancellor, 2009), and to provide timely access to informa-tion requested, subject to any exemptions.

Parallel to enactment of the UK freedom of information laws, the EU developed requirements for providing access to environmental information. The requirements extended the reach of access, not only to public entities but also to the third parties delivering public functions. It is to be noted that in the last 20 years, the UK has changed the divisions between public and private delivery with the development of public-private initiatives (PPIs). Within this context, there has been a public expectation for certain citizen accountability.

In 2010, Lomas (2010) published an article with a UK lens that made the case for information security and records management to work together under the IG umbrella. The most overt UK recognition of the value of multi-disciplinary IG frameworks has and continues to be within the frameworks in place to support the UK's National Health Service (NHS). The NHS was quick to adopt the concept of IG and to develop and deliver an Informa-tion Governance Toolkit in 2003 bringing together compliance requirements from across the health and social care sectors (National Health Service – Department of Health, 2017); it was replaced with a Data Security and

Protection Toolkit in 2018 (NHS Digital, 2018). Lessons learned from this model have been cascaded across national and local governments, with many regions developing IG framework documentation.

Across the UK, there has been an increasing push for openness. The Open Government Partnership has been pushing this agenda framed by an Open Government Manifesto (Open Government Partnership (2019). It considers not only access rights, but new implications for ownership as well. Within the UK, a University College London (2019)-led project entitled MIRRA (Memory-Identity-Rights in Records-Access) has been pushing for new standards for access to records for all care-experienced persons who participated in the creation and ownership of their records through time. As a result of these concerns, ethical considerations implicit in an IG framework are increasingly discussed in terms of balancing organisational and societal concerns.

More generally, there is work on reusing and gaining value from data through time. This relies on IG frameworks to ensure data quality, but in addition to consider the rights and risks to those whose data may be harvested. Initiatives have been developed in this context to manage the issues; for example, the Local Government Association has considered data quality rights and usage in the context of data lakes developed by public administrations (Local Government Association, 2019).

Information and data as assets are now well recognised in the UK with the complex dynamics of citizen delivery and public responsibilities at the fore. Practical tools for identifying and managing information assets properly, such as information asset registers, have been shared (The National Archives, 2017). While not uniformly in place, IG represents a key framework tool to ensure this delivery.

IG research in ITrust

The ITrust project's Team Europe initiated two relevant studies in the field of IG. The first one focused on how to develop an IG policy and the second proposed a model, a method, and a tool for IG maturity assessment to apply in European public administration contexts.

IG policy as a main corporate guide: from vision to operations

The study initiated by Makhlouf Shabou and conducted between 2014 and 2016 aimed at developing an IG policy model (Makhlouf Shabou, 2019). This study analyzed a sample of 13 policies, from different types of institutions (universities and medical, state, and para-state institutions) originating from various countries and continents (America, Europe, and Oceania). It checked 19 indicators divided into four categories: content, format (style, content density, and level of detail), communication (language and mode of spreading, level of visibility), and validation (date of creation and entry into force, validating and review authority, frequency of revisions). This analysis was used as the method of validation of a policy model, which aimed to serve as a template for professionals to develop IG policies adapted to their own organizational context. However, the study determined that having a policy is not an end in itself, and that it does not mean the end of investment in IG.

Maturity model as a key tool for developing and managing IG in a public corporate context

A study conducted between 2016 and 2018 by Makhlouf Shabou and Lomas focused on researching IG within European public administrations and proposed a maturity model (Makhlouf Shabou, Guercio, Katuu, Lomas, & Grazhenskaya, 2019; Makhlouf Shabou & Lomas, 2019). The resulting model includes five levels of maturity and ten dimensions: 1) responsibilities and roles; 2) stakeholder engagement; 3) framework and policy, including risk management; 4) information asset identification, creation, and ownership; 5) information value, quality, and delivery; 6) rights management; 7) records management; 8) information security and resilience; 9) long term preservation; and 10) monitoring and change management. The evaluation criteria relate to people (e.g. leadership, professional expertise, citizen inclusion, etc.), system (e.g. framework design, process development, software and tools, buildings and infrastructures, training, etc.), and ethics (e.g. laws, regulations, directives, standards, obligations, etc.). The assessment performed by the maturity model provides "a clear overview of the corporate information landscape and an accurate characterization of weaknesses and main gaps to be addressed" (Makhlouf Shabou et al., 2019, pp. 106–107) when considering developing an IG.

IG practices and best practices of Swiss public administrations: the case of the canton of Geneva

Context

Another recent project conducted in Switzerland studied the maturity level of IG practices in public administrations (Anderfuhren & Romagnoli, 2018). The case of the canton of Geneva is presented here in more detail. Switzerland, although integrating notions of IG at the federal level – for example the eCH standards in the eGovernment (Association eCH, n.d.) – has the peculiarity of having a great deal of operational independence at the cantonal level, particularly in the field of information management. Although Geneva is no different, as a canton it operates according to two administrative levels – the cantonal and the communal.

At the cantonal level, information management is shared between the eight cantonal departments, all of which operate in an independent manner.

Therefore, everyone has their own information professional. At the communal level, each municipality is also independent of each other. However, document management is rarely entrusted to a professional. It is often managed by the municipal employees, who do not have appropriate training. Moreover, it is important to note that Geneva is at the same time a canton and a city – the administrative organisation of the city resembles that of the canton, with its six departments, each of which has its own information officer/archivist.

Objectives

The purpose of this work was to understand how IG is defined and implemented within Geneva's public administrations. In addition, it reflected on how to better integrate IG to improve the performance of services. More specifically, we: 1) profiled the existing gaps between information management as presented in the literature and as it is experienced in professional practice; 2) proposed a definition of an IG approach for public administration; and 3) proposed a framework to be applied in European public administrations.

Methodology

In order to measure and compare the gap between governance presented in the literature and that experienced by professionals, we adopted a comparative analytical approach: we focused on content analysis, both deductive and inductive. We selected two type of sources: the documentary sources, which represented our theoretical corpus, and the testimony of the information professionals, which covered the practical dimensions. Then we established two collection tools: a reading grid containing our documentary references, and a semi-structured interview guide to collect testimonials of the participants (Figure 5.1).

In order to establish the sample, the target population was defined. It consisted of information professionals active in Geneva public administration,

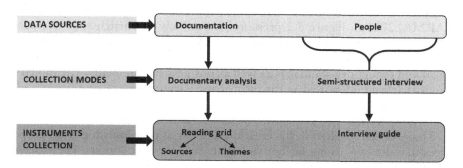

Figure 5.1 Data collection schema

Source: Anderfuhren and Romagnoli (2018, p. 3)

i.e. the archivists. This profile was selected because the archivists plays a strategic role in the IG of organisations. The research was based on the degree of expertise and business skills in the field of information. Only the professionals with a background in information sciences were kept in the final sample. The content analysis of the interviews was undertaken using the NVivo (QSR International, 2020) software.

Results: IG perception and practices as reported by information managers and archivists in public administration in Geneva

The canton of Geneva has two administrative levels: the cantonal level and the municipal level. The perception of what IG represents is not the same at both levels. For cantonal archivists, the emphasis was on the accessibility of information, while governance meant bringing together all the dimensions of an administration as part of a global vision. In their view, it has the elements of ethics and values, reflecting a positive image of the state to the public. For municipal archivists, IG makes it possible to overcome the silos between the different services. Despite these differences, the participants agreed on many points, including the obstacles to the implementation of IG and the risks if it is badly implemented.

The most significant obstacle was employee resistance, as they perceived IG as an attempt to control their actions. The participants observed a refusal on the part of employees to share information with other departments, as there was a consensus that this might result in losing control of skills and essentially a vulnerability, i.e. a pathway to redundancy. This is where the presence of the archivist is necessary because s/he complements development of the skills of each person, which enables them to be involved and provides value. Among the identified risks were the loss of information, the excessively long response times, the lack of traceability of information, and the unauthorised destruction of documents.

During each interview, the participants were asked to self-assess the maturity of their practices according to the ARMA model's five levels of development (substandard, in development, essential, proactive, transformational) (ARMA, 2019a). Figure 5.2 presents an overview of participants' average assessed maturity level for each of the ARMA principles (ARMA, 2019b). The most attributed level was the third – essential – which aligns to meeting legal and regulatory standards as well as business requirements. The dimensions that were identified as the most mature were those of protection and conservation. This is explained by the fact that mandatory laws and regulations govern these two principles, which leaves little freedom in practice.

The research resulted in the creation of a list of proposals for good practices that are easy to implement and adapt to different contexts. They focus mainly on the human and collaborative aspects, because the most resistance was found in these two aspects. In this vein, we strongly recommend considering the following actions

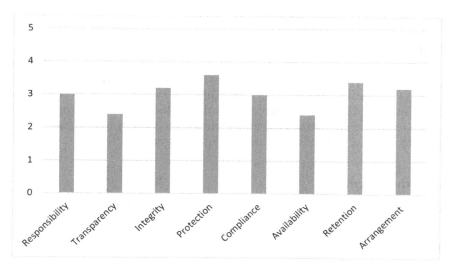

Figure 5.2 Average maturity level for each of the ARMA principles for all participants

- recognize information as a resource
- value information management activity, and to recognize it as useful work that requires specific skills
- involve each stakeholder in the process
- improve transparency and availability of information
- document all your actions
- control access to information
- think as a team, for the team
- analyze the information needs of each department
- go step by step, process by process
- communicate and disclose the governance programme based on feedback and exchanges with other administrations that have undertaken comparable projects
- establish collaborations with other organisations using IG approaches and tools to join a helpful network.

Conclusion

In democratic societies, it is essential that public administrations respond to their main mission, delivering robust and transparent public services that ensure every citizen has the right to reliable, available, protected, and trusted information. Perhaps more so than parts of the private sector, there is a focus on building processes for scrutiny. In addition to improving services and efficiency, public administrations must understand and consider data and information quality as an asset. This requires a range of processes to ensure data quality and respect of citizen data rights.

IG contributes to the continuous search for service improvement and quality. It is a valuable set of mechanisms (principles, tools, processes, and systems) for understanding where services stand in their information practices, as well as a powerful tool for decision-makers. Recently, the ISO TC/46 Committee launched work on a new ISO standard on IG principles and concepts. This initiative recognizes the multidimensional nature of IG approaches and emphasizes the ethical dimension and its importance in the production, use, and reuse of data and information.

Acknowledgements

Many thanks to Aurèle Nicolet for editing help and support.

References

Anderfuhren, S., & Romagnoli, P. (2018). *La maturité de la gouvernance de l'information dans les administrations publiques européennes: la perception de la gouvernance de l'information dans l'administration publique genevoise* [Maturity of information governance in European public administrations: Perception of information governance in Geneva public administration]. Delémont: University of Applied Sciences and Arts Western Switzerland. Retrieved from http://doc.rero.ch/record/323127?ln=fr

ARMA. (2019a). *IG maturity model.* Retrieved from https://www.arma.org/page/PrinciplesMaturityModel

ARMA. (2019b). *The principles (Generally Accepted Recordkeeping Principles).* Retrieved from https://www.arma.org/page/principles

Association eCH. (n.d.). *eCH: e-government standards.* Retrieved from http://www.ech.ch/index.php/fr

Digital Factory of Social Ministries. (2020). *Archifiltre (V 2.1.1)* [App]. Retrieved from https://archifiltre.fabrique.social.gouv.fr/

Directive 95/46/EC of the European Parliament and of the Council of 24 October 1995 on the protection of individuals with regard to the processing of personal data and on the free movement of such data (1995). *OJ L 281,* 23.11.1995, pp. 31–50. Retrieved from https://eur-lex.europa.eu/eli/dir/1995/46/oj

E-ARK Project. (2017). *Summary of activities, Year 3, 1 February 2016–31 January 2017.* Retrieved from https://eark-project.com/resources/annual-summaries/100-annual-project-summary-year-3/E-ARK%20Summary%20Year%203.pdf_%3b%20filename_%3dUTF-8%27%27E-ARK%2520Summary%2520Year%25203.pdf

France Archives. (2020). *Octave (V5.3.0).* [Digital archiving software]. Retrieved from https://francearchives.fr/fr/article/88482499

Franks, P. (2012). Disruptive technologies: Governing them for e-discovery. *Information Management Journal, 46*(4), Hot Topic insert.

Freedom of Information Act 2000. UK Public General Acts. 2000 c. 36. Retrieved from https://www.legislation.gov.uk/ukpga/2000/36/contents/enacted

Gartner Inc. (n.d.). *Information governance.* Retrieved from https://www.gartner. com/it-glossary/information-governance/

General Data Protection Regulation (GDPR), EU 2016/679 (2016).

International Organization for Standardization. (2018). *Information technology – Security techniques – Information security management systems – Overview and vocabulary* (ISO/IEC 27000:2018). Retrieved from https://www.iso.org/obp/ui/#iso: std:iso-iec:27000:ed-5:v1:en

KPMG. (1995). *Hawley Committee: Information as an asset – Checklist and explanatory notes.* London: KPMG.

Local Government Association. (2019). *Better use of data.* Retrieved from http:// www.local.gov.uk/our-support/guidance-and-resources/data-and-transparency/ better-use-data

Lomas, E. (2010). Information governance: Information security and access within a UK context. *Records Management Journal, 20,* 182–198. https://doi.org/10.1108/ 09565691011064322

Lomas, E., Makhlouf Shabou, B., & Grazhenskaya, A. (2019). Guest editorial. *Records Management Journal, 29,* 2–4. https://doi.org/10.1108/RMJ-03-2019-048

Lord Chancellor. (2009). *Lord Chancellor's Code of Practice on the management of records issued under section 46 of the Freedom of Information Act 2000.* London: Ministry of Justice & the National Archives. Retrieved from https://ico.org.uk/ media/for-organisations/research-and-reports/1432475/foi-section-46-code-of-practice-1.pdf

Makhlouf Shabou, B. (2019). An information governance policy is required for my institution, what to do? Practical method and tool enabling efficient management for corporate information assets. In S. Katuu (Ed.), *Diverse applications and transferability of maturity models* (pp. 61–91). IGI Global. http://doi.org/10.4018/978-1-5225-7080-6.ch003

Makhlouf Shabou, B., Guercio, M., Katuu, S., Lomas, E., & Grazhenskaya, A. (2019). Strategies, methods and tools enabling records governance in a cloud environment. In L. Duranti & C. Rogers (Eds.), *Trusting records in the cloud* (pp. 97–116). London: Facet Publishing.

Makhlouf Shabou, B., & Lomas, E. (2019, June). *Un modèle de maturité à l'appui d'une gouvernance informationnelle au sein des organismes publics* [Maturity model in support of information governance within public bodies]. Paper presented at 48th Conference of the Association of Quebec Archivists, Gatineau. Retrieved from http://congres.archivistes.qc.ca/wp-content/uploads/2019/07/V7A_MakhloufShabou_ Lomas.pdf

Maroye, L., Aranguren Celorrio, F., Demoulin, M., De Terwangne, C., Losdyck, B., Soyez, S., Van Hooland, S., & Vanreck, O. (2016). La gestion hybride des documents au sein des administrations fédérales belges sous la loupe du projet de recherche "Hector" [Hybrid document management in Belgian federal administrations under the looking glass of the "Hector" research project]. *Pyramides, 26/27,* 215–230. Retrieved from http://journals.openedition.org/pyramides/1005

The National Archives. (2017). *What is an information asset register?* Retrieved from https://www.nationalarchives.gov.uk/documents/information-management/ info-asset-register-factsheet.pdf

National Archives of Australia. (2017). *Information governance.* Retrieved from https://www.naa.gov.au/information-management/information-governance/

National Health Service – Department of Health. (2017). *Information governance toolkit.* Retrieved from https://web.archive.org/web/20171030112808/http://www.igt.hscic.gov.uk/

Naud, D. (2019, September 30). Trois outils contribuant à l'archivage numérique [Three tools contributing to digital archiving]. *Modernisation et archives.* Retrieved from https://siaf.hypotheses.org/1033

NHS Digital. (2018). *Data security and protection toolkit.* Retrieved from https://www.dsptoolkit.nhs.uk/

Open Government Partnership. (2019). *UK open government manifesto.* Retrieved from https://www.opengovpartnership.org/tag/uk-open-government-manifesto/

Programme Vitam. (2020). *Vitam (V 3)* [Digital archiving software]. Retrieved from http://www.programmevitam.fr/pages/presentation/pres_archivistes/

Public Records Act, Chapter 51 (1958).

QSR International. (2020). *NVivo (V 12)* [Qualitative data analysis software]. https://www.qsrinternational.com/nvivo-qualitative-data-analysis-software/home

Serda. (2019, April). *La gouvernance de l'information numérique dans les organisations. Le temps de la déclinaison opérationnelle* [Governance of digital information in organizations. The time of operational variation]. Paris: Serda Groupe. Retrieved from http://www.serda.com/content/rapport-annuel-gouvernance-2019

Smallwood, R. F. (2014). *Information governance: Concepts, strategies, and best practices.* Hoboken, NJ: Wiley.

State Archives of Belgium. (n.d.). *Hector: Hybrid electronic curation, transformation and organization of records.* Retrieved from http://arch.arch.be/index.php?l=fr&m=nos-projets&pr=hector-hybrid-electronic-curation-transformation-and-organization-of-records

Sundqvist, A., Sahlén, T., & Andreasen, M. (2019). The intermesh of records management principles and enterprise architecture: A framework for information governance in the Swedish context. In P. Bago et al. (Eds.), *Knowledge in the digital age* (pp. 75–85). Zagreb: Department of Information and Communication Sciences, Faculty of Humanities and Social Sciences, University of Zagreb. Retrieved from https://infoz.ffzg.hr/INFuture/images/papers/INFuture%202019%20Proceedings.pdf

Trends Public Sector. (2018). HECTOR gère la numérisation de l'administration [HECTOR manages the digitization of the administration]. *Trends Public Sector,* 26. Retrieved from http://actions.trends.levif.be/actions/trends/publicsector/archive/2018-03/sourcedinspiration.jsp

University College London. (2019). *MIRRA: Memory – Identity – Rights in records – Access.* Retrieved from https://blogs.ucl.ac.uk/mirra/

6 Governmental e-services

Lluís-Esteve Casellas with Hrvoje Stančić

Introduction

The use and development of information technologies applied to the provision of public services are the basis of what we call e-government. The main objective of e-government is to enhance the interaction with citizens, businesses, and industry, and among public administrations, thereby improving their relationships through the simplification of processes and administrative burdens. At the same time, it also promotes greater transparency of government actions and increased citizen participation, thus contributing to the improvement and democratic strengthening of society. In this sense, electronic services (e-services) become a cornerstone of e-government as an enabler of the transformation of the public sector.

Over the last two decades, the EU has promoted the digital transformation of the public sector and, specifically, e-services in several action plans. The objectives of the last 10 years have focused on avoiding a digital divide with citizens, seeking efficiency, making a high impact on key services for citizens and businesses, making key enablers of transformation available, and promoting participation in the processes of decision-making. More recently, the focus has been on achieving a true digital single market by eliminating digital barriers across borders. Nevertheless, success must necessarily be based on the implementation of information governance principles and reliable e-services which are easily accessible, have high user satisfaction, are transparent, facilitate accountability, and reduce administrative burden. At the same time, they should be provided in an adequate, secure, interoperable way and guarantee authenticated access to the whole of Europe. This means enabling security, quality, efficiency, access to information, and, above all, trust in the provision and use of these e-services while also promoting them as a possibility of interacting at distance and also at different levels with public administration. This chapter discusses methods for evaluating these services based on two case studies of the ITrust project addressing the European context.

The e-services for citizens or G2C (Government-to-Citizens) and business or G2B (Government-to-Business) are the focus of the first case study (Stančić et al., 2015a). In order to compare these e-services, the situation in selected European countries was investigated. The aim was to study all aspects that could be important for their implementation as trusted e-services (e.g. technology requirements, data and metadata models, years in operation, brief history, etc.). Furthermore, the degree to which e-services accomplished what they had promised was evaluated.

The second phase of this study (Stančić et al., 2015b) focused on the analysis of the interoperability possibilities of governmental e-services implemented in the EU, taking into account aspects that are important for establishing trusted e-services. This is further discussed in the following chapter.

In contrast, the case study of Girona City Council (Casellas, Oliveras, & Reixach, 2019) focuses exclusively on the aspect of trust in the public sector e-services in Catalonia and Spain, viewed from the perspective of records management and preservation of authenticity of digital records.

Comparative analysis of implemented governmental e-services in the EU

Research methodology

As mentioned, the objective of the study was to evaluate whether the users can trust e-services. The analysis collected information in relation to whether users could consider the e-service as responsible, reliable, accurate, secure, and transparent. In parallel, aspects related to the privacy of the data, duties to remember (i.e. digital preservation), and the right to be forgotten (i.e. safe deletion) were also considered. The results of the study can be useful to design and implement better services, or to improve existing ones. The assessment form was transformed into a checklist (see Appendix 1) which can be used as a method of assessment of public e-services by users, or as a method of self-assessment by e-service creators.

Review of relevant literature and online resources enabled the number of countries involved in the analysis to be narrowed down. However, the availability of online information on e-services was essential for their selection. The research focused on eight European countries: Belgium, Croatia, Denmark, Estonia, Germany, Lithuania, Sweden, and the UK. The e-services analyzed were those from the "representative basket of 20 services" (European Commission, 2010, p. 250), divided into two sections – 12 e-services offered to citizens, and eight e-services aimed at businesses (Table 6.1).

The assessment form consisted of 52 questions divided into six categories:

1   basic service information
2   users
3   business optimization
4   technological solutions
5   storage and long term availability
6   system operation transparency.

Table 6.1 Representative basket of 20 e-services

e-Services for Citizens	e-Services for Businesses
1 Income taxes	1 Social contribution for employees
2 Job search	2 Corporate tax
3 Social security benefits	3 VAT (Value Added Tax)
4 Personal documents	4 Registration of a new company
5 Car registration	5 Submission of data to the statistical
6 Application for building permission	office
7 Declarations to the police	6 Customs declaration
8 Public libraries	7 Environment-related permits
9 Birth and marriage certificates	8 Public procurement
10 Enrolment in higher education	
11 Announcement of moving	
12 Health-related services	

Table 6.2 E-services maturity model showing the research cut-off point

Maturity level	Level	Description
0	No information available	Information is not available online, or the service provider does not have a webpage.
1	Information	Only information about the service is available online (e.g. description of a procedure).
2	One-way interaction	Downloadable forms available online. Empty forms can be filled in using computer or can be printed.
3	Two-way interaction	Forms can be filled in online for which authentication is needed. By submitting online form, a service is initiated.
4	Transaction	A complete service is available online – fillable online forms, authentication, payment, delivery, or other types of complete services.
5	Iteration	Iterative services (e.g. obligatory statistical reporting) which are automatically initiated and create automatic reports on a service being completed.

However, given the high volume of potential responses (8 countries × 20 services × 52 questions = 8,320 responses), questions about the level of computerization was set as a key delimiting question in accordance with the used maturity model: from the value 0 (information not available) to 5 (iterative service) (European Commission, 2010, p. 244), where level 2 (one-way interaction) was used as the cut-off point (Table 6.2).

Findings

The research results are presented according to the six investigated categories.

1   basic service information

- all e-services have been created in the last 15 years, but an early implementation does not necessarily mean higher level of maturity
- information about the level of computerisation is not always offered, or not so that it can be automatically translated into English (e.g. content embedded in Flash)
- the same e-service can offer different levels of maturity depending on the type of transaction, which makes it difficult to determine the level of computerisation.

2   users

- the e-services are used both for external and internal users
- only five cases of mandatory e-services were detected: three for citizens (social security benefits in Sweden, building permission and health-related services in Estonia), and two for businesses (social contribution for employees in Belgium and Croatia)
- materials for users with disabilities were available in 67% of the services.

3   business optimization

- public availability of financial indicators about e-services is extremely scarce
- some e-services report benefits to users (e.g. reduction of process time, or increase in performance), but institutions do not publish information about possible internal reorganisations because of their implementation (e.g. reduction of departments, decreasing the number of employees, etc.).

4   technological solutions

- all e-services require some kind of user authentication
- communications are encrypted in most cases
- the most commonly used signature format is XML Advanced Electronic Signature (XAdES)
- web forms are the usual way of communication and sometimes allow attachments to be added
- there was no information about the kind of technological solution being used (open-source or commercial)
- only in one case does the same institution host the e-service
- no information was found about the use of cloud solutions or if the servers were located in other countries
- only three e-services included reference to ISO 27001 (information security).

5   storage and long term availability

- retention periods vary according to the kind of information, the institution, and the legal requirements, in some cases up to 30 years
- seven e-services reported that data is deleted at the end of the retention period
- the use of long term preservation formats was declared in only one case
- in specific cases, printing transactions on paper is required for personal documents or sensitive data, and the digital form of the information is subsequently destroyed
- no information was found about the use of long term preservation standards or secure digital archiving services
- in 19 services, the institutions provided information on where the data was stored, although only four cases were referring to cloud solutions.

6   system operation transparency

- less than 50% of G2C e-services have online policies, while almost 80% of G2B have them. Particularly noteworthy are policies in the UK regarding the use of personal data limited to the purpose of the e-service
- information about non-disclosure measurements is only available in health-related services
- in general, users can access their data and ask for its correction, but they cannot correct it directly themselves
- about 50% of G2C e-services allow application status tracking, while it is available for most G2B e-services.

Discussion

First, it is necessary to point out the lack of standardized information for conducting comparative analyses like these, at least based on information available online. This is even more complex if one wants to evaluate the level of trust e-services are offering to the users. In this sense, the fact that most of the analyzed e-services are not mandatory and that they coexist with their analogue counterparts could suggest that there is not enough critical mass of users. That may be the reason for the lack of information about these e-services. Therefore, the facts whether a service is obligatory or not, and whether it has achieved critical mass of users or not, should also influence assessment of the implementation success of e-services in the organisations. Having enough relevant information about e-services is undoubtedly of public interest. Their availability could support efficiency of e-services and increase transparency.

In general, the details regarding the information security of the e-services are scarce, and with few references to national or international standards.

Lack of publicly available information on the existence of contingency plans and plans for long term continuity should be noted. This is even more serious in relation to the requirements and processes related to long term preservation or to retention and disposition of information linked to these services.

Finally, based on the research results, it seems that citizens are in a worse position than businesses regarding the (non)availability of information referring to the purpose of data collection. Lack of availability of relevant information about the e-services' operations, at the time of this study, is worrying. Also, introduction of the General Data Protection Regulation (2016) did not motivate e-services to provide more precise information.

E-services between public administrations (G2G): case study of Girona City Council

Research methodology

In the framework of an open digital environment, trust is indispensable. While discussion so far has focused on G2C e-services, here the focus is on e-services between public administrations, i.e. G2G e-services. The objective was to analyze the degree of trust given to services and the authenticity of documents generated or used by them. The analysis aimed at getting the perspective of a municipal administration, here Girona City Council, and, more specifically, from the point of view of records management. The results are being used for implementing internal improvements and trying to influence public e-service providers for better quality e-services. Based on the results, recommendations for planning and designing e-services between public administrations are defined (see Appendix 2).

From the municipal viewpoint, a Catalan city council may have to use e-services from different levels of public administration: the state, the regional government and the provincial government. Additionally, in the case of Catalonia, there is the Consortium of Open Administration of Catalonia (Consorci Administració Oberta de Catalunya, AOC). This consortium consists of different public administrations of Catalonia and its aim is to enable e-government for all Catalan public administrations by the implementation of e-services. One of the most important roles is the intermediation function to facilitate interoperability between any public entity in Catalonia or in Spain. In this sense, the benefit for the municipalities is clear: integration with AOC (*1:1*) simplifies communication and avoids multilateral integration of services with different providers (*n:m*).

On the other hand, there has been a significant increase in e-services since the approval of several legal changes. The key moment was 1 October 2016, when the entire public sector was required to become digital and when the *once-only* principle was introduced. This principle, promoted by the EU and included in the EU eGovernment Action Plan 2016–2020 (European Commission, 2016), allows citizens and companies to provide their information to the public administration once, thus reducing administrative burdens and facilitating digital single market. However, from the records management perspective, the situation is not ideal since no state law requires having a records management system implemented. Until now, regional governments have assumed their regulation solely and unequally (see Chapter 3), and only the Catalan law on archives and records management (2001) established records management as mandatory, although with a limited success (Casellas, 2013). Thus, it can be concluded that digital transformation is not always supported by records management systems.

The research in this study was structured in five phases

1 identification of the services to be evaluated
2 assessment of trust in e-services
3 identification of services that could affect principles of the records management system of the City Council
4 assessment of critical factors related to the authenticity of records
5 proposal for improvements and recommendations.

Previously, an e-service was defined as any technological resource (infrastructure or application) that facilitates access to platforms of business management, information exchange, data interoperability or data validation, and verification. In a more extended meaning, it also covers the provisions of any service to citizens. Under this premise, the first task was to identify the e-services that Girona City Council and municipalities had to use. The analysis focused on the online catalogue of services of the two main public providers: the state and the AOC. In accordance with the criteria for the development of e-government in Catalonia, the AOC provides all e-services between public administrations in Catalonia, but a first revision revealed that both the Catalan and provincial governments did offer some e-services of their own. Therefore, the 89 e-services identified in the two unique catalogues available online, based on their own classifications, were

- Spanish government (59 e-services)

  - e-government and services to citizens (47, grouped in 11 sections)
  - internal management (7)
  - infrastructures (5).

- AOC Consortium (30 e-services)

  - relations with citizens (10)
  - internal management (7)
  - relations between public administrations (5)
  - identity and electronic signature (8).

The trust in e-services was evaluated taking into account basic requirements for private providers defined in the ITrust's case study *Cloud Service Provider*

Contracts (Bushey, Demoulin, How, & McLelland, 2016, 2018). Although the checklist was intended for private providers, the level of requirements for public sector must be at least the same (see also Chapter 4). For public administrations, the analysis focused on published information about e-services' policies and the records of the City Council related to the formalisation of service level agreements. The following aspects were analyzed

- service agreement: legal coverage, terms of use, subcontracting, portability, etc.
- information security: infrastructure security measures, data location, audits and controls, etc.
- confidentiality and data privacy: data ownership, rights of access, intellectual property rights, obligations and responsibilities, audits and controls, etc.
- control of records and data: corporate management (records management functions, retention and disposition, etc.) and characteristics of records.

Due to the scarcity of published online policies, the analysis was complemented by a checklist prepared using the *Digital Records Maintenance and Preservation Strategies (Requirements Set C)* (Hackett, 2008, pp. 24–27) and the information available for each service.

Regarding the effect of e-services on records management, the classifications used by providers in grouping the 89 identified services were not useful for the study. For this reason, services were analyzed from a functional point of view, i.e. the kind of interaction regarding records and information was analyzed. This perspective enabled the following typological approach

1 creation of records, usually by means of a structured template
2 transmission of data and records by submitting or entering to an external system
3 publication of data and records on public platforms, official registries, or official journals
4 verification of data and records which substitutes documents provided by citizens
5 software application for business management, temporary storage, or preservation over time
6 identity and digital signature as a means of access to e-services and records validation.

The impact on presumption of authenticity of records involved in the e-services was evaluated based on this new classification. The criterion for selection of e-services was that it matched at least one of the first four types, given that some of them could be done simultaneously or combined. That is the case of creation and transmission of records and the publication in the official journals. Evaluation was done using two checklists drawn up from two other requirement sets

- *Benchmark Requirements for Supporting the Presumption of Authenticity of Electronic Records (Requirements Set A)* (Hackett, 2008, pp. 15–20) for creation of records or evidence of transactions carried out
- *Baseline Requirements Supporting the Production of Authentic Copies of Electronic Records (Requirements Set B)* (Hackett, 2008, pp. 21–23) for obtaining authentic copies of records when an e-service is used for verification of records or data.

Discussion

The main positive finding is the benefits coming out of integration with a single service provider that performs an intermediary role with other service providers, such as the AOC. However, the fact that several e-services were not integrated in the AOC platform complicates the situation. Next, the absence of an integrated e-service catalogue does not facilitate identification and analysis of each e-service. At the same time, internal management tools such as the catalogue of e-services used, or the registry of authorized interoperating users, are increasingly difficult to keep for at least two reasons: first, because of proliferation and diversity of e-services; second, control of users is usually done per individual e-service and it is difficult to integrate those rights at the level of public administration as a user. If integrated, it could result in a holistic control of the public administration's staff permissions.

Regarding trust in the e-services, this is seriously affected by the absence of specific policies related either to the specific service or to the platform where it is implemented. In general, it could be said that information about e-service implementation is only included in the e-government portal policies, but in a very diffuse way. At a lower level, only the AOC really offers service level agreements, although they are not fully compliant with the reference requirements defined for private providers or preservation strategies that ensure the appropriate measures to prevent the loss or corruption of information.

Regarding the presumption of authenticity of records, all e-services are based on the digital signature and none provides sufficient contextual information to satisfy the presumption of authenticity in the long term. Generally, capturing of the archival bond and the identifier of authoritative record is not planned at the point of creation, incorporation, consultation, or verification of the records. This also hinders integration of management systems with the e-services, integration that in some exceptions is not automated and depends on organizational solutions, e.g. manual downloads of submitted records or transaction evidences, which are usually held on servers of the provider.

Because of the weak traceability of actions and non-integration with the management systems of the public administration as a user, authenticity of the records will be affected in the medium and long terms. This is especially worrying for two reasons. First, only the e-service provider holds control over the management and roles of external users, even though the public administration as a user can interact with it. Second, a relevant number of e-services do not allow users to obtain evidence of the transactions carried out.

Conclusion

The studies presented in this chapter show two models of analysis. They are viewed from different perspectives, but with many similarities in the approach and the results. The analysis approaches and the identification of weak points of the evaluated e-services resulted with the creation of systematic criteria which can, if incorporated, improve design of new e-services, development of their policies and assessment of existing ones, whether by users or service providers.

The weakness of the existing policies related to e-services is highlighted, and especially in those key aspects that generate trust. Broadly speaking, these key aspects are transparency in the provision of the service, guarantees given to the users about the quality of information management, and control that these users may exercise over their records and data. In this sense, records management, storage, long term preservation, and guarantees of authenticity reinforce each of these aspects. However, studies show that the policies in these areas (where they exist) are mostly deficient. In fact, the *e-Safe* building block was also the one that obtained the lowest result (only 37%) in the assessment of horizontal common enablers in the benchmarking of 2010 (European Commission, 2010, pp. 17–18). On the contrary, the *Authentic sources* building block, referring to public registries, achieved the best results (100%). But how was e-authenticity assessed?

Certainly, years have passed since that assessment, but the results show low level of awareness about what really implies an open digital environment and, more specifically, cloud services and solutions. At a broader level, the technological component seems to have weighed much more than the organizational viewpoint in the design and implementation of e-services, and the study on Catalonia and Spain is a good example. Of course, current policies regulating e-services should no longer omit what information is managed, who is managing it, where it is located, when the record was created, for how long it will be retained and how it is managed over time (the W5H criteria – What, Who, Where, When, Why, and How).

As it is deduced from the case study of Girona City Council, it has to be taken into account that the level of maturity of records management systems conditions the view of how e-services should be provided: the more mature and normalized use of the systems, the better quality in the design of e-services. It may seem obvious, but existence of the records management system, whether compulsory by law or not, is not a minor issue at all. Therefore, information governance cannot neglect records management as a key element in its development, in accordance with the dimensions of maturity assessment set out in Chapter 5.

In this sense, implementation of e-services should be considered not only from a collaborative but also from a cooperative point of view. This approach is especially critical in the design of G2G services if the needs of administrations as users are to be taken into account. The same situation is true of G2C and G2B e-services. The user-centred perspective must always have a pre-eminent position so that the user needs and requirements are understood. Undoubtedly, trusted e-services is one of the requirements. Trust should always be assessable, be it through policies or statements of responsibility which are easy to understand by the users, or through the automated visualisation of key performance indicators; for instance, using the assessment methods presented in this chapter as a starting point.

To conclude, trust in e-services neither can be based only on the use of digital signatures nor conceded by default, simply because the provider is a public administration. On the contrary, public administrations should develop e-services taking the "trust by design" approach.

Acknowledgements

We wish to acknowledge the postgraduate students Hrvoje Brzica and Martina Poljičak Sušec, and graduate research assistants Ivan Adžaga, Ana Garić, Kristina Presečki, and Ana Stanković from the Department of Information and Communication Sciences, Faculty of Humanities and Social Sciences, University of Zagreb, as well as Sònia Oliveras and Maria Reixach from the City Council of Girona, who participated in this research.

References

Bushey, J., Demoulin, M., How, E., & McLelland, R. (2016). *Cloud service provider contracts. Checklist* (NA14). InterPARES Trust. Retrieved from https://interpares trust.org/assets/public/dissemination/NA14_20160226_CloudServiceProvider Contracts_Checklist_Final.pdf

Bushey, J., Demoulin, M., How, E., & McLelland, R. (2018). *Cloud service provider contracts* (NA14). InterPARES Trust. Retrieved from https://interparestrust.org/assets/public/dissemination/NA14_final_report_v5-1.pdf

Casellas, L. E. (2013). La Llei d'arxius i documents i la gestió de documents: cinquanta ombres de la llei [The Archives and Documents Act and records management: Fifty shades of the law]. *Lligall. Revista d'Arxivística Catalana, 36*, 21–40. Retrieved from https://www.girona.cat/sgdap/docs/07_CASELLAS-50-ombres-de-la-llei_2013.pdf

Casellas, L. E., Oliveras, S., & Reixach, M. (2019). *Girona City Council in the cloud: Analysis of e-Services between public administrations* (EU06). InterPARES Trust. Retrieved from https://interparestrust.org/assets/public/dissemination/EU06_2020_ GironaCityCouncilAnalysiseServicesPublicAdministrations_FinalReport.pdf

European Commission. (2010). *Digitizing public services in Europe: Putting ambition in action. 9th benchmark measurement.* Retrieved from https://ec.europa.eu/newsroom/dae/document.cfm?doc_id=1926

European Commission. (2016). *EU eGovernment action plan 2016–2020. Accelerating the digital transformation of government.* Retrieved from https://eur-lex.europa.eu/legal-content/EN/TXT/?uri=CELEX:52016DC0179

General Data Protection Regulation (GDPR), EU 2016/679 (2016).

Hackett, Y. (2008). Domain 3 Task Force. Appendix 21: Preserver guidelines – Preserving digital records: Guidelines for organizations. In L. Duranti & R. Preston (Eds.), *International Research on Permanent Authentic Records in Electronic Systems (InterPARES) 2: Experiential, interactive and dynamic records.* Padova, Italy: Associazione Nazionale Archivistica Italiana. Retrieved from http://www.interpares.org/ip2/display_file.cfm?doc=ip2_book_appendix_21.pdf

Stančić, H., Brzica, H., Adžaga, I., Garić, A., Poljičak Sušec, M., Presečki, K., & Stanković, A. (2015a). *Comparative analysis of implemented governmental e-services* (EU09). InterPARES Trust. Retrieved from https://interparestrust.org/assets/public/dissemination/EU09_20160727_ComparativeAnalysisImplementedGovernmentale Services_FinalReport.pdf

Stančić, H., Ivanjko, T., Bonić, N., Garić, A., Lončarić, K., Lovasić, A., . . . Stanković, A. (2015b). *Analysis of the interoperability possibilities of implemented governmental e-services* (EU15). InterPARES Trust. Retrieved from https://interparestrust.org/assets/public/dissemination/EU15_20160727_InteroperabilityGovEServices_FinalReport.pdf

7 Inter-organisational collaboration on e-government

Göran Samuelsson with Hrvoje Stančić

Introduction

In the public sector, information is mainly kept for the current business itself and for legal compliance. Governments have set up e-services for citizens (G2C), for businesses (G2B), and for intragovernmental exchange of information (G2G). Single sign-on (SSO) systems have been implemented for the ease of access to multiple services without the need to log into each of them separately. SSOs, just as the implemented governmental e-services, usually function at the level of a single country. Hence, it is difficult to expect seamless transborder data flow, i.e. the exchange of e-service data. Stančić et al. (2015b) illustrate challenges using the health-related service example of transborder exchange of patients' information between e-health services of different countries when a patient from one country needs treatment in another country. Could the patient limit what information a doctor is allowed to access? Will the possible set-up limitation still be valid when accessing the data using another country's SSO? Should there be an "override" possibility for the set-up limitations in case of an emergency (e.g. when the patient is not conscious)? Can the interconnected e-services from different countries trust each other? In the end, where should the medical record about the incident be stored – in the e-health system of the patient's country, in the e-health system of the country where the incident happened, or in both? Additionally, who is responsible for its long term preservation? This example shows the complexity of interconnecting SSOs to facilitate trusted transborder data flow.

Data, information, and records from governmental e-services are also preserved for cultural and research reasons. The public sector (e.g. in the EU) is about to make significant investments in electronic archiving solutions so that the necessary information can be stored, preserved, and trusted. It will in all cases be necessary to argue for the importance of the information or the benefits among the decision-makers sponsoring such investments, and to prove that the investment has also been realized with the expected and possibly other benefits. To create long term and sustained trust in the digital information not only technical and legal requirements are required, but also a clear vision for sustainability of political, economic, organisational, and technical benefits of the new electronic archiving infrastructures and a focus on communicating the benefits of the preserved information and solutions among the various stakeholders of public preservation services. The aim of this chapter is first to investigate the interconnection possibilities of governmental e-services in the context of trusted transborder data flow, and second to investigate whether and how the selected mode of organisational collaboration when creating electronic archiving solutions may impact the expected benefits from e-government investments.

Long term and sustained trust in digital information

Legal, operational, and/or cultural factors often have a bearing on what type of information is preserved or how much of the information is preserved. It will in most cases be necessary to argue for the importance of information or benefit of preserving it. In the long term, it will also become increasingly important to be able to demonstrate sustainability of skills, finances, or services. Therefore, in order to preserve and rely on information in the future, one should be able to demonstrate the value of both the information objects and the repository. To create a long term and sustained trust in digital information requires not only technical and legal requirements to be met, but also a clear vision for economic sustainability (as further discussed in Chapter 8) and a focus on communicating the benefits of the preserved information among the various stakeholders in public preservation services. Undoubtedly, the study of benefits realization management may be approached from many different angles. In this chapter, the focus is put on modes of collaboration for realizing e-government benefits. E-government aims to improve the efficiency and effectiveness of public organisations and increase the quality of public services through applying information and communication technologies (ICT) (Layne & Lee, 2001; Moon, 2002).

However, several e-government initiatives have provided little impact and the envisaged benefits are not always realized (Millard, 2010). A stream of research argues that potential benefits of IT investments need to be systematically managed in order to secure their realization (Ward, Taylor, & Bond, 1996; Remenyi, Sherwood-Smith, & White, 1997). Benefits realization means "the process of organizing and managing such that the potential benefits arising from the use of IS/IT are actually realized" (Ward & Daniel, 2006, p. 384). Collaboration has been considered as an essential issue for realizing a great many benefits of e-government (Gil-Garcia, 2012). By collaborating, public sector organizations intend to co-create value (Flak, Solli-Saether, & Straub, 2015) and achieve benefits such as economies of scale in IT investments and information integration across government agencies (Gil-Garcia, 2012). In a few countries, such as Sweden, governmental and municipal organisations have traditionally been cooperating only on a voluntary basis, which has hindered benefits realization that could have been reached through stronger collaboration (Grönlund, 2009). While the benefits realization concept and several related methods were introduced in the mid-1990s, empirical studies, especially in the public sector, have remained rare (Ashurst, Doherty, & Peppard, 2008; Päivärinta & Dertz, 2008; Flak et al., 2009). Wider adoption of methods and practices for benefits realization in the public sector has thus emerged only recently, e.g. in Denmark (Hertzum & Simonsen, 2011), Norway (Flak & Solli-Saether, 2013), and Sweden (E-delegationen, 2014). Among the reported cases, e.g. (Flak, 2012), the main focus has been at the level of one organisation.

Flak and Solli-Saether (2013) have addressed the importance of understanding interoperability at the government level and described how a central actor coordinates a portfolio of government service providers through a standardized benefits-reporting approach. There has been an increasing focus on understanding hindrances and incentives for inter-organisational collaboration on e-government initiatives (Gil-Garcia, 2012), and initial speculation on how some collaboration dimensions, such as voluntary versus mandatory (Grönlund, 2009), may impact expected benefits. However, the role of inter-organisational collaboration in relation to benefits realization has remained an under researched issue. Nevertheless, it should be noted that Chapter 6 recommends taking a collaborative and cooperative approach in the development of G2G e-services.

Interoperability of e-services at the government level needs to be realized if the *once-only* principle, requiring businesses and citizens to provide information to the government only once, is to be honoured. If this is taken to a higher, international level of the EU, then one should expect realization of interoperability between national e-services of the EU member state countries. In that case, it would be much easier to establish interoperability between the SSO systems, functioning at national level as a single point of entry to multiple e-services, than trying to make all e-services of all member states interoperable. Taking this approach would also influence the preservation of governmental e-services' records, especially if a collaborative approach is taken at the lower levels. For example, several Swedish governmental and municipal organisations have started collaborating on the acquisition and implementation of systems and services for digital archiving – Rydberg (2014) reported that 117 Swedish government agencies planned to invest approximately €60 million in a shared service for digital archiving; however, this has since been paused. This can be compared to an estimated cost of €140–200 million if each government agency were to implement digital archives independently. Similar initiatives have also started in the municipal sector (Päivärinta, Samuelsson, Jonsson, & Swensson, 2014).

Next, this chapter will investigate interoperability possibilities of implemented governmental e-services and then study the models and benefits of inter-organisational collaboration on e-government.

Interoperability possibilities of implemented governmental e-services

Research methodology

Research into the interoperability possibilities of implemented governmental e-services built upon the results of the comparative analysis of implemented governmental e-services (Stančić et al., 2015a) discussed in the Chapter 6, which detected an absence of publicly available information considering aspects of storage and long term content availability and system operation transparency, which are important for establishing trust in e-services. This research focused on the implemented governmental e-services in the EU in the context of national SSOs in order to identify possibilities for exchanging identification and authentication credentials, thus creating a network of trust between the national systems and enabling citizens to seamlessly use other country's e-services.

Stančić et al. (2015b) divided the research into four stages: identification, data acquisition, analysis, and interpretation. In the identification stage, an environmental scan was done. It identified that in some countries, there are numerous e-services or information about services (not actual e-services) available via governmental portals (e.g. at the time of the research, more than 1,500 in Portugal, 453 in Lithuania, 317 in Estonia) and that it would be impossible to achieve meaningful results if all were assessed. Therefore, as in Stančić et al. (2015a), this research also adopted the "representative basket of 20 services" approach but focused only on 12 G2C services (for more details see Chapter 6, specifically Table 6.1). The SSO systems and their key components were identified in the 28 EU member states. An SSO assessment form was created to standardize data collection. It consisted of 29 questions divided into six categories

1   users
2   legal framework and strategies
3   portals
4   single sign-on
5   trust mechanisms – technical details
6   future plans.

In the data assessment phase, a total of 812 questions were (or tried to be) answered (29 questions × 28 countries). Some questions were unanswered due to the technology-related issues or unavailability of online information. The results were first analyzed by country and then comparatively across countries.

Findings

The results are presented according to the six investigated categories.

1   users

- the percentage of households with a broadband connection (i.e. potential users) ranged from 56%–93%
- the percentage of individuals using the internet for interacting with public authorities (real users) ranged from 10%–84%
- the difference between potential and real users was rather high (≥30%) in some countries.

2   legal framework and strategies (national IT strategy concerning e-government and/or e-government legal texts concerning e-identification/e-authentication)

- most of the analyzed countries have certain legal regulations regarding e-government
- 57% of the analyzed countries had a national IT strategy
- one-third of the analyzed countries have legislation regulating e-government
- certain legal documents regarding e-identification/e-authentication were identified (e.g. data protection acts, legal frameworks for electronic signatures, and associated matters).

3   portals

- all 28 countries have a central e-government portal which can be used as an informative and/or single access point (not necessarily an SSO system) to all e-government services offered from both state and local authorities.

4   single sign-on

- 68% of the analyzed countries had developed SSO system
- on average, seven e-services were connected via an SSO
- the most frequently connected G2C e-services in SSOs are: processes related to social security benefits, application for building permission, announcement of moving/change of address, request and delivery of birth and marriage certificates, and declaration, notification, and assessment of income taxes
- 16 different methods of authentication methods were identified: 64% virtual (e.g. username/password, e-certificate, e-mail, etc.), 36% physical (eID card, smart card, token, etc.)
- six categories of identity data governing bodies were identified: national register, bank, ministry, post, health insurance fund, various administrations.

5   trust mechanisms – technical details on 19 identified SSO systems

- eight SSOs had some information on technical details available, while only three were identified as using SAML. Other identified standards were Liberty Alliance, Shibboleth, and XHTML

- implemented encryption levels/standards were SSL (Secure Socket Layer), TLS (Transport Layer Security), XML Encryption/Signature, and WS-S (Web Service Security)
- six SSOs were part of the (at the time active) STORK (Secure idenTity acrOss boRders linKed) initiative aimed at establishing a European eID Interoperability Platform (STORK, 2019). Today this is realized through the CEF eID building block (eID, n.d.).

6   future plans

- only seven countries provided information on their future plans regarding SSO development. The plans could be categorized into three groups: process optimization (e.g. by simplifying transactions, removing constraints, etc.), security improvements, and technical upgrades (e.g. better compatibility of information systems).

Discussion

Strategically, EU countries have the possibility of improving the situation with governmental e-services, first and foremost in closing the gap between potential users (households with a broadband connection) and real users (individuals using the internet for interacting with public authorities). This would increase the use of e-services. The study of the legal frameworks and strategies shows that it is important not only to view the complexity of SSO implementation from the technical point of view, but also to have defined and clear legal regulations and frameworks on national and transnational levels in order to provide fully functional, safe, and complete interoperability. The eIDAS (2014) regulation has made a significant step in that direction. Interoperability of national e-services through the interoperability of SSOs means that a citizen of one country can use his/her national eID for accessing e-services of another country, i.e. national identification mechanisms are accepted at the EU level. Development of the CEF eID greatly helped this.

The assessment form used, transformed into a checklist (see Appendix 3), can be used by researchers or records managers as a method of assessing SSOs, as a method of self-assessment by the public bodies developing them, or by the EU-level SSO interconnection initiatives. By making enough information available, we believe that SSO users will be able to firmly ground their judgements on whether to trust an SSO system and the interconnected e-services or not.

Inter-organisational collaboration on e-government

Inter-organisational collaboration in the public sector has become more common and today it is more or less considered a self-evident virtue of advanced societies (Hudson, Hardy, Henwood, & Wistow, 1999). Common drivers for collaboration are efficiency, sharing of knowledge, and financial imperatives (Huxham, Vangen, Huxham, & Eden, 2000). The underlying purpose is to achieve collaborative advantage that is not possible to achieve alone (Huxham & Macdonald, 1992). The effect of collaboration increases with complexity, i.e. complex policies are more effectively implemented if agencies collaborate, while easier tasks are better handled without inter-organisational collaboration (Lundin, 2007). However, collaboration is found to be difficult and failures are common (Bryson, Crosby, & Stone, 2006). To succeed with collaboration, trust between partners needs to be built over time (Vangen & Huxham, 2003), where the collaborative capacity indicates how big a change a relationship can bear without the partners losing trust in the relationship (Hudson et al., 1999).

E-government has emerged as an important area for collaboration in the public sector. E-government initiatives are often intended to improve citizen service and administrative efficiency; they require seamless services and sharing of information between authorities and are costly to implement. Moreover, e-government initiatives often require that organisations develop new technical knowledge. The development of e-government has been depicted in maturity models (Australian National Audit Office, 1999; Layne & Lee, 2001; Belanger & Hiller, 2006), where the most mature stages involve horizontal collaboration between organisational levels within a public organisation and vertical collaboration between different public organisations. In an exploratory study of e-government collaboration among Italian municipalities, convention was the most popular way of collaboration, while establishing a new public body was the least common (Sorrentino & Ferro, 2008); see Table 7.1. A convention is a written collaboration agreement between a group of public agencies in which they define the areas and methods of collaboration. A convention is not a legal entity, while a consortium, founded by a group of public agencies, has legal status, only serves its members, and is not allowed to offer services externally. A framework agreement entails a common purchasing contract to which the involved public agencies make individual calls. However, Sorrentino and Ferro (2008) provide few, if any, details on the differences in benefits between the forms or modes of collaboration.

Table 7.1 Forms of municipal collaboration for e-government in Italy

Form of collaboration	*Percentage of municipalities*
Convention	42%
Framework agreement	26%
Consortium	16%
Limited company	4%
New public body	2%
Other	10%

Based on Sorrentino and Ferro (2008, p. 6).

Research methodology

Comparative case studies (Lillis & Mundy, 2005) were conducted to gather information about modes of collaboration. In this research, four cases of Swedish digital archive initiatives were analyzed. The cases were selected since they all focus on one particular type of e-government system (digital archive) and have varying characteristics in regard to collaboration. Secondary data in the form of documentation, mainly project documentation, available from the different digital archive initiatives (the cases) were used as empirical data. The data collected from the cases was complemented with data from a focus group interview and a quantitative survey. The collected data was analyzed through content analysis (Päivärinta, Lönn, Juell-Skielse, & Samuelsson, 2015; Lönn, Juell-Skielse, & Päivärinta, 2016).

Case studies

This section presents the five digital archive cases studies in Sweden.

1   the eARD (e-arkiv och e-diarium, Eng. e-archive or e-diary) initiative had the goal of developing common metadata specifications for digital archives across the Swedish public sector. The project was carried out between 2011 and 2014, but the National Archives of Sweden continues to coordinate and develop the specifications in cooperation with varying public sector organisations (Kristianson, Almalander, & Geber, 2013). Data on the eARD initiative was gathered through secondary sources and the focus group interview

2   in the municipality of Härnösand, the GOINFO project focused on digital preservation and archiving of salary data of municipality employees. According to Swedish legislation, such data needs to be preserved for 70 years, and should be available for inquiries, e.g. to set a citizen's pension. The goal of the project was to make an in-house implementation for receiving salary data from the previous and existing information systems, in which the data had been stored previously (Päivärinta et al., 2014). Data of this case consists of public project reports and workshop notes

3   the Swedish Association of Local Authorities and Regions (SALAR) represents and supports local authorities in Sweden. SALAR conducted a project to establish a framework contract for public procurement of digital archives. The goal with the framework contract was to "offer a common way of working and to facilitate the call-off procedure to adopt, manage and develop a digital archive" (SALAR, 2015). In December 2014, the first municipality made a call-off from the framework contract. Data on the SALAR initiative was gathered through secondary sources and complemented with data from the focus group interview and the survey

4   Sydarkivera is a Swedish municipal association working as a common archival organization for one county and ten municipalities. The

Table 7.2 Case studies' documentation and sources

Case	Documentation
eARD	• notes from focus group interviews • project reports
Härnösand	• project reports and project documentation
Swedish Association of Local Authorities and Regions (SALAR)	• notes from focus group interviews • project description • guidelines for the framework agreement • framework agreement related templates • website • survey
Sydarkivera	• Sydarkivera description • project report • Sydarkivera description and decision support for statement of intent
Swedish National Service Centre (NSC)	• project report • published interview with NSC director-general • press release

association's mission is to act as a joint archive authority and provide a digital archive system for its members (Sydarkivera, 2015). The data in this case study consists of public project reports

5   the Swedish National Service Centre (NSC) is a public authority that provides services for administrative support to national authorities. NSC has been commissioned by the Swedish government to establish a shared service for digital archives in collaboration with the national archives in Sweden. The aim is to facilitate the management of public documentation and to improve the service quality offered to citizens. This is an ongoing project, and the Swedish government has also commissioned seven authorities to participate in the project. The data in this case consists of public project reports and workshop notes. A complete list of documentation studied for each case study is shown in Table 7.2.

Focus group interview

The focus group interview was organized by SALAR together with two Swedish universities, and was conducted during one day for a total of five and a half hours. The aim of the focus group interview was to discuss the benefits of and success factors for digital archives. The focus group participants were selected by purposive sampling (Denscombe, 2010) – participants were to be knowledgeable informants with great experience in digital archives. Participation was voluntary. A total of 16 participants took part. The participants' organisations and roles are shown in Table 7.3.

The interview was audio recorded and the researchers took notes. Also, data was collected through a survey sent out to all 290 municipalities and 20

Table 7.3 Focus group interview participants

Organisation	Focus group interview participants
Municipalities	Seven municipal representatives in the forefront of implementing digital archives in Sweden
West Swedish Municipal Federation	One representative from an organisation coordinating four local government federations
SALAR	Two representatives from Public Procurement, one programme manager from the Centre for e-Society responsible for moderating the discussions
Swedish eDelegation	One representative from the Swedish eDelegation, an expert on benefits realization
Consultant	One consultant with experience in digital archives' implementation
Luleå University	One researcher responsible for moderating the discussions
Stockholm University	Two researchers, responsible for collecting data

county councils in Sweden. The survey included questions about if or when municipalities and county councils planned to implement digital archives, if and how municipalities planned to collaborate on digital archives, and what challenges associated with implementing digital archives they envisaged. The survey was sent to the archival managers and the response rate was 90% (280 responses). The survey helped form a broader understanding of Swedish authorities' perception of collaboration and intention to collaborate in regard to the acquisition and implementation of digital archives.

Data analysis

The data – documentation from secondary sources and notes from the focus group interview – was analyzed using content analysis (Krippendorff, 2012) and then the text (data) was interpreted to extract meaning (Hsieh & Shannon, 2005). The modes of collaboration and benefits were identified and extracted. A process for thematic content analysis was followed to categorize the benefits (Braun & Clarke, 2006).

Results

This section presents the analysis of the four different digital archives use cases in terms of their observed mode of collaboration and the benefits they sought.

The Härnösand initiative

Initiative Härnösand (a Swedish municipality with ca. 25,000 inhabitants) acquired and configured a digital archiving solution of its own in collaboration with a vendor (Päivärinta et al., 2014). A benefits analysis was conducted. The main reason for implementing the system was to ensure compliance with external archiving legislation. Few significant gains from digital interoperability were identified, and the cost savings and other benefits from digital archiving were identified as relatively minor (Päivärinta et al., 2014). The Härnösand case indicates that an in-house archive solution is quick to implement independently by an individual government agency or a municipality that can select a desired system and the vendor independently. The challenge with an in-house development can be ignorance by others (no reuse), and service reorganisation possibilities, as opposed to more standardized and interoperable solutions (Päivärinta et al., 2014). If benefits are to be analyzed and realized only within the scope of one organisation and one software application, the identified cost savings and efficiency gains within the narrow scope of analysis do not necessarily warrant investment in the digital archive.

The Swedish Association of Local Authorities and Regions (SALAR) initiative

The SALAR initiative has established a framework agreement to simplify public organisations' procurement of digital archives. A framework agreement forms a general level basis for future procurement. Public organisations can procure a digital archive as a product or a service and associated consultant services, and make call-offs from the agreement. A total of 535 government agencies and municipalities are entitled to make call-offs from the agreement, and the survey showed that (in 2014) 22% of the organisations intended to do so. Delivery models, payment models, and terms and conditions for future procurement have been established by SALAR and negotiated with several digital archive suppliers on behalf of a large number of public organisations. This collaboration initiative thereby promotes economies of scale, aiming to lower administration costs for procurement. SALAR possesses negotiation competence and skills which, in combination with negotiating for a vast number of organisations, contributes to negotiation power and a strong position with the suppliers. SALAR can thereby negotiate favourable prices for digital archives, which is another aspect of how economies of scale are promoted through this initiative. Making a call-off by following SALAR's guidelines for procurement, individual organisations can ensure they are compliant with the public procurement laws. In this initiative, a requirements specification for digital archives was developed by SALAR. One important system requirement is that the supplier system should be compliant with integration standards for data input. The framework thereby promotes interoperability of delivering data to the digital archives.

The Sydarkivera initiative

In the Sydarkivera initiative, a jointly owned association governed by a board, was formed by several public organisations. Each association member organisation has a board representative. The board has been assigned to act as a common archiving authority for its members – it allows a shared archiving responsibility, while the association can take over legal responsibility for archiving from its members. The organisation thus provides a digital archive as a service and some other archiving authority functions as a service(s) for its members. This collaboration initiative promotes economies of scale in regard to reduced IT operation costs, reduced archiving costs, and reduced IT procurement costs. The association takes over the responsibility for the final storage and preservation of digital public documentation from its member organisations. The member organisations can thereby reduce their own IT operations cost by terminating IT systems, saving costs for technical operation and licences, improving IT architecture, and reducing costs of information handling when changing systems. The member organisations, i.e. municipalities, split the costs for the service based on their population size. The shared organisation focuses on the core archiving activities.

By managing archived information from several organisations, the cooperative organisation can offer the same information to external stakeholders regardless of the information's origin, thereby fostering the concept of open data.

The Swedish National Service Centre (NSC) initiative

The Swedish National Service Centre (NSC) is a public organisation developing digital archives as a service offered to all authorities at the national state authority level. The digital archive service is an intermediate archive used before archiving at the National Archives of Sweden. In this concept, an authority using the service is still the responsible archiving authority and thereby retains the information owner responsibility. NSC's archiving service fosters economies of scale, in the short and long term, both for individual authorities and the national administration. The acquisition, operation, maintenance, and development of digital archive systems are centralized. It is a cost-effective alternative because of better use of resources when a number of authorities share a service. In the short term, it is more cost effective to establish one common digital archive as a service centrally since the investment cost for digital archiving can be reduced. Besides offering a digital archiving system as a service, NSC also offers services related to all aspects of the archiving process, customer service, and possibly other support services and consultancy services. Authorities can source this competence and capabilities from NSC.

Analysis of collaboration modes

In this section, the five derived collaboration modes are discussed (Päivärinta et al., 2015, pp. 13–15).

In the *in-house collaboration mode,* an archive is developed and maintained by the individual public organisation, either through in-house development or through a software development company. In this mode, there is no collaboration connected to procurement, implementation, and operation of IT systems among public organisations, although collaboration in the form of information sharing can exist. Benefits with in-house development are that complete autonomy can be kept, and a customized system can be implemented rather quickly responding to the primary purpose at hand. However, the scale of benefits identification (and later on benefits realization) may remain at a low level, forgetting the larger-scale benefits that could be reaped from interoperability and the potential of data use for secondary purposes beyond the primary requirement of legislative compliance.

In the *vendor-driven collaboration mode,* a standard IT system is developed by a vendor and offered as a product or service to several public organisations. Benefits with this collaboration mode are related to economies of scale, tested experiences, and knowledge from previous implementations, keeping up with technical advancements and a broad skill-base provided by vendors. However, if the dominating vendors would not follow open standards, potential benefits from digitally archived data beyond the vendor's solution sphere could be hindered.

In the *cooperative technology collaboration mode,* a public organisation establishes a framework agreement with conditions for acquisition of IT systems and negotiates with one or several vendors. Public organisations can procure IT systems (as a product or service) and related support services by making call-offs from the agreement. The benefits of this collaboration mode are mostly related to simplified procurement through pre-negotiated conditions for procurement, support, and standard procedures for making call-offs. It also promotes economies of scale since procurement is carried out centrally leading to reduced costs for procurement and IT systems. Another benefit that can be achieved in this mode is simplified development of requirements for public organisations.

In the *cooperative authority service mode,* a jointly owned organisation governed by a board or committee (association) manages a specific area of responsibility and IT support system for its member organisations. The association can form an independent common authority enabling the association's organisation to take over the legal responsibility (partially or fully) for a specific area from its member organisations. This collaboration mode promotes economies of scale due to a shared service whereby costs for IT procurement, operation, and maintenance can be reduced. In this mode, common capabilities can be developed and focused on a specific area. It allows for an effective and specialized organisation with capabilities that can be sourced from its member organisations. This collaboration mode can also promote interoperability, information quality, availability, and open data.

In the *public organisation service mode,* an independent public organisation provides an IT system as a service to a number of authorities. In this mode, the operation, maintenance, and development of the IT system is centralized. This mode shares many of the benefits of the cooperative authority service mode – economies of scale, interoperability, and information quality and availability. The main difference is that in this mode, the organisation responsible for the service is independent, as the customers are not co-owners of it. Further, the organisation is not a common authority and thereby does not take over partial or full responsibility for a specific area. Thereby, even though legal and regulatory compliance can be fostered, the service organisation does not take over legal responsibilities.

Discussion

The research findings show how inter-organisational collaboration (or non-collaboration) modes for acquiring and implementing digital archive solutions and services vary. Some of the modes resemble the forms of collaboration in the Italian context (Sorrentino & Ferro, 2008). For example, the *cooperative technology mode* is similar to their *framework agreement*. The *cooperative authority service* is a combination of *new public body* and *consortium*, but also includes provisioning of a software service. Sorrentino and Ferro (2008) report on vendor-driven solutions, but do not consider it a form of collaboration, as this research does in the *vendor-driven mode*. The research in the Swedish context did not identify a mode similar to the *limited company*. On the other hand, the *public organisation service mode* does not resemble any of the Italian modes.

The analysis shows how benefits expected from digital archiving initiatives vary and can be, to some extent, related to the chosen mode of collaboration. That is, the chosen collaboration mode may have impact on which benefits are sought in the first place, or the expected benefits may have impact on the choice of collaboration mode. While the research findings do not provide clear hypotheses in this regard, initial observations inspire future research plans aiming to explore relations of chosen collaboration modes and expected (and realized) benefits in more detail.

Analysis of digital archiving development cases and collaborations in the Swedish context represents a rare opportunity of simultaneously studying several cases of one particular type of e-government system with different modes of collaborations for acquiring and implementing such systems. This makes possible theorizing of relationships between varying modes of collaboration and benefits to be realized. Therefore, this research brings the aspect of collaboration modes into the discussion in connection with benefits realization methods, practices, and strategies in the public sector, which have been so far largely focused on the level of one organisation (Flak, 2012), or only on one mode of collaboration, whereas a dominant actor in a public sector coordinates overall development of e-government services in one domain (Flak & Solli-Saether, 2013).

Conclusion

This chapter investigated whether and how the interconnection of SSO systems and e-services, as well as the selected mode of collaboration, may impact the expected benefits from e-government investments and trust in the e-services. The results of the research and its approach can be applied in the research of benefits realization in the context of other types of e-services. Here, an emerging theory in the field of digital archiving, which in our mind represents an infrastructural e-government investment, could be further refined and validated through replication studies in other domains of infrastructural e-government programmes. It could even be applied to the benefits realization modelling in the case of SSO usage and interconnection between EU member states. The aspect of trust in the developed e-services, i.e. the possibility of the national e-identity usage beyond the borders (computational trust between the SSO systems and consequently between the e-services), could also be applied because it indirectly influences usage of e-services and therefore realization of the expected benefits. Special attention should be given to the transborder data flow since in some cases, such as e-health services, sensitive records and personally identifiable information may be transferred (Lončarić & Stančić, 2016). Enough information about how those situations are handled – i.e. if and how much of the data is transferred, where it is stored, who can access it, if it is preserved, and if it is safely deleted – influence the overall trust in the e-services and SSO systems.

Finally, one important area of benefits realization is identification of the costs of collaboration, or (SSO) coordination costs, and how they are affected by the mode of collaboration (Huxham et al., 2000). It should be taken into account that the federated approach to storage and digital preservation, or to e-services' interconnection in general, may prove to have financial benefits. Therefore, economic models for cloud storage are discussed in the next chapter.

Acknowledgements

We wish to acknowledge Tomislav Ivanjko and graduate research assistants Nikola Bonić, Ana Garić, Ksenija Lončarić, Ana Lovasić, Kristina Presečki, and Ana Stanković from the Department of Information and Communication Sciences, Faculty of Humanities and Social Sciences, University of Zagreb, as well as Tero Päivärinta from Luleå University of Technology, and Carl-Mikael Lönn and Gustaf Juell-Skielse from Stockholm University, who participated in the research studies mentioned in this chapter.

References

Ashurst, C. A., Doherty, F. N. D., & Peppard, J. P. (2008). Improving the impact of IT development projects: The benefits realization capability model. *European Journal of Information Systems, 17*, 352–370.

Australian National Audit Office. (1999). *Electronic service delivery, including internet use, by Commonwealth Government agencies.* Canberra, Australia: Auditor General, Australian National Audit Office.

Belanger, F., & Hiller, J. S. (2006). A framework for e-government: Privacy implications. *Business Process Management Journal, 12,* 48–60.

Braun, V., & Clarke, V. (2006). Using thematic analysis in psychology. *Qualitative Research in Psychology, 3,* 77–101.

Bryson, J. M., Crosby, B. C., & Stone, M. M. (2006). The design and implementation of cross-sector collaborations: Propositions from the literature. *Public Administration Review, 66,* 44–55.

Denscombe, M. (2010). *The good research guide: For small scale social research projects* (4th ed.). Buckingham, UK: Open University Press.

E-delegationen. (2014). *Vägledning i nyttorealisering* [Guidance in benefits realization]. Retrieved from https://docplayer.se/2098360-Vagledning-i-nyttorealisering.html

eID. (n.d.). Retrieved from https://ec.europa.eu/cefdigital/wiki/display/CEFDIGITAL/eID

eIDAS. (2014). *Regulation (EU) No 910/2014 of the European Parliament and of the Council of 23 July 2014 on electronic identification and trust services for electronic transactions in the internal market and repealing Directive 1999/93/EC.* Retrieved from https://eur-lex.europa.eu/legal-content/EN/TXT/?uri=uriserv%3A OJ.L_.2014.257.01.0073.01.ENG

Flak, L. (2012). *Gevinstrealisering og offentlige IKT-investeringer* [Profit realization and public ICT investments]. Oslo: Universitetsforlaget.

Flak, L., Dertz, W., Jansen, A., Krogstie, J., Spjelkavik, I., & Ølnes, S. (2009). What is the value of e-government – And how can we actually realise it? *Transforming Government, 3,* 220–226.

Flak, L., & Solli-Saether, H. (2013). Benefits realization in e-government: Institutional entrepreneurship or just hype? In *HICSS '13: Proceedings of 46th Hawaii International Conference on System Sciences* (pp. 2062–2071). Washington, DC: IEEE Computer Society. https://doi.org/10.1109/HICSS.2013.114

Flak, L., Solli-Saether H., & Straub, D. (2015). Towards a theoretical model for co-realization of IT value in government. In *HICSS '15: Proceedings of 48th Hawaii International Conference on System Sciences* (pp. 2486–2494). Washington, DC: IEEE Computer Society. https://doi.org/10.1109/HICSS.2015.297

Gil-Garcia, J. R. (2012). Towards a smart state? Inter-agency collaboration, information integration, and beyond. *Information Polity, 17,* 269–280.

Grönlund, Å. (2009). "It's the economy stupid" – Why the Swedish e-Government action plan will not deliver better government, and how it could. *International Journal of Public Information Systems, 2009,* 61–75.

Hertzum, M., & Simonsen, J. (2011). Effects-driven IT development: Specifying, realizing, and assessing usage effects. *Scandinavian Journal of Information Systems, 23,* 3–28.

Hudson, B., Hardy, B., Henwood, M., & Wistow, G. (1999). In pursuit of interagency collaboration in the public sector: What is the contribution of theory and research? *Public Management an International Journal of Research and Theory, 1,* 235–260.

Huxham, C., & Macdonald, D. (1992). Introducing collaborative advantage: Achieving inter-organizational effectiveness through meta-strategy. *Management Decision, 30.* https://doi.org/10.1108/00251749210013104

Huxham, C., Vangen, S., Huxham, C., & Eden, C. (2000). The challenge of collaborative governance. *Public Management an International Journal of Research and Theory, 2,* 337–358.

Hsieh, H. F., & Shannon, S. E. (2005). Three approaches to qualitative content analysis. *Qualitative Health Research*, 15, 1277–1288.

Krippendorff, K. (2012). *Content analysis: An introduction to its methodology.* Thousand Oaks, CA: SAGE Publications.

Kristianson, G., Almalander C., & Geber M. (2013). *E-arkiv och e-diarium (eARD) översiktlig beskrivning* [E-archive and e-diary (eARD) overview description]. Version 2.0. Stockholm: Riksarkivet.

Layne, K., & Lee, J. (2001). Developing fully functional e-government: A four-stage model. *Government Information Quarterly*, 18, 122–136.

Lillis, A. M., & Mundy, J. (2005). Cross-sectional field studies in management accounting research – Closing the gaps between surveys and case studies. *Journal of Management Accounting Research*, 17, 119–141.

Lončarić, K., & Stančić, H. (2016). Mogućnost interoperabilnosti elektroničkih usluga tijela državne uprave na međunarodnoj razini [Nteroperability possibilities of governmental electronic services at the international level]. *Arhivska praksa*, 19, 322–329.

Lundin, M. (2007). When does cooperation improve public policy implementation? *Policy Studies Journal*, 35, 629–652.

Lönn, C., Juell-Skielse, G., & Päivärinta, T. (2016). Modes of collaboration for realizing e-government benefits. In *HICSS '16: Proceedings of 49th Hawaii International Conference on System Sciences* (pp. 3031–3040). Washington, DC: IEEE Computer Society. https://doi.org/10.1109/HICSS.2016.380

Millard, J. (2010). Government 1.5 – Is the bottle half full or half empty. *European Journal of ePractice*, 9, 1–16.

Moon, M. J. (2002). The evolution of e-government among municipalities: Rhetoric or reality? *Public Administration Review*, 62, 424–433.

Päivärinta, T., & Dertz, W. (2008). Pre-determinants of implementing IT benefits management in Norwegian municipalities: Cultivate the context. In M. A. Wimmer, H. J. Scholl, & E. Ferro (Eds.), *Electronic government.* Lecture notes in Computer Science (Vol. 5184, pp. 111–123). Berlin: Springer.

Päivärinta, T., Lönn, C. M., Juell-Skielse, G., & Samuelsson, G. (2015). *Benefits realization management* (EU14). InterPARES Trust. Retrieved from https://interparestrust.org/assets/public/dissemination/EU14_20151109_BenefitsRealization_FinalReport_Final.pdf

Päivärinta T., Samuelsson G., Jonsson E., & Swensson E. (2014). *Nyttorealisering av FGS:er* [Benefits Realisation as common specifications]. eARD, Delprojekt 2. Stockholm: Riksarkivet.

Remenyi, D., Sherwood-Smith, M., & White, T. (1997). *Achieving maximum value from information systems: A process approach.* Chichester, UK: John Wiley & Sons Ltd.

Rydberg, O. (2014). *Staten bygger e-arkiv för en halv miljard* [The state builds an e-archive for half a billion]. Retrieved from https://www.idg.se/2.1085/1.578793/staten-bygger-e-arkiv-for-enhalv-miljard

SALAR. (2015). *E-arkiv* [E-archive]. Retrieved from https://www.sklkommentus.se/upphandling-och-ramavtal/vara-ramavtal-och-upphandlingar/ramavtal-och-avtalskategorier/digitala-tjanster/e-arkiv/

Sorrentino, M., & Ferro, E. (2008). Does the answer to e-government lie in intermunicipal collaboration? An exploratory Italian case study. In M. A. Wimmer, H. J. Scholl, & E. Ferro (Eds.), *Electronic government. EGOV 2008.* Lecture Notes in Computer Science (Vol. 5184, pp. 1–12). Berlin Heidelberg: Springer.

Stančić, H., Brzica, H., Adžaga, I., Garić, A., Poljičak Sušec, M., Presečki, K., & Stanković, A. (2015a). *Comparative analysis of implemented governmental e-services* (EU09). InterPARES Trust. Retrieved from https://interparestrust.org/assets/public/dissemination/EU09_20160727_ComparativeAnalysisImplementedGovernmental eServices_FinalReport.pdf

Stančić, H., Ivanjko, T., Bonić, N., Garić, A., Lončarić, K., Lovasić, A., . . . Stanković, A. (2015b). *Analysis of the interoperability possibilities of implemented governmental e-services* (EU15). InterPARES Trust. Retrieved from https://interparestrust. org/assets/public/dissemination/EU15_20160727_InteroperabilityGovEServices_ FinalReport.pdf

STORK. (2019). *About secure identity across borders linked.* Retrieved from https:// joinup.ec.europa.eu/collection/secure-identity-across-borders-linked-stork/about

Sydarkivera. (2015). *Nyttorealiseringsplan. Etapp 1 år 2015–2016* [Benefits realization plan. Stage 1 2015–16]. Retrieved from https://www.sydarkivera.se/?mdocs-file=780

Vangen, S., & Huxham, C. (2003). Nurturing collaborative relations: Building trust in interorganizational collaboration. *The Journal of Applied Behavioral Science, 39*, 5–31.

Ward, J., & Daniel, E. (2006). *Benefits management: Delivering value from IS & IT investments.* Chichester, UK: John Wiley & Sons Ltd.

Ward, J., Taylor, P., & Bond, P. (1996). Evaluation and realization of IS/IT benefits: An empirical study of current practice. *European Journal of Information Systems, 4*, 214–225.

8 Economic models for cloud storage

Julie McLeod with Hrvoje Stančić

Introduction

Offering a flexible strategy for platform, infrastructure, and software services, improved access to and sharing of records and data, increased security, increased potential for long term preservation, the advantage of economies of scale and (potential) cost savings, worldwide expenditure on cloud IT infrastructure (on- and off-premises) is anticipated to exceed that on non-cloud IT infrastructure (International Data Corporation, 2019). Service providers and consultancy companies highlight the economic benefits of using cloud services for the storage of digital information. As more data and records are generated and stored in the cloud, either as part of an intentional archives storage programme or by default in business systems, there is evidence that records professionals are increasingly using the cloud for the storage of digital collections (Stuart & Bromage, 2010; Zander, 2014; Oliver & Knight, 2015). Cost presents a significant pull toward cloud storage, but cost is ongoing. Although some users may argue the cloud is too expensive, they rarely calculate TCO (total cost of ownership) in full for on-premises solutions. It should, for example, include setting up the server room (quality of wire installations, etc.), setting up the testing room (new equipment needs to be unpacked and tested before it is plugged into the secure system in the server room), cost of electricity, internet costs, costs of firewalls and other hardware and software protection and security solutions, licences, cost of backup (local and remote), cost of personnel (application of patches, working around problems, lifelong education), and vendor support fees (it is likely that the companies will outsource some parts of the overall system functionality – server room fire protection and power supply backup need maintenance). All this is included in the cost of cloud storage which, if used, might leave the organisation's IT personnel more time to focus on how they could help increase the organisation's revenue. Although organisations may employ various methods to estimate cost, using a generally accepted model can help systematize what is a highly complex decision-making process to arrive at a decision in which decision-makers can have more confidence. This chapter presents findings from two research studies, one that explored the use of models for costing cloud storage services and another that explored issues of trust in adopting such services, claiming that trust should be looked upon as a combined socio-technical set of requirements, roles, rules, policies, procedures, best practices, responsibilities, and responsible governance.

Existing work on models for digital storage costs

Since 2009, a small body of complementary work on modelling the cost of cloud storage has been published in the computer science/information systems and library/archives disciplines, with one in economics (McLeod & Gormly, 2015, 2018). Beginning with the application of a pre-existing buy-or-lease business decision model (Walker, 2009), subsequent work addressed perceived weaknesses in this model and led to the use and development of different models, which sought more comprehensive coverage of the costs to consider and/or ways to handle uncertainty. Four different financial or management accounting theories, with some variations, underpin the models presented in the work, including a toolkit that considers a range of qualitative factors rather than purely cost. These are

1 discounted cash flow including net present value, differential net present value, and internal rate of return (Walker, Brisken, & Romney, 2010; Mastroeni & Naldi, 2011a, 2011b; Khajeh-Hosseini, Greenwood, Smith, & Sommerville, 2012; Wang et al., 2012. See also: D. C. Rosenthal et al., 2012; Rosenthal & Vargas, 2012; Naldi & Mastroeni, 2013, 2016)
2 Monte Carlo models and Kryder's Law (D. S. H. Rosenthal et al., 2012; Rosenthal & Vargas, 2012)
3 full cost accounting including total cost of ownership (Reichman, 2011; Dutta & Hasan, 2013)
4 acquisition interval: length of time in acquiring additional storage (Mazhelis, Fazekas, & Tyrväinen, 2012; Laatikainen, Mazhelis, & Tyrväinen, 2014).

Their key characteristics are summarised in Table 8.1.

The DCF models are potentially less useful for modelling digital storage costs over the longer term, as they rely on historical data (Walker et al., 2010). Their more sophisticated versions (DNPV, IRR) can be useful as they account for unknown or random changes (e.g. leasing price and disc failure) and incorporate risk measures. Monte Carlo models are also helpful for longer term cost modelling as their probabilistic algorithms account for unknown changes (e.g. interest rates). Kryder's Law (Walter, 2005), which states that storage density of discs doubles every two years but is widely translated into the exponential decrease in digital storage cost, is relevant here. Work on projecting cloud storage costs and the impact of Kryder's Law, amongst other factors, reveals that cloud storage pricing has not decreased in accordance

Table 8.1 Summary characteristics of costing models used in a cloud storage context featuring in the literature

Model / financial theory	Characteristics
Discounted cash flow (DCF) including: • Net present value (NPV) • Differential net present value (DNPV) • Internal rate of return (IRR)	**DCF:** based on the principle of the value of money (spent or invested) over time; i.e. a unit of money today having a different value in the future, taking account of inflation, interest rate (the discount rate) and returns. Standard economic techniques but sometimes criticized because they assume the interest rate is constant rather than variable over time. **NPV:** sum of the present values of all the cash flows relating to a project, i.e. cash inflows (earned) and cash outflows (spent). A positive NPV indicates a profit, a negative NPV a loss. In a buy-or-lease scenario, if NPV (buy) is greater than NPV (lease), then the decision should be to buy. Considers factors such as capital costs (e.g. purchase, interest rate), operating costs (e.g. energy, personnel), and other relevant costs for the context (e.g. disc price trends, disc replacement rates, and hardware salvage value). **DNPV:** considers the difference between the two NPVs rather than their absolutes; easier to calculate. **IRR:** the interest rate required for the NPV to be zero.
Monte Carlo/stochastic models and Kryder's Law	**Monte Carlo models:** based on Monte Carlo or other stochastic methods, i.e. algorithms that use statistical probability to handle uncertainty (e.g. future storage costs or volumes). **Kryder's Law:** states that storage density of discs doubles every two years; widely translated into the exponential decrease in digital storage cost.
Full cost accounting (FCA) including total cost of ownership (TCO)	**FCA:** recognises a wider range of costs than standard financial cash flow methods, e.g. economic, social, and environmental costs. **TCO:** sum of all expenditures of a project or system (e.g. power, personnel, hardware), accounting for direct and indirect costs, including overheads, but not for the time value of money. Can be used in FCA.
Acquisition interval	Length of time between intervals at which an organisation evaluates its storage needs (including predicting demand for storage) and acquires additional in-house storage.

with this law (D. S. H. Rosenthal et al., 2012; Rosenthal & Vargas, 2012). Pricing of some of the major cloud storage providers was shown to have dropped at most by 3% per year or remained the same, in comparison with a 30% per year drop in disc prices over a 30-year period. TCO is difficult to use accurately in practice and "a more pragmatic approach is to compare only the costs that change between the two scenarios, known as relative cost of operations" (Reichman, 2011, p. 13). Changing factors include storage acquisition cost, storage utilisation, redundancy copies, service life of storage, maintenance, and data migration, personnel, and infrastructure cost (facilities and energy). As the name suggests, acquisition interval theory accounts for the length of time between evaluating and acquiring additional storage, considered by some to be critical in analyzing storage cost. For further details, see McLeod and Gormly (2015, 2017).

Although a range of increasingly sophisticated models have been developed to understand and compare the cost of storing data and information in the cloud versus in-house, since Johnson and Lewellen's (1972) seminal paper on modelling the buy-or-lease decision, they all have limitations.

Use of models for cloud storage costs in practice

From 2010–2015, only 11 case examples of the adoption of economic models in practice have been identified. They are summarised in Table 8.2. The "real" case examples are all based on university departments or services (Khajeh-Hosseini et al., 2012; Mazhelis et al., 2012; Dutta & Hasan, 2013; Laatikainen et al., 2014). The hypothetical scenarios all consider the relative size of the organisation (small, medium, large), regardless of sector, and make comparisons (Walker et al., 2010; Mastroeni & Naldi, 2011a; Reichman, 2011; D. S. H. Rosenthal et al., 2012; Naldi & Mastroeni, 2016). The other scenarios all use actual service providers' pricing structures (Rosenthal & Vargas, 2012; Wang et al., 2012; Naldi & Mastroeni, 2013). Most examples include at least one caveat – for example, additional factors to consider or risk assessment – in drawing conclusions.

In 2015–2016 McLeod and Gormly (2016, 2017) explored records professionals' use of models to inform their decision-making and business case preparation for using cloud storage services. In their small but international survey, about 25% (15) of respondents indicated that their organisation had used a costing model in the decision-making process, of which ten were using cloud storage. The most popular models used were relative cost of operations (10), defined in the survey as the "comparison of costs that change between in-house and cloud, including service life of storage, redundancy copies, personnel and infrastructure," and non-financial factors (9) defined as "technology suitability, stakeholder impact, socio-political benefits, risks, responsibilities." Few had used the more sophisticated models identified in the literature. This raises questions about the adequacy of their cost modelling, although two-thirds had used two or more models which compensates

Table 8.2 Summary of case examples and scenarios presented in the literature

Case example/scenario	Conclusion (buy vs. lease; cloud vs. in-house)
1 Discounted cash flow including net present value, differential net present value, and internal rate of return	
Three scenarios – a single-user computer, medium-size, and large organisations	**Single-user computer**: cloud is more cost effective for storage of less than four years, purchase is recommended for long term storage. **Medium-size organisations**: cloud storage is the best option. **Large organisations (over 1,000 servers)**: cloud is cost effective for up to nine years, purchase is more economical for longer periods
Pricing comparison of providers: Dropbox, SugarSync, IDrive, Google Drive, Carbonite, Symform, Mozy, Amazon	Two types of pricing: tapering pricing ("declining block rate charge") and bundling (or "quantity discount"). All providers surveyed, except Amazon, use bundling. For individual users, Google Drive and IDrive are the best options. For businesses, Amazon, Carbonite, and SugarSync appear to offer the best plans, though Dropbox is also a contender when factors beyond the calculation are considered.
Hypothetical "simulation scenario" with values for each parameter in the model (based on current costs, etc.) and size of company (small, large)	Larger companies looking toward storage over the long term (10+ years) will benefit from a buy decision. For smaller companies, the cost of an insurance policy to protect against the risk of making the wrong decision is "affordable" over the shorter time, according to their pricing formula.
Scenarios: medium and large companies	Cloud storage has greater cost benefits for medium-sized than for large-sized companies, and for long term rather than short term investment. They assess the risk of making the wrong lease-or-buy decision, employing the value-at-risk risk measure, to demonstrate that risk is greatest when the possible profits from both buy and lease decisions are close to equal.
Hypothetical scenarios using Amazon S3 (advertised pricing)	Cloud storage is more beneficial for small organisations (annual storage growth rate of 1 TB) than for large organisations (annual storage growth rate of 10 TB)
School of Computer Science University of St. Andrews, UK compared with Amazon Web Services (AWS)	Little difference between in-house (buying servers) and cloud storage costs, but need to consider factors beyond financial considerations, such as organisational change.

(Continued)

Table 8.2 (Continued)

Case example/scenario	Conclusion (buy vs. lease; cloud vs. in-house)
2 Monte Carlo models and Kryder's Law	
Hypothetical scenarios with values for each parameter in the short and long term models based on current costs	Pricing models of cloud storage services (at the time) mean that the cloud is not an appropriate option for long term storage.
LOCKSS boxes using Amazon S3 (simple storage service)	Local disk storage is cheaper for long term storage because cloud storage pricing has not decreased according to Kryder's Law. Proposed adjustments to Amazon S3, to make the service more cost effective, are vindicated by the introduction of Amazon Glacier, but, if Glacier pricing follows that of S3, it will be a more expensive long term option than local storage.
3 Full cost accounting including total cost of ownership	
Computer and Information Science Department Data Centre (small), University of Alabama Birmingham, USA compared with Amazon S3 (advertised pricing)	Cost for storing 1 byte per year: • in-house = 71.51×10^3 picocents • Amazon S3 = 88.37×10^3 picocents (1 US picocent = $\$1 \times 10^{-14}$) The costs are relatively similar but factors such as pricing, scale of operation, and data redundancy should be considered.
Generalised comparison between internal and cloud storage of 100 TB of data	Demonstrates a 74% reduction in cost with the cloud, but cautions about other issues involved in using the cloud.
4 Acquisition interval – length of acquisition of additional storage	
Oxford University Computing Services compared with Amazon S3 (advertised pricing)	In a typical case of exponentially growing storage demand, (public) cloud storage is more cost effective when the intervals between assessments of private storage are longer. However, the acquisition interval at which private storage becomes more financially beneficial is also affected by other factors: the utility premium charged by the cloud provider, necessary storage redundancy, and the costs of transferring data to and from the cloud.

somewhat. Interestingly, less than half of the respondents whose organisation had chosen cloud storage for economic reasons had actually used an economic model in making their decision (10 of 25 respondents).

In the organisations that both used cloud storage and an economic model (10), the most popular reason for using a model was to estimate costs as part of the adoption decision-making process, but they were also used as part of a business case for cloud adoption and also to monitor costs post-adoption. Three case studies explored in more detail how costing models were used in practice. One organisation compared the cost of in-house versus cloud storage for a records collection and considered how in-house storage services might develop and affect the cost of that option. Modelling showed that the cloud was by far the most economic option over an eight-year period, and they had assured themselves that cloud services could meet the archival requirements. No formal review of the original modelling against current reality had been conducted, but costs were in line with expectations. Another organisation compared a number of services in terms of cost but did not use a purely financial model. They also evaluated non-financial factors, particularly technology suitability (i.e. functionality/features, industry/collaborator trends), stakeholder impact, risks, and responsibilities, as their main concerns were scalability and meeting future needs. The cloud adoption decision-making process was informal and based on past vendor experience. The third organisation used total cost of ownership to model the cost of software applications, which was proving to be challenging in the cloud context, as Reichman (2011) indicates. Also, on-premises solutions often had not included hidden costs, especially the people costs to "get something done." Non-financial factors were also being considered.

Although the small size of the sample limits any conclusions regarding the use of economic models, the data appears to indicate a preference for the simpler, perhaps more commonly used, ones. Given the development of complex models, because simpler cost comparisons were found to be inadequate, this is concerning. However, in the two case examples when financial models were used, the recordkeeping professionals interviewed were very aware of the shortcomings of the models used.

A number of issues emerged from this study (McLeod & Gormly, 2017). First, models for estimating the cost of storing records in the cloud are not widely used and, while recordkeeping professionals are often, but not always, involved in the cloud storage decision-making process, they are often not the leading voice. This is a concern given the functional requirements for records storage. Second, what is the potential impact of moving from capital to ongoing operating expenditure in using cloud storage services, and the potential risks to data and information if storage costs were to show an unsustainable increase? Third, cost modelling is context and use specific; therefore, a full understanding of the scenario is required. Finally, existing models need further development. They can be effective in supporting the business case but are inadequate for estimating longer term storage costs. Additionally, it is essential to identify *all* costs, not just technical ones, particularly the hidden costs of people's time, yet existing models do not explicitly capture some costs (e.g. tight access and security controls for federated systems).

Issues of trust in the decision-making process

McLeod and Gormly's study (2017) found that the most significant issues of trust in using a cloud service were concerns about the continued delivery of a sustainable and also economically viable service, and the ability of the service to meet records requirements. Trust in CSPs (cloud service providers) is important and lack of trust in them can adversely affect the cloud adoption decision, reflecting the suggestion by Leverich, Nalliah, and Suderman (2015) that trust in the service provider is relatively more important than trust in the technology. These issues can be addressed through a robust decision-making process which involves all relevant stakeholders, identifies and prioritizes requirements, investigates and assesses options, identifies responsibilities and stakeholder impact, and manages risk.

Views of the risks of using cloud services vary. Some organisations consider the risks as similar to those faced on premises, although recognise that the magnitude of the consequences should a risk materialise may be significantly greater, depending on the risk, since they are not wholly in the organisation's control. Others manage risk based on the criticality of the content, as well as the business actions and access restrictions necessary, choosing to store only certain classes of records and/or cloud services. This strategy follows the conclusions of Stuart and Bromage (2010), who describe cloud adoption as a "risk-based decision" (pp. 223–224) in which the risks differ between organisations and between records of different values. Risk management enables organisations to reap the benefits of cloud services while minimizing any risks.

Issues of trust in cloud service providers

In addressing issues of trust in CSPs offering IaaS (Infrastructure-as-a-Service), we argue that trust should be looked upon as a combined socio-technical set of requirements, roles, rules, policies, procedures, best practices, responsibilities, and responsible governance.

Research methodology

The research presented here was part of the ITrust's study *Ensuring Trust in Storage in Infrastructure-as-a-Service* (Stančić, Buršić, & Al-Hariri, 2015), and was divided into four stages: identification, data acquisition, analysis, and interpretation. The research was limited to the EU region, with the focus on Croatia.

In the research, Stančić et al. (2015) looked for the minimum amount of information providing trust in the service and also positioning service providers as trusted ones. For the purpose of research, the NIST (National Institute of Standards and Technology, USA) definition of cloud computing was adopted specifying that it is

> a model for enabling ubiquitous, convenient, on-demand network access to a shared pool of configurable computing resources (e.g. networks, servers, storage, applications, and services) that can be rapidly provisioned and released with minimal management effort or service provider interaction. This cloud model is composed of five essential characteristics, three service models, and four deployment models.
>
> (Mell & Grance, 2011, p. 2)

Aligning with Mell and Grance (2011), Stančić, Rajh, and Milošević (2013) differentiate between three service models: SaaS (Software-as-a-Service), PaaS (Platform-as-a-Service), and IaaS (Infrastructure-as-a-Service). They also differentiate between four deployment models: private, community, public, or hybrid cloud. Also following Mell and Grance (2011), the Records in the Cloud project (Duranti, 2014) identifies five essential characteristics of cloud solutions: on-demand self-service, broad network access, resource pooling, rapid elasticity, and measured service (Table 8.3).

The ITrust terminology database defines *trust* as "confidence of one party in another, based on alignment of value systems with respect to specific actions or benefits, and involving a relationship of voluntary vulnerability, dependence and reliance, based on risk assessment" (Terminology Database, n.d.). Therefore, the users of cloud services should have enough information on a service, e.g. stated in the terms of service, to be able to trust it. The SLA (service-level agreement) signed between users and CSPs should treat both parties equally. To better understand whether this is the case, a questionnaire containing 36 questions was developed and used for surveying ten CSPs operating at a national level in Croatia. The fact that only three responded in full shows that either the issue of trust is not the focus of the seven CSPs that did not respond (which would be worrying), or that they were not able to respond to the majority of questions (thus they did not want to reveal the low level of trust the users should have in their services), or the survey asked too complicated questions for one person to answer (this is the risk the research team was aware of before sending the survey). Nevertheless, the CSPs that responded provided enough detailed information to give a glimpse of the situation.

Inspired by Jansen and Grance (2011, pp. 14–36), the questionnaire was organized in ten categories:

1 general information
2 governance

Table 8.3 Cloud service models, deployment models, and characteristics

Service models	SaaS	Application delivery through client software. User is neither aware of nor controls physical infrastructure, nor can configure other applications than the delivered one.
	PaaS	Environment delivery (e.g. operating system). User can control and configure the delivered environment, but is neither aware of nor controls physical infrastructure nor can configure application-hosting environment.
	IaaS	Virtual data centre delivery where user can configure and deploy virtual environments/components.
Deployment models	Private	Built for, provisioned for, and used by one organisation. Usually service-oriented and ideal for users having specific requirements.
	Community	Built for, provisioned for, administered by, and used by several organisations forming a community and sharing same requirements and goals.
	Public	Built for rent by a cloud service provider.
	Hybrid	Two or more deployment models combined – physically separated but connected by mutually portable data or applications.
Characteristics	On-demand self-service	Users can access as many computing capabilities as they need.
	Broad network access	Access is enabled from any device with an internet connection.
	Resource pooling	The underlying infrastructure enables multi-tenancy, i.e. multiple users can use the same infrastructure at the same time without interfering with each other.
	Rapid elasticity	Users can increase or decrease the amount of computing resources (processor power, storage, etc.) they use at any time.
	Measured service	Pay-as-you-go model allows users to pay only for what they have used. The amount of used resources is precisely measured.

3 compliance
4 trust
5 architecture
6 identity and access management
7 software isolation
8 data protection
9 availability
10 incident response.

The developed questionnaire was later transformed to a checklist (see Appendix 4) and translated into Spanish (Stančić, Buršić, & Al-Hariri, 2016) so that any user wanting to assess and compare IaaS cloud services can use it and determine whether an IaaS service can or should be trusted.

Research results

The selected research results are grouped according to the survey categories (Stančić, Al-Hariri, & Buršić, 2014; Stančić et al., 2015).

General information

The set of questions in this category aimed at gathering general information. The surveyed CSPs provide all standard service models (SaaS, PaaS, and IaaS) both to legal and natural persons. They use verified hardware companies for redundant storage and server solutions they implement. Predominantly IaaS is rented as infrastructure, but one CSP stands out with a bundle of free additional services such as virtual server, console access, preinstalled images, daily backup, traffic monitoring, twice-yearly safety scanning, the possibility to expand resources, and a help-desk service. All respondents provide total separation of clients and reservation of guaranteed resources.

Governance

(Information) governance is one of the key factors in assuring data security, relying on implemented policies and procedures. The survey asked whether users can verify data integrity and, if so, how they can be sure that the data from other users is not mixed with theirs. The respondents stated that clients have complete autonomy and responsibility over data in their own virtual servers, while virtualisation prevented logical and physical mixing of the data. International standards are followed, e.g. ISO 27001 on information security management.

Compliance

For a user considering IaaS, it might be important to know with which laws a CSP is aligned, where geographically the data is stored, and if any part of the service is subcontracted. All respondents claimed they are aligned with the relevant national and international legal regulations. The data is stored in Croatia, but one CSP offers storage on their partners' premises outside of Croatia though still within the EU. All respondents reported that no part of their service was subcontracted.

Trust

This category is central for users choosing a trustworthy CSP. In relation to risk management, two out of three respondents referred to ISO 27001 (2005).

On the question of physical and logical security of virtual servers and applications only, one respondent mentioned separation at disc level and different layers of network infrastructure. CSPs regulate data ownership by contracts or by terms of service if the service is provided free of charge. Another trust-related concern was whether the users can trust the CSP employees. It seems that they can, since all CSPs claimed they have a clause about data confidentiality in their employment contracts. In terms of certificates, one of the respondents stands out by having NATO and EU certificates. However, the ANSI/TIA-942, a telecommunication infrastructure standard for data centres, was not mentioned. The surveyed CSPs provide fair protection against various attacks (e.g. DoS [Denial of Service], DDoS [Distributed DoS], etc.) but one provider did not have protection against DoS attack, making the service rather vulnerable.

Architecture

Hardware and software architecture for cloud service provision can have significant influence on overall security. The respondents claimed they limit and monitor access to hypervisors. Protection is maintained on the CSP side, while only one offers client-side protection on request. The architecture security measures were investigated, e.g. protection against attacks on hypervisor, or implementation of virtual machine image management. Two out of the three CSPs use virtual machine image management. Although respondents provided limited answers about usage of encryption, types of encryption, and protocols used on SSL (Secure Sockets Layer) and TLS (Transport Layer Security) levels, they did say that encrypted (symmetrical and asymmetrical) network exchange is used.

Identity and access management

Data sensitivity and privacy of information have always been an area of concern for organisations. The identity proofing and authentication aspects of identity management entail the use, maintenance, and protection of PII (personally identifiable information) collected from users. Therefore, this ancillary data should be protected, and organisations should be given assurance of protection. All the respondents use some kind of data isolation, either by using a stand-alone system or by limiting access to administrators only.

Software isolation

CSPs achieve flexibility of on-demand services through multi-tenancy. In an IaaS cloud computing environment, this is typically done by multiplexing execution of virtual machines from different users on the same physical server. Multi-tenancy in virtual machine-based cloud infrastructure can be open to different sources of threat such as a man-in-the-middle attack. All respondents claimed they use some sort of protection such as complex cryptographic algorithms, personal PKI (public key infrastructure), or protection through SSL. The provider-side server attacks are prevented by using IPS (intrusion prevention systems).

Data protection

The research team examined protection of data-in-transit and data-at-rest. It was found that one provider does not use encryption, while others use high end disc systems which provide several types of encryption. Test attacks on the systems are done to determine overall security. All CSPs can retrieve (un) intentionally deleted data.

In a public cloud computing environment, the data from one client is physically collocated with other clients' data, which can complicate things with regards to safe deletion of data. In many cases it was possible, by using proper skills and equipment, to recover sensitive information from the used drives bought at online auctions. In the research, the CPSs mention that data sanitization is the client's responsibility. Several deletion methods are used on the provider-side, such as zero fill or virtual volume deletion. One provider specified: "(We) overwrite all addressable locations with a character, its complement, then a random character and verify."

Availability

In the year 2012, the Megaupload file sharing servers were raided and all assets were seized. The US government insisted that all user data, even the legitimate data, should be destroyed. More than 50 million users were at risk of losing their data (Megaupload Data, 2012). This example shows that users and their legitimate businesses can be at risk because of (illegal) decisions made by the service provider. Also, CSPs can suffer damage or loss due to natural disasters or human errors. Or, they can run out of business, go bankrupt, or have other kinds of financial difficulties. The mentioned threats and risks could be addressed from two sides – by enforcing a CSP-side policy or by setting up a user-side contingency plan, including solutions to prolonged and permanent system disruptions, especially with mission-critical operations, until restoration of the service.

In case of a court order requiring a user's hardware and/or data, all surveyed providers are obliged to provide either hardware, which would be removed from the data storage facility, or a copy of the user's volume. The first solution could potentially affect other users, since their data (not covered by the court order) could become "collateral damage," while the latter is considered a more practical solution for providing all needed information. However, if a physical server indeed is seized, CSPs would reallocate resources to maintain service at the highest possible level for other clients. If the CSPs were to run out of business, go bankrupt, or suffer other financial difficulties, they claimed that they would most certainly give the latest copy of the data to the users. One provider mentioned that some elements of this scenario are covered by the SLA, specifically in the case when users are using dedicated infrastructure. In that case, clients would be offered to opportunity to purchase the infrastructure and the price would be set by the national tax administration.

Incident response

Incident response involves an organized method for dealing with the consequences of an attack against the security of a computer system. The cloud provider's role is vital in performing incident response activities, including incident verification, attack analysis, containment, data collection and preservation, problem remediation, and service restoration. In the case of a security incident, all providers can track compromised data and undertake corrective actions to reduce possible damage. Also, all respondents record forensic data, and one of the CSPs is preserving them. Users of all CSPs have access to the forensic data relevant for their service.

Discussion

The set of 36 questions divided into ten categories was sufficient to provide enough information on the IaaS model of a cloud service offered by CSPs so that users can assess whether they could trust the service or not, i.e. whether they can consider the service as responsible, reliable, accurate, secure, transparent, and trustworthy, as well as whether it considers privacy issues, duties to remember (i.e. digital preservation), and the right to be forgotten (i.e. safe deletion).

On reflection, it was not easy to get feedback from the CSPs and the response rate was lower than expected. Despite that, the results are indicative. Before they were surveyed, the CSPs were focused on the business side of their operations and were not considering recordkeeping- or archival science-related requirements or trust-related issues. Therefore, the survey has achieved an unforeseen educational benefit. Some CSPs commented that the survey "made them think" about offering more information online. Indeed, trust between users and CSPs should be based on enough information made available by CSPs and the possibility for users to negotiate the type and functionalities of the provisioned service. CSPs should also demonstrate their operational sustainability and conformance to the relevant standards. Therefore, the trust in CSPs offering IaaS should be looked upon as a combined socio-technical set of requirements, roles, rules, policies, procedures, best practices, responsibilities, and responsible governance.

Conclusion

Records are, arguably, the most complex form of recorded information organisations have to manage and, increasingly, are being stored in the cloud either by design or default. It is, therefore, important to make well-informed decisions about using cloud services for their creation, capture, and preservation, to understand the risks and benefits, and to be able to trust in CSPs. In this chapter, we have focused on the economic aspect of the decision-making process and trust in CSPs offering IaaS. In relation to economics, the vast majority of respondents surveyed had not used any kind of costing model in the decision-making process, including those who had chosen cloud storage for economic reasons and, when they had, they had used the less sophisticated models that exist in the literature. Records professionals need to be aware of and understand the various costing models and ensure the most appropriate ones are used in the decision-making process. Checklists and guides for cloud usage aimed explicitly at recordkeeping professionals can help with awareness raising. However, existing ones do not explicitly address the economic issue – meaning that there is an opportunity to add it. Checklists can also be used as part of the process of assessing and choosing a trustworthy CSP (Appendix 4) and, as has been demonstrated, to raise awareness and educate CSPs, since not all of them perceive the concept of trust in their service as their concern. However, "trust in the service provider is a far greater consideration than trust in the technology" (Leverich et al., 2015, p. 4). Trust is complex and should be based on CSPs communicating adequate information and clients negotiating the functionality required. It comprises cognition (e.g. judgements based on first impressions or experience), relational (from the relationship over time, such as contractual terms and service sustainability), and calculated trust (e.g. cost savings, economic viability) (Leverich et al., 2015; McLeod & Gormly, 2017). Trust is therefore a mutual concern and responsibility of both CSPs and clients, and should be seen as a combined socio-technical set of requirements, roles and responsibilities, and responsible governance (including rules, policies, procedures and best practices).

Acknowledgements

We wish to acknowledge graduate research assistant Brianna Gormly, from the School of Information, University of British Columbia, as well as post-graduate student Edvin Buršić and graduate research assistant Adam Al-Hariri from the Department of Information and Communication Sciences, Faculty of Humanities and Social Sciences, University of Zagreb, who participated in this research.

References

Duranti, L. (2014). *Records in the cloud: Detailed description.* Retrieved from http://www.recordsinthecloud.org/secure/documents

Dutta, A. K., & Hasan, R. (2013). How much does storage really cost? Towards a full cost accounting model for data storage. In J. Altmann, K. Vanmechelen, & O. F. Rana (Eds.), *Economics of grids, clouds, systems, and services. GECON 2013.* Lecture Notes in Computer Science (Vol. 8193, pp. 29–43). Cham: Springer. https://doi.org/10.1007/978-3-319-02414-1_3

International Data Corporation. (2019, June 20). *Cloud IT infrastructure revenues continue to expand despite slow down in spending in 2019.* Press Release. Retrieved from https://www.idc.com/getdoc.jsp?containerId=prUS45293719

Jansen, W., & Grance, T. (2011). Guidelines on security and privacy in public cloud computing. *Special Publication 800–144.* Gaithersburg: National Institute of Standards and Technology. Retrieved from http://csrc.nist.gov/publications/nistpubs/800-144/SP800-144.pdf

Johnson, R. W., & Lewellen, W. G. (1972). Analysis of lease-or-buy decision. *Journal of Finance, 27,* 815–823.

Khajeh-Hosseini, A., Greenwood, D., Smith, D. W., & Sommerville, I. (2012). The cloud adoption toolkit: Supporting cloud adoption decisions in the enterprise, *Software: Practice and Experience, 42,* 447–465. https://doi.org/10.1002/spe.1072

Laatikainen, G., Mazhelis, O., & Tyrväinen, P. (2014). Role of acquisition intervals in private and public cloud storage costs. *Decision Support Systems, 57,* 320–330. https://doi.org/10.1016/j.dss.2013.09.020

Leverich, M., Nalliah, K., & Suderman, J. (2015). *Historical study of cloud-based services* (NA11). InterPARES Trust. Retrieved from https://interparestrust.org/assets/public/dissemination/NA11_20150109_HistoricalStudyCloudServices_InternationalPlenary2_Report_Final.pdf

Mastroeni, L., & Naldi, M. (2011a). *Storage buy-or-lease decisions in cloud computing under price uncertainty.* Paper presented at the 7th EURO-NGI Conference on Next Generation Internet (NGI), Kaiserslautern.

Mastroeni, L., & Naldi, M. (2011b). Long-range evaluation of risk in the migration to cloud storage. In *13th IEEE Conference on Commerce and Enterprise Computing (CEC 2011)* (pp. 260–266). Luxembourg: IEEE.

Mazhelis, O., Fazekas, G., & Tyrväinen, P. (2012). *Impact of storage acquisition intervals on the cost-efficiency of the private vs. public storage.* Paper presented at the 5th IEEE International Conference on Cloud Computing (CLOUD), Honolulu, HI. https://doi.org/10.1109/CLOUD.2012.101

McLeod, J., & Gormly, B. (2015). *Economic models for storage of records in the cloud (StaaS): A critical review of the literature* (EU18). InterPARES Trust. Retrieved from https://interparestrust.org/assets/public/dissemination/EU18_20150713_Cloud EconomicsLitReview_FinalReport.pdf

McLeod, J., & Gormly, B. (2016). *Economic models for cloud storage decision-making: An investigation into the use of economic models for making decisions about using the cloud for records storage* (EU20). InterPARES Trust. Retrieved from https://inter parestrust.org/assets/public/dissemination/EU20_20160609_CloudEconomic Models_EUWorkshop8_FinalReport.pdf

McLeod, J., & Gormly, B. (2017). Using the cloud for records storage: Issues of trust. *Archival Science, 17*(4), 349–370. https://doi.org/10.1007/s10502-017-9280-5

McLeod, J., & Gormly, B. (2018). Records storage in the cloud: Are we modelling the cost? *Archives and Manuscripts, 46*, 174–192. https://doi.org/10.1080/01576 895.2017.1409125

Megaupload Data 'To Be Destroyed In Days'. (2012, January 30). *Sky News*. Retrieved from https://news.sky.com/story/megaupload-data-to-be-destroyed-in-days-10481354

Mell, P., & Grance, T. (2011). The NIST definition of cloud computing. *NIST special publication 800–145*. Gaithersburg: National Institute of Standards and Technology. Retrieved from https://nvlpubs.nist.gov/nistpubs/Legacy/SP/nistspecialpublication 800-145.pdf

Naldi, M., & Mastroeni, L. (2013). Cloud storage pricing: A comparison of current practices. In *Proceedings of the 2013 International Workshop on Hot Topics in Cloud Services (pp. 27–34)*. Prague: Association for Computing Machinery. https://doi.org/10.1145/2462307.2462315

Naldi, M., & Mastroeni, L. (2016). Economic decision criteria for the migration to cloud storage. *European Journal of Information Systems, 25*, 16–28. https://doi. org/10.1057/ejis.2014.34.

Oliver, G., & Knight, S. (2015). Storage is a strategic issue: Digital preservation in the cloud. *D-Lib Magazine, 21*(3/4). Retrieved from https://www.dlib.org/dlib/ march15/oliver/03oliver.html

Reichman, A. (2011). *File storage costs less in the cloud than in-house*. Retrieved from http://media.amazonwebservices.com/Forrester_File_Storage_Costs_Less_ In_The_Cloud.pdf

Rosenthal, D. C., Rosenthal, D. S. H., Miller, E. L., Adams, I. F., Storer, M. W., & Zadok, E. (2012). *Toward an economic model of long-term storage*. Retrieved from http://static.usenix.org/events/fast/poster_descriptions/Rosenthaldescription.pdf

Rosenthal, D. S. H., Rosenthal, D. C., Miller, E. L., Adams, I. F., Storer, M. W., & Zadok, E. (2012). *The economics of long-term digital storage*. Retrieved from https://www.lockss.org/locksswp/wp-content/uploads/2012/09/unesco2012.pdf

Rosenthal, D. S. H., & Vargas, D. L. (2012). *LOCKSS boxes in the cloud*. Retrieved from https://www.lockss.org/locksswp/wp-content/uploads/2012/09/LC-final-2012.pdf

Stančić, H., Al-Hariri, A., & Buršić, E. (2014). Archival approach to IaaS cloud services. In T. Hunjak, S. Lovrenčić, & I. Tomičić (Eds.), *Proceedings of 25th Central European Conference on Information and Intelligent Systems* (pp. 216–222). Varaždin: Faculty of Organization and Informatics. Retrieved from http://archive. ceciis.foi.hr/app/public/conferences/1/papers2014/683.pdf

Stančić, H., Buršić, E., & Al-Hariri, A. (2015). *Ensuring trust in storage in Infrastructure-as-a-Service (IaaS)* (EU08). InterPARES Trust. Retrieved from https://interpares

trust.org/assets/public/dissemination/EU08_20160727_EnsuringTrustStorage IaaS_FinalReport_Final.pdf

Stančić, H., Buršić, E., & Al-Hariri, A. (2016). *Asegurar la confianza en el almacenamiento de un servicio de infraestructura en la nube (IaaS)* [Ensuring trust in storage in Infrastructure-as-a-Service (IaaS)] InterPARES Trust. Retrieved from https://interparestrust.org/assets/public/dissemination/EU08_20161110_IaaS-Checklist_v1-2_Spanish.pdf

Stančić, H., Rajh, A., & Milošević, I. (2013). "Archiving-as-a-Service": Influence of cloud computing on the archival theory and practice. In L. Duranti & E. Shaffer (Eds.), *The memory of the world in the digital age: Digitization and preservation* (pp. 108–125). Vancouver: UNESCO.

Stuart, K., & Bromage, D. (2010). Current state of play: Records management and the cloud. *Records Management Journal, 20*, 217–225. https://doi.org/10.1108/09 565691011064340

Terminology Database. (n.d.). *Trust.* InterPARES Trust. Retrieved from http://arstweb.clayton.edu/interlex/en/term.php?term=trust

Walker, E. (2009). The real cost of a CPU hour. *Computer, 42*(2), 35–41.

Walker, E., Brisken, W., & Romney, J. (2010). To lease or not to lease from storage clouds. *Computer, 43*(4), 44–50.

Walter, C. (2005). Kryder's law. *Scientific American, 293*, 32–33.

Wang, J., Hua, R., Zhu, Y., Xie, C., Wang, P., & Gong, W. (2012). *C-IRR: An adaptive engine for cloud storage provisioning determined by economic models with workload burstiness consideration.* Paper presented at the 7th IEEE International Conference on Networking, Architecture and Storage (NAS). Xiamen: IEEE. https://doi.org/10.1109/NAS.2012.13

Zander, O. (2014). *Preserving 40 terabytes per day: On-premises, cloud . . . or both?* Paper presented at the 2nd Annual Conference of the International Council on Archives, Girona.

9 Conclusion to Part I

Part I of the book on the one hand identified a set of skills the information managers, records managers, and archivists should have, while on the other hand, recognized many gaps in skillsets, knowledge, policies, legal regulations, etc., that will need to be filled. It also detected employee resistance, in the case of the introduction of new information governance models, caused by perceptions that innovative approaches were an attempt to control their actions. This shows that the fast change of public administration needs to be adapted to the "(not so) slow and steady" approach if it wants to, at least partially, keep pace with fast ICT development. However, not only is it necessary to keep the pace, but also to keep the records authentic and preserved in the long term, even if they are entrusted to new models of cloud storage. Complexity and fragmentation of the legislative framework on cloud computing for electronic recordkeeping and digital preservation were detected. It was recommended that a common effort to create a homogeneous regulatory framework specifically dedicated to these aspects may be truly beneficial.

Understanding and considering the data and information quality as an asset is beneficial to public administrations. By taking this path, they can offer better e-services to citizens and businesses, but also to themselves. By implementing the *once-only* principle, public administration can improve the services. Inter-organisational collaboration, interconnection of e-services and sharing data, information, and records between public administration e-services among the EU member states will create new value and make way for more efficient government. However, trust in transactions and actors, as well as trustworthiness of the records created, should be protected and preserved if public administration wants to create trusted e-services. The key aspects of such services are transparency in their provision and the level of control that the users may exercise over their records and data. Taking not only cooperative and collaborative approaches, but federated approaches, too (e.g. to storage and digital preservation), may prove to have beneficial financial effects. Benefits expected from such initiatives vary, and they are partly dependent on the chosen mode of collaboration. However, understanding how to best utilize cloud services for records creation, capture, and preservation, and what it takes to trust a CSP, helps in making well-informed decisions – both financial and organisational. The checklists developed as a result of the research can help public administration to better understand the requirements, deriving from the records management profession and archival science, on what is needed to create trusted e-services and preserve their records in the cloud as authentic, trusted, and verifiable sources of evidence.

Part II
Citizens

10 Introduction to Part II

Part II of the book takes the citizens' perspective on the challenges related to entrusting records to the cloud. Citizens rely on public bodies to operate transparently and make not only documents and records openly available, but data as well. Datasets, derived from the underlying records, should be available in reusable formats either by request or according to publication schemes. This falls under the citizens' "right to data" principle. Therefore, this part starts by addressing the issues of open data in relation to privacy, followed by the discussion around quality of the data derived from the *citizen-state* interaction, inextricably connected to the participating citizen, and maintenance of the authenticity and integrity during any process of data extraction. The questions of whether it is possible to make anonymity an intrinsic property within an individual level dataset, whether the concept of privacy is diametrically opposed to government openness, and whether lack of clarity in purpose and lack of transparency in an e-service lead to loss of public trust in online records in general are discussed. Next, the way in which individuals experience and understand the documents delivered to them by internet connection is explored. The ways in which they judge such material to be authentic and "the real thing" show the citizens' level of understanding and the importance they associate with the fundamental archival concepts we hold so dear. On the other hand, quality and intuitiveness of the electronic records management systems user interfaces lead to better usability – critical to efficient searching for and using the authentic (open) data and records. To that end, this part proposes a heuristic evaluation method that can detect many usability issues at minimum cost. Finally, this part discusses a key factor in the *citizen-state* interplay, the education of records managers and archivists, who are responsible for making open data possible.

Part II of the book presents research results based on the investigation of the relevant body of literature, case studies, interviews, studies in user perceptions, usability studies, and studies of educational policies, practices, and curricula.

11 Open data and privacy

James Lowry and Anna Sexton

Introduction

Defining "data politics," Ruppert, Isin, and Bigo (2017) wrote that data politics is concerned "with not only political struggles around data collection and its deployments, but how data is generative of new forms of power relations and politics at different and interconnected scales" (p. 2). One clear thread in data politics is openness, with notions of open societies and open environments sharing a dependency on access to information – the former for informed participation and the latter for control using data. These affordances of data are often viewed as being in tension in government openness and individual privacy, where the data is deemed to be neutral, but its uses are political. Mindful that "raw data is an oxymoron" (Gitelman, 2013) – that data, like archives and records, are never neutral – this survey takes a high-level look at data protection and data reuse policy and activism in the UK in the context of open data to identify where and how privacy and openness connect.

The social and political significance of this topic cannot be overstated, as the recent difficulties of the Open Society Foundations (OSF) show. OSF's work on information and digital rights seeks to "curb overly broad and unaccountable surveillance, make major internet platforms more accountable to the public, and expose and challenge problems caused by algorithmic decision-making" (Open Society Foundations, n.d.). Post-2011, OSF has been banned in Russia, shut down in Pakistan, and driven out of Hungary and Turkey under government pressure and interference, demonstrating that information activism around privacy and access is perceived by some governments as a threat to their hegemony.

The political will behind the open data movement in the United Kingdom was chiefly commercially motivated, with the Cameron government citing innovation as a driver for the foundation of the Open Data Institute in 2011. In the same year, the UK co-founded the Open Government Partnership, an international organisation seeking to promote transparency and public participation in government. The year 2011, then, marks an important moment in the UK's open data movement, and this study of the literature therefore begins at this date. The literature review will focus on British sources, rather than European sources more generally. While this is primarily due to the limits of space, we recognize that we are writing as the UK moves towards Brexit, and the benefits of European work on privacy, and other areas of information policy and human rights that have been experienced in the UK, may soon fall subject to the agendas of domestic political actors. With this in mind, we have looked at privacy "from above," in the sense of laws, regulations and policies instigated by UK central government, and privacy "from below," in the sense of information activism from British civil society. The chapter draws on the ITrust's literature reviews *Open Government Data* (Lowry, 2015) and *Recordkeeping, Open Government Data and Privacy* (Sexton & Shepherd, 2017).

Privacy from above

According to Bates, the open government data (OGD) agenda in the UK rests on the notion that non-personal data "produced by public bodies should be opened for all to re-use, free of charge, and without discrimination" (Bates, 2014, p. 389). Since the election of the coalition government in 2010 in the UK, there has been a marked political focus on the potential to generate income from opening up public sector information, in part as a reaction to the global financial downturn and the introduction of austerity measures. This included, in 2011, a £10 million pledge by the government, to be delivered over five years, for the establishment of the Open Data Initiative. The Chancellor of the Exchequer gave this pledge in his Autumn 2011 statement to parliament with justifications that were tied into catalyzing "new markets and innovative products and services" (Chancellor of the Exchequer, 2011, p. 40). In a speech in December 2011, the Prime Minister employed a subtly different rhetoric which spoke to notions of collective action, solidarity, and citizen participation. Despite this glaze, it is clear from the Chancellor's earlier positioning that the UK's OGD agenda is as much connected to what Keen, Calinescu, Paige, and Rooksby (2013, p. 229) describe as "practical neo-liberalism" as it is to participatory citizenship. In "practical neo-liberalism," it is the relationship between the state and the private sector that takes precedence, and which is ultimately reinforced.

Despite central government drives to open up data as a reusable asset, there is in reality a series of stumbling blocks to any realisation of exploiting citizen-state data held in publicly maintained systems through open data initiatives. There are fundamental questions on usability and usefulness that are linked to the quality of the underlying records from which the data to be opened is drawn, as well as the extent to which data can maintain its authenticity and integrity during any process of extraction (Lowry, 2014). Keen et al. contend that datasets generated from public sector records are generally both incomplete and inaccurate. There is also a fundamental problem with any assumption that the state has the right to decide the "ifs, how, and when" in relation to opening up data derived from citizen interaction with state services. The assumption that they *do* have this right runs counter to growing trends of public feeling in the UK that emphasise citizen rights to control access to their data (Keen et al., 2013, p. 229).

To be published as wholly open data without restrictions, datasets must be anonymized (de-identified). Anonymisation is a process that "prevents all parties from singling out an individual in a dataset, from linking two records within a dataset (or between two separate datasets) and from inferring any information in such a dataset" (Article 29 Working Party, 2007). It might be assumed on the surface that this then solves the problem of citizen control: if individuals are no longer identifiable, then the data is surely no longer "theirs." This is an assumption that is reinforced in data protection law, as data protection is only applicable to *identifiable* data, with no data subject rights over data that has been de-identified. Yet the simple acceptance that anonymisation (de-identification) solves any issues that the citizen might have with the creation of open datasets that are derived from their interaction with the state is problematic. It is simply not possible to make anonymity an intrinsic property within an individual level dataset, because identifiability is context dependent and depends on what other data is available to the individual seeking to make an identification. Data derived from citizen-state interaction is in fact always inextricably connected to the participating citizen and the community from which they derive, and therefore those who have participated in the creation of the data retain a deeply vested interest in its ongoing use. However, the notion that they should have a say in supposedly anonymized open data reuse is not currently supported in law, policy, or regulation around open data.

Controlling the levels of detail (the granularity) in the data is one relatively effective way to manage the risk of identification, but the less detailed the data, the less commercially valuable, or otherwise useful (i.e. to researchers), the dataset becomes. Keen et al. (2013) suggest that it is "not clear" if or how "the circle of data protection and commercially valuable publication can be squared" (p. 238). Proponents of the OGD agenda often frame open data as a direct benefit for the citizen. As taxpayers, citizens should have access to data relating to the services that they help to pay for, to re-use with as few restrictions as possible. Yet clearly, as the preceding discussion begins to tease out, positing open data as a "citizen's right" can be in direct tension with the protection of the citizen's more fundamental rights, freedoms, and interests. For these reasons alone, the aspirations of the "open government agenda" are contentious.

While *sharing* data may lie at the heart of the OGD agenda, from a privacy perspective, the *limitation* of sharing personal information is not only seen as positive; it is cast as a fundamental human right. However, its reach is viewed in law as "non-absolute" and its application is therefore weighed against its functioning in society. A number of high-level overlapping legal measures exist to protect privacy, including privacy rights, which guarantee freedom from interference; rules of data protection, which control the processing of personal data; and duties of confidentiality, which protect against unauthorized or unreasonable breaches of confidence (Nuffield Council on Bioethics, 2014). Across these legal measures, a balance is sought between privacy and public interest, including where the boundary of privacy lies in relation to other fundamental human rights and interests.

An examination of the complexity of how these balances have been translated into the legal framework around data sharing can be opened up through a consideration of practices around more granular, person-level data generated through citizen-state interaction. This kind of data is often made accessible by government departments not as fully open data but as pseudonymized data. In these instances, artificial identifiers replace personal identifiers in a way that still enables the tracking of an individual across linked datasets. Pseudonymized data of this kind does fall under the Data Protection Act; however, the procedural mechanisms and possibilities surrounding its reuse are also controlled by an overlapping web of more specific and context-dependent laws and regulations. In exploring the extent to which the consent of the data subject plays a role in the release and reuse of government administrative data, Sexton, Shepherd, Duke-Williams, and Eveleigh (2018) examined processes for data release by UK government departments in relation to health, education, transport, and energy. This study revealed that while the General Data Protection Regulation (GDPR) and related UK Data Protection Act uphold the consent of the data subject as the primary procedural mechanism underpinning the fair and lawful processing of personal data, it is by no means the only permissible mechanism for authorizing data release. In place of explicit consent, it is possible for researchers and data providers to rely on alternative legal gateways, on privacy notices, and on offering opt-outs to data subjects.

The primary influencing factor on the centrality (or otherwise) of consent of the data subject is the specificities of the legislative framework governing the collection and processing of the data. For example, school data collection is made mandatory under specific legislation and regulation including the Education Act and the Children's Act. In line with provisions made in this legislation, collection and reuse of school data relies on the display of privacy notices in schools and on local authority websites, with only limited opt-out arrangements. School data is therefore routinely aggregated into a large dataset known as the National Pupil Dataset, which is made available by the Department for Education in varying degrees of granularity and identifiability. While scrutiny by a panel and various other safeguards are in place to control the release and reuse of this dataset, the consent of pupils or parents is not a component in the governance model.

In understanding the legislative framework underpinning the open government agenda, it is also necessary to highlight the impact of the EU's Re-use of Public Sector Information (PSI) Directive 2013/37/EU (Directive, 2013/37/EU), which has been transposed, in the English context, into The Re-Use of Public Sector Information Regulations 2015 (2015). For the purposes of the

Regulations, public sector information is defined as any information (content) whatever its medium (form) – including print, digital or electronic, and sound recordings – produced, held or disseminated by a public sector body, with a public body defined as being both central and local government or any other public body including cultural sector bodies.

In the UK context, The National Archives is the principal body offering guidance on the implementation of the regulations, which includes best practice on standard licences, datasets and charging for re-use. Documents holding personal data are not excluded from reuse under regulations, but such reuse has to be in accordance with the EU and national rules on the processing of personal data. This means that data may be derived, for example, from medical records or from patient interactions with services and made available for reuse as long as disclosure risk is effectively safeguarded through robust anonymisation.

As explored by Janssen (2011), the web portal data.gov.uk was launched in January 2010 to provide a single access point to open data varying from information about school locations, house prices, and tax receipts, to commuting statistics and public transport routes and timetables. The UK push towards open data and reuse has also finally been cemented by the introduction of a "right to data" by the Protection of Freedoms Bill, amending the Freedom of Information Act 2000, to include an obligation for public bodies to publish datasets available for reuse in a reusable format either in response to a request or through their publication schemes.

The UK PSI Regulations are designed to enforce mandatory reuse permission for all information produced, held, or disseminated within the course of a public task unless reuse is otherwise restricted or excluded (with some exceptions for the cultural sector). The aim is to ensure that as much public sector information is made available for reuse as possible under transparent and unrestrictive conditions, and at marginal cost. To ensure compliance, public bodies must, among other things, be proactively aiming to make information and metadata open and machine readable, under open licences and for free where possible.

As noted by Janssen (2011), in its 2010 Digital Agenda (European Commission, 2010), the European Commission "emphasised the importance of the availability of public sector data for stimulating markets for online content" (p. 446). In its introductory guide to the amended PSI Directive, The National Archives UK also connects this ethos of economic benefits and employment opportunities across Europe by stating that "re-use of public sector information stimulates the development of innovative new information products and services in the UK and across Europe, thus boosting the information industry" (The National Archives, 2019). Janssen (2011) describes the PSI Directive "as a direct result of the European Commission's concern about the underdevelopment of the European information market and its inability to compete with the United States," a concern fuelled by the Commission's view that federal level data was widely available across the

United States at low cost (p. 447). The purpose of the Directive was there-fore twofold:

> on the one hand, enabling the availability of public sector data to third parties at low prices and unrestrictive conditions, and on the other hand, ensuring a level playing field between public bodies that operate in the information market in competition with the private information industry.
>
> (Janssen, 2011, p. 447)

However, in relation to exploitation of commercial value, the push towards openness at no (or marginal) cost effectively prevents the public sector itself from profiting from the information industry that it feeds. The promotion of openness necessarily entails a loss of control, and the negative implications are therefore felt by those who profited from the control mechanisms that were originally in place. The PSI Directive's attempts to "level the playing field" are actually designed to ensure that the private sector is not at a dis-advantage to the public sector. Janssen (2011) summarizes how the directive is in fact designed to prevent public sector bodies from locking "their data in exclusive deals with one private company or to maximise short term rev-enues by abusing their market power as monopolists" (p. 448). The directive is also designed to mitigate any

> risk that public sector bodies fund (part of) their market activities with public tax money in order to keep their market prices low, and in this way use cross-subsidisation to distort the market.
>
> (Janssen, 2011, p. 448)

This is achieved through the insistence that the re-use of public sector infor-mation has to be "non-discriminatory for comparable categories of re-use" (Directive, 2003/98/EC).

The underpinnings of the regulations are therefore more in favour of enabling the private sector to profit from public sector information than protection of the public sector's ability to monetize the information it holds. Mustill (2019) also explores the processes of capital accumulation associ-ated with the release of open data and interrogates how open government data has become a "means by which public wealth can be transferred to private capital" through what he describes as "non-rivalrous enclosure" where the guise of openness obfuscates the reality that the usability of the data is "restricted at any given time to those in possession of the necessary tools" (p. 18).

This reinforces the point that "openness" is not wholly "good" for all sections of society, all of the time. It is argued by those who see OGD as a form of neo-liberalism that the private sector in fact stands to benefit over and above both the citizen and the public sector. With regards to the citizen, commercial exploitation raises strongly held privacy and security concerns, as well as concerns about unfair treatment realized through biases in how data is both created and then reused. Can either the private sector (or, indeed, the public sector) be trusted to act in the citizen's best interest? And for all citizens fairly, without marginalisations occurring? Rumours that the insurance industry may have used data released by the Health and Social Care Information Centre's (HSCIC) predecessor body to fix the costs of insurance provides plenty of fodder for the notion that the citizen, the public sector, and the private sector often have competing interests, with OGD placing the balance most firmly in the hands of the latter.

Coming back to the question of how privacy and openness interconnect in national legislation, regulation, and policy – the rules on reuse of public sector information must be applied in full compliance with data protection legislation, and this is made explicit in the text of the regulation. However, a 2018 impact assessment commissioned by the European Commission on the implementation of the EU PSI Directive by member states draws out that while the importance of compliance with GDPR and national data protection legislation as a precedent over the reuse of information is well understood, there has been uncertainty across member states on facilitating reuse while ensuring data protection compliance in cases when public registers or datasets also contain personal data (e.g. car registration databases, or hospital records). Significantly, the impact assessment reveals that concerns were raised by member state representatives around the "suitability of techniques that can be used for anonymisation or ways by which purpose limitation can be ensured" (European Commission, 2018). This highlights how, despite the drive towards open data and the introduction of legislation to both force and support data sharing, the fundamental tensions between privacy and openness are still seen by implementers as difficult to resolve.

Privacy from below

In this setting, where law, regulation, and policy, together with technical and procedural issues of data management and curation, continue to be contested, privacy activism within UK civil society is energetic. This activism is led by a handful of organisations, chiefly Privacy International, Big Brother Watch, Liberty, and the Open Rights Group. Though state funded, the Open Data Institute (ODI) has also supported privacy activism, providing a base for the UK's Open Government Partnership (OGP) civil society forum, fostering research and leading projects on topics such as data ethics, policy design, and standardisation. Privacy figures in the ODI's data ethics work, including its Data Ethics Canvas (Open Data Institute, 2019), which is a tool to help users design and run data projects that are ethical and have positive impacts. Although the term "privacy" does not feature in the Canvas itself, the supporting documentation shows that ODI evolved its tool with reference to pre-existing data ethics frameworks including privacy frameworks.

The following summary of civil society priorities around privacy illuminates the range of ways in which privacy is threatened in the open environment, but also shows that much privacy activism is not directly concerned with privacy in public sector information reuse as envisaged by government advocates of OGD. Instead, covert data collection and opaque practices with closed and shared data appear to be the primary concerns.

Privacy International (PI) is a UK registered charity that exists to "promote the human right of privacy throughout the world" (Privacy International, n.d.). It does this through advocacy and policy work, legal action, technical analysis, investigation, and research, and by fostering an "international privacy movement." Its current campaigns focus on a range of topics including advertising technologies, secret global surveillance networks, critiquing identity systems, monitoring the role of the Internet of Things (IoT) in court cases, and protecting migrants at borders. PI produces a range of resources, including "long reads," case studies, "explainers" (illustrated FAQs), advocacy documents, and videos. PI has also produced numerous reports, some of which focus on particular countries or regions, others of which have a wider scope. Reports of the latter type include *The Global Surveillance Industry*, which traces the history of the development of surveillance technologies and looks at their international trade (Privacy International, 2016). In 2018, with the International Committee of the Red Cross, PI published *The Humanitarian Metadata Problem: "Doing No Harm" in the Digital Era*, which is intended to inform humanitarian workers about the data risks associated with certain technologies, and discusses the "do no harm" principle in this context (Privacy International and the International Committee of the Red Cross, 2018). Also in 2018, PI published *Digital Stop and Search: How the UK Police Can Secretly Download Everything from Your Mobile Phone*, which responds to the potentially unlawful use of mobile phone extraction tools by UK police, and argues for changes such as an independent review of the practice and the development of new official guidance (Privacy International, 2018). PI also participated in the UK's OGP civil society forum that drafted commitments for the national action plan.

Big Brother Watch describes itself as a "cross-party, non-party, independent non-profit organisation leading the protection of privacy and civil liberties in the UK" (Big Brother Watch, 2019b). Its campaigns include "Face Off," which opposes the use of facial recognition technology in public surveillance, and "Free Speech Online," which is concerned with the haphazard censorship of online speech by social media companies, as well as the possibility of government regulations to control speech over social media. Much of Big Brother Watch's online content is about mobilizing the public, but it also publishes briefing notes, blogs, opinion pieces, and factsheets. The organisation has produced parliamentary briefings and evidence, submissions, and letters, which it makes available on its website. Its research reports cover topics such as classroom management software, body-worn cameras, and police access to digital evidence. Its most recent report, *Digital Strip*

Searches: The Police's Data Investigations of Victims, discusses the seizure of digital information from crime victims' phones, police use of artificial intelligence to analyze the data, and these practices in relation to current laws and the legal concept of consent (Big Brother Watch, 2019a). Importantly, the report surfaces victims' experiences, and includes a section written by the director of the Centre for Women's Justice. Big Brother Watch's *The State of Surveillance in 2018* report covers a range of current issues, including the effect of surveillance on the right to freedom of assembly, blacklisting practices, the impact of state surveillance on investigative journalism, accountability in school surveillance and data sharing, and immigration enforcement (Big Brother Watch, 2018).

Liberty is an independent membership organisation that was established in 1934 to help defend human rights in the UK (Liberty, n.d.). The membership consists of campaigners, lawyers, and policy experts who work to defend rights through public campaigning, test case litigation, Parliamentary work, policy analysis, information sharing, and the provision of free legal advice. Of its seven current campaigns, four are explicitly about privacy, with campaigns around facial recognition software in public places, data sharing in immigration enforcement, mass surveillance, and police spying. Though Liberty does produce reports, much of its written output is in the form of written evidence and policy briefings. In relation to information issues, these briefings cover the use of algorithms in the justice system, official secrecy, and freedom of expression in universities, etc.

The Open Rights Group (ORG) is a UK-wide campaigning organisation with two stated aims: to challenge: 1) threats to "privacy by both the government through the surveillance of our personal communications and private companies, who use our personal data to increase their profits"; and 2) threats to "free speech through the criminalisation of online speech, online censorship and restrictive copyright laws" (Open Rights Group, n.d.). The group's current campaigns related to privacy target the hoarding of personal data by political parties for the purposes of targeted advertising, involve GDPR complaints about adtech, push back on age verification technologies on the basis that they breach rights to privacy, and considering the implications of Brexit for privacy. The ORG claims several legal victories in its efforts to push back on state surveillance, including a successful challenge (with Privacy International and others) in the European Court of Human Rights to the UK's mass surveillance programmes exposed by the Edward Snowden leaks, and their involvement in the UK Court of Appeal challenge to the "Snooper's Charter" provisions found in the Data Retention and Investigatory Powers Act 2014. ORG also develops tools to support the right to privacy, most notably the Data Rights Finder, developed with the Information Commissioner's Office and a technology studio IF, which allows users to access jargon-free explanations of organisations' privacy policies.

ORG works on a number of privacy policy issues, but of most relevance to this chapter, ORG is the only civil society actor in this space to focus directly, rather than incidentally, on open data. It finds a number of problems with the UK government's move to "open by default," seeing privacy as the most contentious,

> especially in the area of healthcare, where pharmaceutical companies want access to patient health data to aid research. Claims that such personal and sensitive data can be successfully "anonymized" ignore evidence of the very real threats that individual records can be reidentified.
>
> (Maguire, 2012)

ORG states that it works on open data through the OGP and groups across Europe and has had three initiatives relevant to the scope of this survey. First, it worked against government plans to privatize aspects of data creation and management in the areas of weather, land, and mapping as part of the formation of a Public Data Corporation, which worked under several names before being folded into a board within the Department for Business, Innovation, and Skills. Second, ORG works to identify privacy risks around the commercialisation of "anonymized" public services data. Finally, ORG has been concerned with historic data and in particular opening it to the family history "sector" in a programme called "Open Genealogy" (Open Rights Group, n.d.).

With this important exception, this survey has shown that in the activist space, there is very little overt connection between open data and privacy. Instead, there is a clear concern for data gathering (particularly in relation to covert techniques) and cross-agency data sharing. The involvement of organisations like Privacy International and the ORG in the UK's Open Government Partnership civil society forum shows that the relevant actors are alert to the privacy issues connected with open data and open government more broadly, but, outside of ORG's work, the problems and corrective efforts appear to concern data collection and opaque sharing practices, rather than publication and redaction. Gray has suggested that an

> ambitious politics of data would have to move beyond programmes to make data public or keep data private through various attendant technical, policy and legal systems that facilitate or inhibit the flows of data in society. . . . This would entail opening up spaces for democratic deliberation and social participation around the creation of data and around processes of datafication.
>
> (Gray, 2016)

Arguably, this is the direction in which civil society actors are trying to drive the privacy regime, so that individual agency is not necessarily focused on preventing dataveillance, but is instead fully informed and empowered to co-create (or not) data for civic purposes.

Conclusion

The ITrust research in this space and the relevant literature since 2011 demonstrate the complex and contentious interactions of the privacy and openness agendas in the UK. Law, regulation, and policy behind OGD have been driven by neoliberal aspirations to data-fuelled economic growth, as well as by concerns for government transparency and participatory governance. Privacy in this context is not simply diametrically opposed to government openness – the two are entangled together, along with private sector interests, technological developments, and community concerns. Yet, with the notable exception of ORG, UK privacy activists are rarely directly concerned with open government data, and more often concerned with data gathering practices and sharing across government bodies and private sector actors.

It is interesting to note a recent development in data activism in the United States. A "manifest-no" has been built from a feminist standpoint perspective utilizing the power of "no" to make a series of refusal statements on data sharing and reuse. These statements challenge the assumption that the harm associated with data practices are the same for everyone, when historic and systemic patterns of exploitation produce differential vulnerabilities for communities. The statements also highlight how current data practices are normalizing a drive to both monetize and hyper-individualize the human experience. Thus, the manifest-no acts as a form of resistance to this status quo by instead centring collective forms of life as a means to exceed neoliberal logic (Cifor et al., 2019). Such ways of thinking, conceptualizing, and practising data are important to draw in here, because they provide a means to not only question but begin to actively refuse the logic bound up in high-level policy, regulation, and law at the intersection of openness and privacy. This is a kind of communal statement of data politics not yet seen in the UK.

References

Article 29 Working Party. (2007). *Working document on the processing of personal data relating to health in electronic health records (EHR)*. Retrieved from https://ec.europa.eu/justice/article-29/press-material/public-consultation/ehr/2007_ehr/ms-national/dept_health_and_children_ie_en.pdf

Bates, J. (2014). The strategic importance of information policy for the contemporary neoliberal state: The case of open government data in the United Kingdom. *Government Information Quarterly, 31*(3), 388–395. https://doi.org/10.1016/j.giq.2014.02.009

Big Brother Watch. (2018). *The state of surveillance in 2018*. Retrieved from https://bigbrotherwatch.org.uk/wp-content/uploads/2018/09/The-State-of-Surveillance-in-2018.pdf

Big Brother Watch. (2019a). *Digital strip searches: The police's data investigations of victims*. Retrieved from https://bigbrotherwatch.org.uk/wp-content/uploads/2019/07/Digital-Strip-Searches-Final.pdf

Big Brother Watch. (2019b). *Big brother watch's written evidence to the Joint Committee on Human Rights on the Right to Privacy (Article 8) and the Digital*

Revolution inquiry. Retrieved from https://bigbrotherwatch.org.uk/wp-content/uploads/2019/06/Big-Brother-Watch-written-evidence-to-JCHR-The-Right-to-Privacy-and-the-Digital-Revolution-Inquiry-Feb-2019-II.pdf

Chancellor of the Exchequer. (2011). *Autumn statement*. HM treasury. Retrieved from https://assets.publishing.service.gov.uk/government/uploads/system/uploads/attachment_data/file/228671/8231.pdf

Cifor, M., Garcia, P., Cowan, T. L., Rault, J., Sutherland, T., Chan, A., . . . Nakamura, L. (2019). *Feminist data manifest-no*. Retrieved from https://www.manifestno.com/

Directive 2003/98/EC of the European Parliament and of the Council of 17 November 2003 on the re-use of public sector information. (2003). Retrieved from https://eur-lex.europa.eu/legal-content/en/ALL/?uri=CELEX%3A32003L0098

Directive 2013/37/EU of the European Parliament and of the Council of 26 June 2013 amending Directive 2003/98/EC on the re-use of public sector information. (2013). Retrieved from https://eur-lex.europa.eu/legal-content/EN/TXT/?uri=CELEX%3A32013L0037

European Commission. (2010). *A digital agenda for Europe*. Retrieved from https://eur-lex.europa.eu/LexUriServ/LexUriServ.do?uri=COM:2010:0245:FIN:EN:PDF

European Commission. (2018). *Impact assessment*. Working document. Retrieved from https://eur-lex.europa.eu/legal-content/EN/TXT/HTML/?uri=CELEX:52018SC0127&rid=4

Gitelman, L. (Ed.). (2013). *Raw data is an oxymoron*. Cambridge, MA: MIT Press.

Gray, J. (2016). *Datafication and democracy: Recalibrating digital information systems to address societal interests*. Retrieved from https://www.ippr.org/juncture/datafication-and-democracy

Janssen, K. (2011). The influence of the PSI directive on open government data: An overview of recent developments. *Government Information Quarterly*, 28(4), 446–456. https://doi.org/10.1016/j.giq.2011.01.004

Keen, J., Calinescu, R., Paige, R., & Rooksby, J. (2013). Big data + politics = open data: The case of health care data in England. *Policy & Internet*, 5, 228–243. https://doi.org/10.1002/1944-2866

Liberty. (n.d.). https://www.libertyhumanrights.org.uk

Lowry, J. (2014). Opening government: Open data and access to information. In J. Lowry & J. Wamukoya (Eds.), *Integrity in government through records management* (pp. 161–171). London: Routledge. https://doi.org/10.4324/9781315589077

Lowry, J. (2015). *Open government data literature review project* (EU02). Inter-PARES Trust. Retrieved from https://interparestrust.org/assets/public/dissemination/EU02_20151210_OpenGovernmentDataLiteratureReview_FinalReport.pdf

Maguire, L. (2012). *Open data*. Retrieved from https://web.archive.org/web/20200423170117/www.openrightsgroup.org/issues/opendata

Mustill, E. (2019). Understanding How open government data is used in capital accumulation. Towards a theoretical framework. In S. E. Wood, J. Lowry, & A. J. Lau (Eds.), *Information/control: Control in the age of post-truth. Special Issue. Journal of Critical Library and Information Studies*, 2(2). https://doi.org/10.24242/jclis.v2i2.63

The National Archives. (2019). *Why PSI must be re-useable*. Retrieved from https://www.nationalarchives.gov.uk/information-management/re-using-public-sector-information/about-psi/psi-must-re-usable/

Nuffield Council on Bioethics. (2014). *The collection, linking and use of data in biomedical research and health care: Ethical issues*. Retrieved from https://www.nuffieldbioethics.org/publications/biological-and-health-data

Open Data Institute. (2019). *Data ethics canvas*. Retrieved from https://theodi.org/article/data-ethics-canvas/

Open Rights Group. (n.d.). *Who we are*. Retrieved from https://www.openrights group.org/who-we-are/

Open Society Foundations. (n.d.). *Our work*. Retrieved from https://www.opensociety foundations.org/what-we-do/themes/information-and-digital-rights

Privacy International. (n.d.). *About*. Retrieved from https://privacyinternational.org/about

Privacy International. (2016). *The global surveillance industry*. Retrieved from https://privacyinternational.org/sites/default/files/2017-12/global_surveillance_0.pdf

Privacy International. (2018). *Digital stop and search: How the UK police can secretly download everything from your mobile phone*. Retrieved from https://privacyinter national.org/sites/default/files/2018-03/Digital%20Stop%20and%20Search%20 Report.pdf

Privacy International and the International Committee of the Red Cross. (2018). *The humanitarian metadata problem: 'Doing no harm' in the digital era*. Retrieved from https://privacyinternational.org/sites/default/files/2018-12/The%20Human itarian%20Metadata%20Problem%20-%20Doing%20No%20Harm%20 in%20the%20Digital%20Era.pdf

The re-use of public sector information regulations 2015. (2015). Retrieved from https://www.legislation.gov.uk/uksi/2015/1415/contents/made

Ruppert, E., Isin, E., & Bigo, D. (2017). Data politics. *Big Data & Society*, 4(2). https://doi.org/10.1177/2053951717717749

Sexton, A., & Shepherd, E. (2017). *Recordkeeping, open government data and privacy* (EU21). InterPARES Trust. Retrieved from https://interparestrust.org/assets/public/dissemination/EU21Recordkeepingfinalreport.pdf

Sexton, A. K., Shepherd, E. J., Duke-Williams, O. W., & Eveleigh, A. (2018). The role and nature of consent in government administrative data. *Big Data and Society*, 5(2). https://doi.org/10.1177/2053951718819560

12 Public trust in online records

The case of the UK *care.data* programme

Julie McLeod with Sue Childs

Introduction

This chapter explores the issue of public trust in online records using the example of the United Kingdom (UK) *care.data* programme. Announced in 2013, *care.data* was a National Health Service (NHS) initiative that aimed to collect and ultimately link health data from different care settings for monitoring, planning, researching, and improving services. What lessons about trust in online records (not stored in the cloud) can be drawn from a study of this high-profile, contemporary case example, which was unsuccessful and closed in 2016? Beginning with a brief overview of the *care.data* programme and the authors' approach to the study, it discusses the key findings and draws conclusions about building public trust in online records in an open digital environment.

The *care.data* programme

The *care.data* programme was an initiative by NHS England, an executive non-departmental public body working with the Department of Health and Social Care by overseeing the budgeting, planning, delivery, and day-to-day operation of the commissioning of NHS services in England. The aim of the programme was to "improve the safety and care of patients" by linking "information from different NHS providers to give healthcare commissioners a more complete picture of how safe local services are, and how well they treat and care for patients across community, GP and hospital settings" (NHS England, 2013). The Health and Social Care Information Centre (HSCIC) was the organisation responsible for implementing this programme and acting as the safe haven for the data. HSCIC (now NHS Digital) is an executive non-departmental public body working with the Department of Health and Social Care as "the national information and technology partner to the health and social care system" (NHS Digital, 2020).

The HSCIC was responsible for managing a wide range of healthcare datasets, including hospital episode statistics (HES), which provide information on all admissions, outpatient appointments, and accident and emergency attendances at NHS hospitals in England. The *care.data* programme involved collecting datasets from general practices (i.e. primary care practices), where the general practitioner (GP; i.e. primary care physician) sees patients with non-emergency healthcare problems and provides the main access into the NHS, and linking this general practice data to HES. Although GPs were providing aggregated data, *care.data* proposed to extract individual patients' personal and clinical data, comprising their unique NHS number (used in all NHS transactions), date of birth, postcode, gender, and coded clinical information. Such GP data is identifiable personal and sensitive data about an individual patient. The GP data also includes the whole population as nearly everyone is registered with a GP from birth to death, and GP care is 24/7. Hospital activity only covers a small proportion of the population at any one time and is episodic, i.e. only when a person visits hospital.

The study

The study (Childs & McLeod, 2015; McLeod & Childs, 2018), conducted from January–May 2015, aimed to identify issues of trust in managing digital records that contain personal data, and to contribute to the research objectives of ITrust in the context of access to information. A purposive sample of publicly available online sources – documenting stakeholder views and providing contemporary, topical information between 2011 and April 2015 – was analyzed. The sources included government, health professional and campaign group sources, as well as the mass media and online health media. The sample enabled a 360° view of the range of stakeholders' perspectives. In addition to developing a timeline and summary of key events, a thematic analysis of the content of the sources was conducted to identify subject themes (i.e. *what* is said), followed by a discourse analysis of a small sample of the sources (i.e. the *way[s]* things are said). The study discovered what was done and said and when, but not necessarily *why*. For a full picture, interviews and focus groups would have been required. See Childs and McLeod (2015) for full details of the methodological approach.

Figures 12.1 and 12.2 provide a chronology of the key events and decisions relating to *care.data*.

Emergent themes

The key issues to emerge related to the purpose of *care.data*, governance, consultation and communication, informed consent processes, and data security procedures are discussed next.

The purpose

While there are clear benefits of a single, population-wide database, e.g. tracking clinical conditions, improving services and supporting health research to discover better treatments, lack of clarity about the purpose of

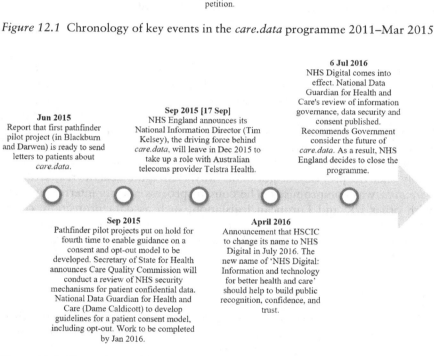

Dec 2011
Government consultation to automatically include patient data in clinical research with patients able to opt-out.

Jan-Dec 2013
Privacy groups and health professionals are concerned and start action & lobbying. National and professional press coverage exposing problems and concerns.

Feb 2014
NHS England postpones *care.data*.

Mar 2015
Roll out postponed until after the UK general election in May 2015.

Dec 2012
care.data listed in NHS England planning guidance to surprise of health professionals.

Jan 2014
Flawed public leaflet campaign. Concern and discussion of problems goes mainstream, e.g. 38 Degrees national petition.

Feb-Oct 2014
Inquiries held; advisory groups set up.

Figure 12.1 Chronology of key events in the *care.data* programme 2011–Mar 2015

Jun 2015
Report that first pathfinder pilot project (in Blackburn and Darwen) is ready to send letters to patients about *care.data*.

Sep 2015 [17 Sep]
NHS England announces its National Information Director (Tim Kelsey), the driving force behind *care.data*, will leave in Dec 2015 to take up a role with Australian telecoms provider Telstra Health.

6 Jul 2016
NHS Digital comes into effect. National Data Guardian for Health and Care's review of information governance, data security and consent published. Recommends Government consider the future of *care.data*. As a result, NHS England decides to close the programme.

Sep 2015
Pathfinder pilot projects put on hold for fourth time to enable guidance on a consent and opt-out model to be developed. Secretary of State for Health announces Care Quality Commission will conduct a review of NHS security mechanisms for patient confidential data. National Data Guardian for Health and Care (Dame Caldicott) to develop guidelines for a patient consent model, including opt-out. Work to be completed by Jan 2016.

April 2016
Announcement that HSCIC to change its name to NHS Digital in July 2016. The new name of 'NHS Digital: Information and technology for better health and care' should help to build public recognition, confidence, and trust.

Figure 12.2 Chronology of key events in the *care.data* programme Jun 2015–Jul 2016 (after the end of the study)

care.data raised significant concerns among health professionals and campaign/consumer groups. Of particular concern was the lack of transparency about what identifiable patient data would be included, who would be using it, and for what purposes. Would the users be the NHS or private healthcare providers, public researchers or commercial researchers, other government departments or private sector organisations? Would the data be used for administration, public good, commercial gain, or political reasons?

Governance

Governance issues were not identified and addressed in the early stages of *care.data*, so appropriate procedures were not developed in time for the programme's proposed implementation. The problems included poor and inadequate consultation and communication with the public and other key stakeholders, poorly explained and complex informed consent procedures and options, and poorly thought through data security. All of these raised significant concerns with the public whose data was to be collected and with the GPs who were tasked with providing it. These issues were either obvious from the outset or could have been easily identified through early consultation with patient representatives and other stakeholders.

Informed consent

With personal data, particularly sensitive health data, the issue of informed consent is critical and revolves around the opt-in/opt-out debate. Giving citizens the choice to opt-in is ethically preferred; however, fewer people will choose to opt-in than opt-out, leading to incomplete, biased datasets. Researchers prefer an opt-out approach, which results in a more complete dataset. Opt-out was intended for *care.data*. However, many people asked to opt-out in the early stages of the roll-out of *care.data*, with more likely to apply once the programme got under way. Hence, the benefits realisation of *care.data* was compromised. The consent process and its interrelationship with other UK and European legislation, such as data protection, confidentiality, and mental capacity, were not properly considered. The opt-out process was not clearly explained, the approach was very complex, and procedures were not fully developed.

Data security

GPs faced the dilemma of upholding conflicting duties: 1) to ensure their patients' records are kept secure under the Data Protection Act (1998, Principle 7) and in line with their professional ethics of patient confidentiality; and 2) to transfer records to HSCIC as legally required by the Health and Social Care Act (2012). Data linkage would be required to combine the GP and hospital data to realise the benefits. Therefore, either identifiable or pseudonymised data (using a unique identifier that does not reveal a person's true identity) would be required. However, pseudonymized data has the potential to re-identify individuals by combining different elements of information. The unique NHS ID is an insecure way to pseudonymize data. When combined with the patient's postal code (unique to one or a few houses) and date of birth, it can easily re-identify a person. Though pseudonymization within the GP practice before the data passed to the HSCIC was suggested, this was not pursued.

An alternative is for identifiable data to be held only within a safe haven where data linkage would occur, with outputs being anonymized or aggregated as applicable. HSCIC was the safe haven for *care.data*, but the history of data releases by its predecessor (Batten, 2014) without adequate security provisions had damaged its reputation. A safe haven must be a trusted body, and safe haven procedures must be strong and clearly and publicly described. Such procedures did not appear to have been properly developed at the time of *care.data*. Although at the time people raising data security fears were accused of scaremongering, such fears are genuine and must be addressed.

Summary

All of these issues had a negative impact on building public trust in the government, NHS England and *care.data*. These findings match those of similar research published after the completion of the study, although that research focused on public policy rather than issues of trust (Presser, Hruskova, Rowbottom, & Kancir, 2015).

Stakeholder trust

The *care.data* programme occurred at a time of increasing public distrust of the government's handling of the NHS (with concerns about privatization of health services), wider mistrust in the government's increasing use of private companies to provide public services linked to distrust of the probity of these private companies, and a wider concern about the misuses of personal data by governments and private companies. *care.data* crystallized all of these existing trust issues into one initiative that health professionals, campaigners, and citizens could focus their concerns on and could challenge. As the poor conduct of *care.data* itself became more apparent, this only increased people's concerns and distrust and strengthened their resolve to challenge it. The *care.data* programme therefore became a crisis of public trust.

The trust environment in which *care.data* operated comprised both trusted individuals and organisations

- the NHS – a commonly used quote (attributed to the Conservative politician Nigel Lawson) is "the NHS is the closest thing the English have to a religion"
- health professionals, particularly GPs
- researchers, whether NHS, university, or not for profit

and mistrusted individuals and organisations

- the government
- MPs, particularly because of the scandal over their expenses claims (Lewis, 2019)
- private companies contracted to provide public services and a number of resulting scandals
- Department of Health and Social Care and NHS England, particularly because of the reorganisation of the NHS and fears over privatisation (Health and Social Care Act, 2012)
- HSCIC, particularly because of the past behaviour of its predecessor, and its *care.data* subcontractor Atos (and the scandal over "fit to work" tests) BBC (2014)
- private healthcare providers
- other public bodies accessing sensitive personal health data (seen as mission creep of *care.data*)
- private organisations accessing sensitive personal health data (seen as mission creep of *care.data*).

As a trusted group – GPs and other health professionals – had serious concerns about *care.data* and lobbied against it, the distrust of campaigners and citizens towards *care.data* was strengthened. However, lack of trust can become contagious. GP bodies and health research charities feared the distrust created by *care.data* would lead the public to mistrust them, too. Once trust is lost, it takes a long time to rebuild.

The end of the *care.data* programme

As the crisis developed, the government and NHS England began to demonstrate a realisation of the importance of trust issues and that trust had become eroded.

In September 2015, the Secretary of State for Health (Secretary of State for Health, 2015) said:

> Exciting though this all is, we will throw away these opportunities if the public do not believe they can trust us to look after their personal medical data securely. The NHS has not yet won the public's trust in an area that is vital for the future of patient care.

The Secretary of State for Life Sciences commissioned two parallel reviews. The first was a review of information governance, data security and consent, undertaken by the National Data Guardian for Health and Care. The second was a review of data security, undertaken by the Care Quality Commission (CQC).

The National Data Guardian for Health and Care (2016) review set out ten data security standards, covering people, process, and technology aspects, and recommended that the government consider the future of *care.data*, in particular the consent and opt-out model to ensure that people could make informed choices about how their data was to be used. The Foreword stated:

> Everyone who uses health and care services should be able to trust that their personal confidential data is protected. . . . Unfortunately, trust in the use of personal confidential data has been eroded and steps need to be taken to demonstrate trustworthiness and ensure that the public can have confidence in the system. . . . The trust needed for effective information sharing cannot be ensured without secure systems and easily understood explanations of how information and privacy are protected.
>
> (p. 2)

The CQC review (Care Quality Commission, 2016) assessed whether personal health and care information was being used safely and was appropriately protected in the NHS and made recommendations to improve practice. The Foreword noted: "As confidential data is held and accessed in fresh ways through new technology, the risks change and so must the response if both security and public trust are to be maintained" (p. 3).

These reviews led to the cancellation of *care.data* on 6 July 2016. However, the government was "absolutely committed to realising the benefits of sharing information, as an essential part of improving outcomes for patients," would work to "retain public confidence," and noted that *care.data* would be "invaluable" in moving forwards" (Department of Health and Social Care and Parliamentary Under-Secretary of State for Life Sciences, 2016). Additionally, the Life Sciences Minister announced a formal government consultation to seek the views of the public and professionals on its two main proposals – the data security standards and the consent/opt-out model. The minister stated: "To achieve our ambition of a fully digital NHS, it is vital that the public trusts health and care staff to keep their personal data safe and secure" (Department of Health and Social Care and Parliamentary Under-Secretary of State for Life Sciences, 2016). This consultation was carried out in September 2016 and resulted in a Department of Health (2017) report which contained "commitments to ensure the health and social care system in England realises the full benefits of sharing data in a safe, secure and legal way, and, that complements the existing Caldicott principles" (p. 4). The report outlined procedures and actions to build and maintain public trust.

Understanding trust

The *care.data* case example can be understood in terms of Zucker's three modes of trust production (Thomas, 1998, pp. 178–184; Zucker, 1986, pp. 59–65) and Thomas' three broad conceptions of trust (Thomas, 1998, pp. 169–178). It should be noted that public trust is as much subjective and attitudinal as it is objective.

The three modes of trust production are: 1) process based, dependent on a "record" of past exchange and reciprocity, which can be directly experienced or be second-hand, e.g. via an organisation's reputation or "brand"; 2) characteristic based, using information based on social similarity, such as family or cultural grouping; and 3) institutional based, using formal mechanisms such as professional status and accreditation of a person or an organisation and use of intermediaries such as contracts and insurance. These are all-important and coexist. For *care.data*, the process-based and institutional-based modes were important. The NHS is a trusted "brand" in the UK. Health professionals are highly trained and accredited through organisations such as the British Medical Association and the Royal College of General Practitioners. One of the proposed benefits of *care.data* – use of the data for research purposes – is dependent on people (the donors of their personal and health data) considering it part of the gift exchange underlying process-based trust production, receiving in return future improved healthcare and the satisfaction of contributing to the public good. To realize the research benefits of big health data requires public involvement, acceptance, and trust (via mechanisms such as publicly available summaries of research findings and healthcare improvements), transparency and explanations of research methodology, transparency and visibility of data use, people themselves controlling access to their data on a more granulated basis than blanket opt-in/opt-out controls, and data security via safe havens (van Staa, Goldacre, Buchan, & Smeeth, 2016).

> The ultimate solution, however, must combine new technologies with clear accountability, transparent operations, and public trust. In addition, data stewardship is not just about physical and digital security: staff training, standard operating procedures, and the skills and attitudes of staff are also important. This combination of data protection (safe havens) and culture of best practice not only underpins a trustworthy research environment but also a learning health system.
>
> (van Staa et al., 2016, p. 2)

There are three broad conceptions of trust. Fiduciary trust is an asymmetrical relationship whereby the powerful person or organisation has to be trusted to carry out their duties without taking personal advantage of their privileged position. Examples are professionals such as doctors and lawyers, and government agents such as MPs and public officials. The mechanisms to ensure the appropriate behaviour include professional ethical standards, organisational rules of behaviour, laws, and regulations. Welch, Hinnant, and Moon (2005, p. 376) note that IT could both increase fiduciary trust (through the greater availability of information for the citizen) and decrease it (through inflexible, bureaucratic electronic systems). Mutual trust is dependent on more symmetrical interpersonal relationships, though the mutual trust in the individual, such as a patient to the GP, might then extend to the organisation, such as the GP practice concerned. Welch et al. also note that "officials who utilize the one-to-one or one-to-many interactive capabilities of information technologies to acknowledge and respond to citizen communications may be addressing the concept of mutual trust" (Welch et al., 2005, p. 376). Social trust, a form of "social capital," is the end result of all the micro level interactions between individuals. Trust is fundamental to all the interactions between humans, though it is taken for granted until it is betrayed in a specific circumstance. Social trust cannot be separated from the other forms of trust – it is generated from, and supportive of, mutual trust and underpins fiduciary trust. The NHS is a prime example of social capital in the UK. However, *care.data* predominately functioned within the concept of fiduciary trust, which was perceived by the public and some health professionals to have broken down. The concept of mutual trust has been weakened in the NHS as people no longer have a lifelong relationship with a specific "family" doctor, but with a group practice where the patient sees whichever GP is available.

Welch et al. (2005, pp. 373–374) note various factors that could cause a decline in public trust in governments. Those that seem relevant to *care.data* are: reaction to scandal (e.g. private contractors and the handling of public service contracts), inefficient performance (e.g. the expensive failure of the National Programme for IT [NPfIT], which was cancelled at a probable expenditure of at least £10 billion, with no significant benefits being delivered [Syal, 2013]), policy failure (e.g. continuous reorganization of the NHS under successive governments), and economic issues (e.g. the government's austerity programme from 2008 to the current day).

Thomas (1998, p. 185) notes that trust can be lost in times of organizational reorganization, from lying and from misuse of power, all of which were conditions that existed, or were perceived to exist, in the wider sociopolitical context of *care.data*. Zucker (1986, p. 59) notes that when trust is breached there is confusion, shock and anger, but not necessarily distrust: "To distrust . . . implies an attribution of intentionality that continues throughout all interactions or exchanges, at least of a particular type." The *care.data* programme did not at the beginning generate distrust itself. Rather, existing distrust of the government and NHS England, and their handling of the NHS, were transferred to the *care.data* programme. However, as the problems with the management of *care.data* became apparent, distrust in *care.data* itself resulted.

Conclusion

The *care.data* programme showed that the poor handling of a government initiative about managing sensitive personal health data can result in a breakdown in public trust, despite the community benefits in terms of health research and improved healthcare management that could have resulted from the merging of GP and hospital data. Emerging as the core of the trust issue were lack of clarity about the purpose of *care.data*, lack of transparency about the users and uses of the data, poorly thought through procedures for ensuring data security, and complex and poorly explained consent procedures for the public to use. Good governance, consultation and communication, appropriate and clear informed consent processes, access and use controls, and data security procedures are all key to achieving trust.

Additionally, the wider socio-political context of a breakdown in trust of the government's handling of the NHS as a whole turned this breakdown in public trust of *care.data* into a crisis. The *care.data* crisis demonstrates the criticality of context when making any recommendations or providing guidelines for other organisations and/or scenarios. Trust issues in the wider socio-political context have worsened and are therefore more likely to become a factor that has to be considered.

Regardless of this wider distrust, *care.data* might not have become a target for campaigners if there had been good governance from the beginning, and it is somewhat surprising that there was not. The health sector, and the NHS specifically, is credited with the earliest foray into information governance, having launched its Information Governance Toolkit (n.d.) in 2003–2004. The toolkit assessed healthcare organisations against information governance policies and standards, particularly the Caldicott Principles protecting patient identity (Department of Health, 1997, 2013). In 2018, it was replaced by a Data Security and Protection Toolkit (2020) providing assessment against the National Data Guardian's (2016) ten data security standards.

Despite the closure of the *care.data* programme, an end result was improved governance of health data within the NHS, with a number of reviews and reports being produced and implemented in addition to the already existing governance framework.

References

Batten, I. (2014, March 3). *Contract and risk assessment for release of HES data to PA Consulting*. Retrieved from https://www.whatdotheyknow.com/request/contract_and_risk_assessment_for

BBC. (2014, March 27). *Fit-to-work tests: Atos contract to end*. Retrieved from https://www.bbc.co.uk/news/uk-26766345

Care Quality Commission. (2016). *Safe data, safe care. Report into how data is safely and securely managed in the NHS*. Retrieved from https://www.cqc.org.uk/sites/default/files/20160701%20Data%20security%20review%20FINAL%20for%20web.pdf

Childs, S., & McLeod, J. (2015). *A case example of public trust in online records – the UK care.data programme* (EU 17). InterPARES Trust. Retrieved from https://interparestrust.org/assets/public/dissemination/EU17_20150802_UKCareData Programme_FinalReport_Final.pdf

Data Protection Act. (1998). Retrieved from https://www.legislation.gov.uk/ukpga/1998/29/contents/enacted

Data security and protection toolkit. (2020). Retrieved from https://www.dsptoolkit.nhs.uk/

Department of Health. (1997). *The Caldicott Committee. Report on the review of patient-identifiable information.*

Department of Health. (2013). *Information: To share or not to share. The information governance review.* [Caldicott Review, 2013]. Retrieved from https://www.gov.uk/government/publications/the-information-governance-review

Department of Health. (2017, July). *Your data: Better security, better choice, better care. Government response to the National Data Guardian for Health and Care's review of data security, consent and opt-outs and the Care Quality Commission's review 'Safe data, safe care'.* Retrieved from https://www.gov.uk/government/uploads/system/uploads/attachment_data/file/627493/Your_data_better_security_better_choice_better_care_government_response.pdf

Department of Health and Social Care and Parliamentary Under-Secretary of State for Life Sciences. (2016, July 6). *Written statement to Parliament. Review of health and care data security and consent.* Retrieved from https://www.gov.uk/government/speeches/review-of-health-and-care-data-security-and-consent

Health and Social Care Act. (2012). Retrieved from https://www.legislation.gov.uk/ukpga/2012/7/contents/enacted

Information governance toolkit. (n.d.). Retrieved from https://web.archive.org/web/20171030112808/http://www.igt.hscic.gov.uk/

Lewis, W. (2019). MPs' expenses: A very British scandal. *New statesman.* Retrieved from https://www.newstatesman.com/politics/uk/2019/05/mps-expenses-very-british-scandal

McLeod, J., & Childs, S. (2018). Public trust in online records: The case of the UK Care.data programme. In A. Anderson, I. C. Becker, & L. Duranti (Eds.), *Born digital in the cloud: Challenges and solutions, presentations at the 21st Archival Sciences Colloquium of the Marburg Archives School* (pp. 43–64). Marburg: Marburg Archives School.

National Data Guardian for Health and Care. (2016). *Review of data security, consent and opt-outs.* Retrieved from https://www.gov.uk/government/publications/review-of-data-security-consent-and-opt-outs

NHS Digital. (2020). *About.* Retrieved from https://digital.nhs.uk/about-nhs-digital

NHS England. (2013, October 16). *News. NHS England sets out the next steps of public awareness about care.data. Care.* Retrieved from https://www.england.nhs.uk/2013/10/care-data/ [Note the remaining contemporary online *care.data* official information]

Presser, L., Hruskova, M., Rowbottom, H., & Kancir, J. (2015, Aug 11). Care.data and access to UK health records: Patient privacy and public trust. *Technology Science.* Retrieved from http://techscience.org/a/2015081103

Secretary of State for Health. (2015). *Speech at NHS Innovation Expo.* Retrieved from https://www.gov.uk/government/news/health-secretary-outlines-vision-for-use-of-technology-across-nhs

Syal, R. (2013, September 18). Abandoned NHS IT system has cost £10bn so far. *The Guardian.* Retrieved from https://www.theguardian.com/society/2013/sep/18/nhs-records-system-10bn

Thomas, C. W. (1998). Maintaining and restoring public trust in government agencies and their employees. *Administration and Society, 30*(2), 166–93.

van Staa, T. P., Goldacre, B., Buchan, I., & Smeeth, L. (2016). Big health data: The need to earn public trust. *BMJ, 354*(i3636). https://doi.org/10.1136/bmj.i3636

Welch, E. W., Hinnant, C. C., & Moon, M. J. (2005). Linking citizen satisfaction with e-government and trust in government. *Journal of Public Administration Research and Theory, 15*(3), 371–391. https://doi.org/10.1093/jopart/mui021

Zucker, L. G. (1986). Production of trust: Institutional sources of economic structure, 1840–1920. *Research in Organizational Behavior, 8*, 53–111.

13 User perceptions of born-digital authenticity

Jenny Bunn

Introduction

In the first two chapters of this section, the citizen-state relationship is writ large, primarily in terms of the role citizens expect and are willing to accept that the state should play in regulating the use (by other parties or the state) of data held about them. In this chapter, the state and that relationship fades from view and we start instead to see the citizen, an individual, in relation to documentary form. Recordkeepers (archivists and records managers among them) have long been involved in serving up documents on demand to individuals. Sometimes those demands cannot be met, e.g. to protect the privacy of others, but generally providing access to documentary forms is regarded as a core function of recordkeepers within Europe and across the world. In recent years, the forms that recordkeepers are presenting to individuals have changed to digital ones, and the way in which those forms are delivered has also changed. No longer is it necessary to visit a search or file room to collect paper or parchment documents from counters or cabinets. Rather, you can sit anywhere in the world with internet access and click on a link such that the document you require appears in front of you on whatever screen you are using. This chapter reports on a project that explored how individuals experience and understand the documents delivered in this way, and in particular how they judge such material to be authentic and "the real thing."

Authenticity has been a central issue in all four phases of the InterPARES project. In the first phase, research into the authenticity of electronic records led to the creation of sets of requirements for assessing authenticity and producing authentic copies of electronic records (Duranti, 2005, Appendix 2). This research was informed by Diplomatics, an established body of thought with origins traced back to 17th century Europe. Subsequent consideration has also highlighted the constructed nature of the concept of authenticity and the creation of guidelines for the creators of documents to help them with constructing authenticity, at least in its nature as "reliable evidence of what you have done" (Duranti & Preston, 2008, Appendix 20). It is in this form that recordkeepers are most concerned with authenticity, because they are also concerned with trust. Trust is the glue that holds individuals, societies, and nations together and it has been defined within the ITrust project as

> Confidence of one party in another, based on alignment of value systems with respect to specific actions or benefits, and involving a relationship of voluntary vulnerability, dependence and reliance, based on risk assessment.
>
> (Pearce-Moses, 2018, s.v. Trust)

Confidence between parties (e.g. between citizen and state) grows through an ongoing relationship in which values are aligned and the parties demonstrate that they can rely on each other and that they will fulfil their promises to the other party, do what they say they would do and be what they purport to be. Maintaining "reliable evidence of what you have done" (Duranti & Preston, 2008, Appendix 20) is vital to both parties' ability to hold themselves to account with respect to how they have acted and to allow them to reflect on and learn from their mistakes or mis-steps. Sometimes it is hard to face up to our mistakes, and in our minds and memories, there is perhaps always a tendency to put a positive gloss on our actions. Accurate and systematic recordkeeping helps to keep us all honest – it supports the conditions that make trust possible.

Recordkeepers (particularly those who have undergone a period of professional training in the Western tradition) are well versed with authenticity in the sense previously discussed. It remains of vital concern to them because it defines one way in which they can serve (and hopefully be valued in return for serving) the public good. It is not, however, their only concern, because in common with the whole world, recordkeepers are also facing up to an ever-changing digital landscape where what is technically possible is rapidly expanding at what seems like a faster pace than we have ever experienced before. Seeking to deal with and adapt to this change was a key driver in the initiation of the InterPARES projects in 1999, and it has remained an undercurrent throughout. The research described in this chapter was designed to face this undercurrent head on, by also asking questions about how these changes might be impacting not just on our constructions of authenticity, but also on our constructions of reality. For in the digital world of parallel physical, virtual, and augmented reality, the nature of such constructions is becoming much more complicated.

At first glance, this may seem like quite a leap, but the connections are there. "Authentic" is, after all, a synonym of real and the questions "is this the real thing?" and "is this authentic?" can be seen, at least in the English language, as essentially interchangeable. The Oxford English Dictionary defines reality as "what is real rather than imagined or desired" (Reality, 2019) and the way in which accurate and systematic recordkeeping can help us to keep it real, rather than to succumb (singularly or collectively) to our imagined or desired recollections of our actions and behaviours has already been mentioned. On a theoretical level, it was these connections that the project sought to explore, but on a practical level, what was done during the ITrust study will now be described in more detail.

User perceptions of born-digital authenticity

For the study (Bunn, Brimble, Obolensky, & Wood, 2016), original data was collected via a series of nine interviews. The majority of the interviewees were in the 18–24 age group, although there were also individuals in older age groups, with the oldest interviewee being in the 40–49 age group. The majority of the interviewees were students in programmes run by the Department of Information Studies at University College London; others were experienced recordkeeping practitioners. The oldest participant reported that s/he had first regularly used a computer or other digital device in early adulthood, while the others reported that they had done so either at primary school (ages 5–11) or secondary school (ages 12–18). During each interview, the participants were asked to access four documents. They were then asked: 1) to describe what they thought they were looking at; 2) whether or not they thought it was the real thing; and 3) why they held that opinion. Finally, they were also asked to reflect on their ideas about authenticity and to articulate why they thought these documents were being kept as digital archives. The order in which the documents was accessed was reversed in some interviews as a precaution against responses being conditioned by any one particular order.

The documents under consideration were briefly described to the participants (in pre-interview communication) in the following terms

1   e-mail messages between work colleagues, 2001
2   Metroblogging London Website, 2005
3   memo to the SCM (Structured Capital Markets) Approval Committee of Barclays Bank seeking approval for Project Faber, 2007
4   press notice detailing the response of Lord Nolan to the House of Commons' response to the first report of the Select Committee on Standards in Public Life, 1995.

At the interview, they were given instructions in order to access them and in so doing, it became apparent to them that the documents were located in a variety of different "archives," namely The National Archives (4), the British Library's UK Web Archive (2), the 9/11 Digital Archive (1) and WikiLeaks (3). Two of the documents were born digital, but their form imitates more traditional analogue counterparts – (3) and (4), although (3) also included the "tracked changes" of a word processed document, betraying its born-digital origins, and (4) consisted of both the press notice and a page of metadata detailing its born-digital origins. The other two documents did not imitate traditional analogue forms – (1) being an e-mail conversation, and

(2) a website. Finally, two of the documents were quite dry administrative records (3) and (4), and two were more immediate personal records, generated as a result of traumatic events (1) and (2).

The interviews were transcribed, checked with the participants, and then coded against a framework adapted from the work of K. F. Latham (Latham, 2015). Latham's study was interested in understanding how museum visitors understood their experience of the real thing (TRT) and was based on interviews with 21 visitors from five museums who were asked to walk through their visit to an exhibit and consider questions such as "*What does 'the real thing' mean to you?*" and "*What if museums went completely online?*" (Latham, 2015, p. 4, italics in original). The framework developed was based on Latham's finding of "four qualitatively different ways of understanding TRT in the museum," making these different ways of *self, relation, presence,* and *surround,* the main codes against which analysis was conducted. Within each of these main codes, subcodes were created for the various ideas identified by Latham, resulting in 25 codes in total. The decision to use this framework was taken on the grounds that it offered a way to blur the lines between questions of authenticity and those of reality or at least real-ness, in accordance with the aims of the study. A more detailed description of the coding process can be found in the final study report (Bunn et al., 2016), but in retrospect, what became apparent in revisiting the study for the purpose of writing this chapter is the way in which the lines were not so much blurred as drawn during that process.

The way in which the four main codes of *self, relation, presence,* and *surround* were interpreted and applied betrayed a focus (whether in the data or in the coder's head, or both) on the following ideas

- *self*: the terms in which people expressed themselves when explaining their judgements on the degree to which the documents were the real thing or not
- *surround*: the sense in which these documents seemed not to be seen as sharing an environment with the participants, but nonetheless had presence somewhere
- *presence*: the nature of the presence of these documents, more somewhere than here and in relation to time
- *relation*: the people imagined or known who were discussed in relation to the individual documents and the roles they were assigned.

In the next stage of the initial analysis, however, these ideas were grouped around two further codes, *judgements of authenticity* and *digital presence,* thereby drawing a very clear line between participants' constructions of authenticity and of reality. As soon as this line was drawn, consideration of connections started to be lost. And so, for the purposes of this chapter, the data has been revisited and re-analyzed with a view to looking for connections and insight in the overlap rather than the distinction between these two high-level codes.

Constructing both authenticity and reality

The two codes that were brought together around the theme of judgements of authenticity were *self* and *relation*, whereas *presence* and *surround* were connected within the theme of *digital presence*. It was noted, however, that the two ideas started to blur together around what was termed *conflation of then and now*. This idea found form initially under the theme of *judgements of authenticity* in the observation that in making such judgements, the interviewees often imagined and made reference to the creators and current holders of these documents, but rarely so imagined previous users of these documents or those responsible for getting the document from the creator to the current holder. By way of the exception proving the rule, on one rare occasion and in relation to the e-mail messages from the 9/11 Digital Archive, an interviewee spoke of how

> obviously this has been edited because it's here, so *someone* took it out of some organisation's server, edited it to portray, to convey this message of how people were trying to find each other in the chaos.
>
> (Interviewee 6)

An awareness of the absence of imagined intermediaries resonated with an idea that Latham had raised with regards to the original coding around presence, where it had been noted that "this actual thing that was once in the space with another person at another time holds something different than anything that has not followed the same path" (Latham, 2015, p. 10).

In the museum context discussed by Latham, the idea of *presence* was also discussed in conjunction with ideas of *evidence*, *aura*, and *truth*, suggesting that *presence* carries connotations not just of "the actual presence of a physical thing that is in the space with the experiencer," but also connotations of authority, of standing as proof of another place and time. *Presence* is actual then not just in a physical sense, in physical experience here and now, but also as an act of actualizing, of making real, another time and place. Here again then was the theme of *conflation of then and now*, but this time, not in conjunction with *judgements of authenticity*, but with that of *digital presence*.

Although interviewees were asked whether or not they believed that the documents they were being shown were "the real thing," they were not directly asked whether or not they believed that they were "actual" things. In coding for *presence* and *surround*, however, attention was paid to the places and times in which the documents were said to be, and any discussion of how they brought the past to life. For example, there was not much of a sense expressed of these documents being *in* the same space as either the participants or anyone else; rather, they were spoken of as being located *on* somebody's computer or *on* this or that website or platform. The sense that people had of a past existence for the documents seemed therefore to be less about where they had been, and more about when they had been. Dates and times were frequently mentioned, e.g.

> I'm looking at the date first, to see *when this document was conducted.*
> (Interviewee 7)

> Everything has got an author and *a time stamp from when it was posted.*
> (Interviewee 2)

And there was also a sense in which some of the documents, at least, could make the past real and bring it to life. For example, of the e-mail messages from 9/11, participants spoke of how

> the time is very close, it seems very quick response and I think it's, they are, they work in the same company, maybe it's in the building that was destroyed so *I can feel that, . . . people's anxiety.*
> (Interviewee 8)

> The human side of it, I mean yes it adds to it because I can imagine what it would be like you know you're trying to find out where all of your colleagues [are].
> (Interviewee 9)

In the overlap between the themes of *judgements of authenticity* and *digital presence*, then, the idea of the *conflation of then and now* drew attention to the idea of a *path from then to now*, of a gap that could be opened up and examined or closed and brought to life. Time could be unfolded around these documents or within them, or both, but it was primarily a temporal and not a spatial path that defined these documents' presence.

Unfolding time

Attention having been drawn to the unfolding of time, further consideration was given to the ways in which this was discussed by the participants. For example, it has already been noted that time and date stamps were often mentioned and also that in the case of the e-mail messages, it was the short time elapsed between the messages that help to bring the anxiety of that time to life. This was not, however, the only document within which time unfolded. For example, in respect of the Barclays Bank memo (with its tracked and timestamped changes making evident the process of editing over at least a week), someone spoke of how it's usually from a source from within the company. So, how else would someone have got this document while it was in process? It must be legitimate to an extent because it's obviously not a finished item.

> (Interviewee 1)

Then again, in the case of the blogging site (which contained a series of blog posts made and time and date stamped on the website around the time of the July 2005 terrorist attacks in London), a participant spoke of

> the authenticity of reaction, the immediacy of the reactions, perhaps of the individuals involved in making these comments.
>
> (Interviewee 4)

In both cases, this unfolding of time also seems to be associated with idea about closeness (in temporal terms) to the process or triggering event. Indeed, in response to the question "And of the four documents, then, which one would you say is the most real or feels the most real?" one participant responded

> the e-mail exchange and the blog because they're not highly formatted. No one's gone through like ten drafts of it to produce it. It feels more close to what somebody actually thinks and what someone might actually say if you just stopped them in the street.
>
> (Interviewee 9)

Within one document however, an unfolding of time took place that did not engender closeness, but rather distance. Document 4, the press notice, came from The National Archives as a single PDF file that contained the press notice and a page of metadata which included the original file name and directory, author, and creation and last printed on dates of 2 July 1998. This was noted by a number of participants, particularly in relation to the date on the press notice, which was 19 July 1995.

> The metadata is just about when it was made. This says 1998 but it was in 1995, so does that mean it's been digitized?
>
> (Interviewee 1)

> I think it's odd that it's 1998 that it was last printed, that might have significance.
>
> (Interviewee 9)

> It says creation date is this file. It seems not to match.
>
> (Interviewee 8)

> Looking now at some of the information about the creation dates, which is obviously a few years after the document was dated 1995 . . .

I'm going by the creation date 1998 and that it's possibly a digitized document from 1995 if it's an authentic document.

(Interviewee 4)

This last quote shows how this mismatch brings the document's authenticity into question a bit more. The inclusion of the metadata and its time to the document and its time leads to time unfolding not just within the document, but also outside it. An additional process outside the process attested to by the press notice becomes visible, and as another participant put it

when I was looking for that page it was archives, so it's like another layer between me and the information so there is another step there was someone involved in the process which can add some uncertainty.

(Interviewee 6)

On the one hand, therefore, the presence of this metadata can be seen to be working against a judgement of authenticity. The original coding showed how in these judgements, the judgements actually being made (in this case) were mostly about the motivations and intentions of others, and primarily the creators and current holders/those presenting the documents as authentic.

It is created by someone like you or me and that something can be shown on the material, but it doesn't mean it's very objective it doesn't mean it completely records the truth.

(Interviewee 8)

I don't know why people would do some fake things in this particular thing because I think it's a serious topic.

(Interviewee 6)

I mean having been to The National Archives I think they haven't got enough time on their hands to have like some major conspiracy going on.

(Interviewee 9)

I guess it's interesting that it's on the WikiLeaks page because *they* are known for digging up the truth, so it makes me sort of think it's authentic because it's a file that they have brought up to say this thing has been going on and everybody needs to know.

(Interviewee 2)

The addition of metadata to this document means that the time unfolding within the document conjures up not just time unfolding the process and events to which it refers, but also time unfolding outside and around the document itself. The question of how that document got from then to now is opened up for examination, leaving a lot more time in which to imagine other agencies acting, not to create it in the first place or present it to you now, but to transport and facilitate movement between the two and through time.

Then again, however, in this surfacing of time unfolding outside and around the document itself, of agency needed to transport it through time, the presence of this metadata could also be said to be seen to be supporting a judgement of realness, of presence, of this document having an "actual" existence and persistence separate from the participant's current experience of it on their screen. The Oxford English Dictionary defines real as "having an objective existence; actually existing physically as a thing" (Real, 2019) and the metadata gives the press notice an objective existence. It exists physically as a thing, not because we can physically touch it, but because it requires physical agency (on behalf of someone or some other thing) to endure. In turn, it is this judgement or sense of objective existence that supports judgements of authenticity, since without it, how can it be seen to be bringing the past to life, to have been close to past events.

Conclusion

The study reported here sought to explore a possible connection between questions of authenticity and those of reality. None of these questions have been answered, but connections have been drawn between the way in which a document is perceived to be a thing (to have a presence in the sense of actual existence) and the way in which it is perceived to be authentic. These connections have been found in the ideas of a *conflation between then and now* and of how time can be seen as unfolding within our reading of documents as representative of past events or outside it with our reading of them as documents (which have an existence of their own). Latham (2015) wrote that "this actual thing that was once in the space with another person at another time holds something different than anything that has not followed the same path" (p. 10). Could not this path be both one through time, but also one in time, establishing this actual thing as something different?

These conclusions are theoretical ones, and they will not translate easily into practice or offer any simple solutions to the question of trust and records in an open digital environment. A connection has been drawn between the way in which a document is perceived to have a presence and that in which it is perceived to be authentic or real. Within this connection, a distinction has also been drawn, that between time unfolding in real time (as the participants read and inhabit the world and events the documents represent and bring to life) and time unfolding in the passage of time around us and all the other things (people and documents) that thereby can be seen to have an objective existence. No one would deny that our reality is changing, that it is becoming amongst other things an open digital environment. Perhaps then, it is worth considering that with a change in reality must also come a change in how we conceptualize and more importantly actualize and trust in our sense of what is real, of what is authentic.

Acknowledgements

The author would like to thank all the participants who agreed to be interviewed for this study and to acknowledge the contribution of research assistants Sara Brimble, Selene Obolensky, and Nicola Wood.

References

Bunn, J., Brimble, S., Obolensky, S., & Wood, N. (2016). *Perceptions of born digital authenticity* (EU28). InterPARES Trust. Retrieved from https://interparestrust.org/assets/public/dissemination/EU28_20160718_UserPerceptionsOfAuthenticity_FinalReport.pdf

Duranti, L. (Ed.). (2005). *The InterPARES project: The long-term preservation of authentic electronic records: The findings of the InterPARES project.* San Miniato: Archilab.

Duranti, L., & Preston, R. (Eds.). (2008). *International Research on Permanent Authentic Records in Electronic Systems (InterPARES) 2: Experiential, interactive and dynamic records.* Padova, Italy: Associazione Nazionale Archivistica Italiana.

Latham, K. F. (2015). What is 'the real thing' in the museum? An interpretative phenomenological study. *Museum Management and Curatorship, 30*(1), 2–20, https://doi.org/10.1080/09647775.2015.1008393

Pearce-Moses, R. (Ed.). (2018). *InterPARES Trust terminology.* Retrieved from https://interparestrust.org/terminology/term/trust

Real. (n.d.). *Oxford English Dictionary.* Retrieved from: https://www.oed.com/

Reality. (n.d.). *Oxford English Dictionary.* Retrieved from: https://www.oed.com/

14 Usability of electronic record management systems

Sevgi Koyuncu Tunç with Özgür Külcü

Introduction

Rapid digitisation leads to exponential growth of business data and content. Every day, corporations are creating large numbers of business documents, contracts, offers, sales announcements, marketing materials, human resources (HR) guides, training guides, etc. These documents are usually scattered on different digital devices. The McKinsey report, published in 2012, states that employees are spending on average 1.8 hours per day for searching and collecting information and that employees cannot access correct documents due to the time/location barrier (Chui et al., 2012). According to the *Definitive Guide to America's Most Broken Processes* (Nintex, 2018), 49% of the people interviewed had problems finding documents, 43% experienced problems in document approval and sharing processes, and 33% had document versioning problems. This motivated the ITrust study (Külcü & Koyuncu Tunç, 2015) to investigate and determine the factors affecting usability of ERMS. The heuristic evaluation (HE) method, which depends on the usability principles, guidelines, and criteria, was applied. The study explained HE method application steps, revealed its advantages and disadvantages, and identified improvement areas. Therefore, this study can be used both as a resource and a tool showing how to test the usability of ERMS.

Literature review

Heuristic evaluation is a low-cost, effective, and fast usability assessment method developed by the usability expert Jakob Nielsen (Geng & Tian, 2015). The method is defined as "evaluation through experts" since there is no user involvement in the evaluation process (Dix, Finlay, Abowd, & Beale, 2004). One or more usability experts undertake predefined tasks using the software system and observe the interaction against a checklist of usability principles to evaluate the usability of the software (Blandford, Keith, Connell, & Edwards, 2004; Gray & Salzman, 1998; Preece, 1993). HE can be applied on any software domain like online learning,

ERMS, HR, etc. A balanced evaluation team should consist of usability experts and domain experts. Experts who have both proficiencies are called "double experts" (Karoulis & Pombortsis, 2003). If there is more than one expert, they should evaluate the system independently so that evaluations can be fair and objective (Nielsen, 1993). Output of the HE is a list of usability problems organized according to the usability principles (Dix et al., 2004).

Research methodology

The premise of this research is that the source of usability problems related to the ERMS software lies in the fact that these systems are being developed without considering principles of good human-computer interaction (HCI) and usability principles. Therefore, the main research question was: "what are the factors which affect usability of an ERMS, and how can these factors be investigated?" The research steps are shown in Figure 14.1.

The heuristic walkthrough is a cost effective and easy-to-apply usability evaluation method. HE allows us to analyze a system according to the usability principles. In the study, first the literature review was done, then all the detected important criteria were gathered to form a single list. The usability evaluation criteria highlighted in the most cited usability-related publications in the literature were organized in six groups: efficiency, effectiveness, user satisfaction, easiness to learn, easiness to remember, and error management. Finally, a list of 18 items to investigate was created (usability evaluation checklist) and used in the heuristic walkthrough

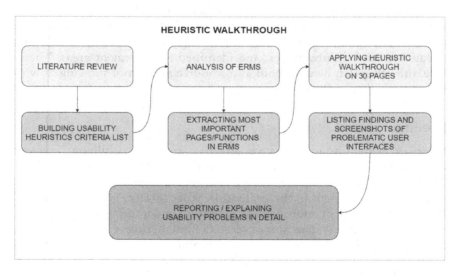

Figure 14.1 The research process involving heuristic evaluation method

1   system state visibility
2   user control and freedom
3   consistency
4   preventing errors
5   flexibility and efficiency
6   aesthetic and simple design
7   error messages
8   help and documentation
9   shortcuts and tips
10   undoing transactions
11   following standards by design principle
12   readability of user interface (UI) text
13   compatibility between forms (supporting faster user learning)
14   distinctiveness of signals (eliminating confusion)
15   similarity of images and icons with the objects they represent
16   information access cost efficiency
17   size and position of clickable screen elements
18   availability of additional information.

After the research, an additional six criteria were added (see end of the following section).

In the process of the ERMS usability evaluation, the ERMS was analyzed and all functions and their screens (pages) listed. The 30 most important and most often used screens were selected for the evaluation process.

The test data has been created in the ERMS for test users set up by the university management, and the 30 pages which are important for the ERMS were evaluated in two iterations using the identified 18 items from the usability criteria list. Detailed findings and screenshots of the problematic user interfaces were compiled, analyzed, and discussed (Külcü & Koyuncu Tunç, 2015).

Findings

The main purpose of the HE method is to identify the problems in the user interface design of a system through a list of criteria. The ERMS of Hacettepe University was analyzed with four different types of test users (faculty secretary, faculty dean, department chair, and department secretary). The 30 selected ERMS pages were analyzed using HE, and each page was assessed against the usability evaluation checklist. Usability issues detected in the system are shown in the Table 14.1.

As a result of the heuristic evaluation, 83 user interface errors that need to be improved in terms of usability and human-computer interaction were determined. Out of those, 45 errors should be corrected urgently, 26 errors should be corrected in the medium term, and 12 errors (regarding the appearance of the pages) should be further considered to be corrected.

Table 14.1 Number of identified ERMS issues according to the usability evaluation checklist

Heuristics	Number of detected issues
Shortcuts and tips	9
General usage design principles	8
Error messages	8
User control and freedom	8
Preventing errors	7
Aesthetic and simple design	6
Distinctiveness of signals (eliminating confusion)	5
Availability of additional information	4
Consistency	4
Readability of UI texts	4
Similarity of images and icons with the objects they represent	4
System state visibility	4
Size and position of clickable screen elements	3
Flexibility and efficiency	2
Help and documentation	2
Information access cost efficiency	2
Undoing transactions	2
Compatibility between forms (supporting faster user learning)	1

According to the results of the heuristic assessment applied in this study, to increase the usability of the ERMS the following improvements are required

- warning and information messages should be added to prevent data loss before exiting unsaved forms
- in the form verification, an incorrectly filled field should be directly pointed at, while the general warning messages such as "check fields" should be avoided
- items on the pages should be arranged to guide users correctly, and system should prevent users from performing actions contrary to the busines rules and standards (e.g. distribution/archiving of documents without filing should not be allowed)
- a special error page should be used for unhandled exceptions and errors to guide the users
- users should be able to achieve their goals with a minimum number of steps (e.g. departments should be listed as soon as the department selection window is opened, and no extra button should need to be clicked)
- the items on the screen should be legible and clearly visible
- the pictures on the icons must indicate the meaning of the function of the UI element
- the UI elements that perform the same function should have the same design, thus making it easier for users to remember using it

- the appearance of active and passive page elements should be designed to reflect the difference.

After the heuristic evaluation study, it was concluded that the following six new criteria should be added to the ERMS usability evaluation checklist

1 automatic suggestion of the standard file plan (for incoming/newly created documents)
2 "search in all fields" capability (available from document search page)
3 visibility of elements according to the type of user (unnecessary/ unauthorized page elements must be invisible)
4 terminology usage (it should be clear, understandable, and standardized)
5 list of recently used documents
6 availability of document tagging option (to improve search capabilities).

Discussion

According to the findings of the usability evaluation conducted within the scope of this study, the most important factors affecting the usability of ERMS are lack of simplicity of the document creation screens, lack of guidance, poor search capability, insufficient information to perform transactions, poor navigation capabilities, non-instructional error messages, and the possibility of non-standard processing of information. Next, a set of recommendations are given and discussed.

Document creation

In the process of creation of official documents with a large number of information types, data entry must be carried out from simple to detailed, and with as simple an interface as possible. The user should be guided by a design which enables the user to fill in mandatory information in steps and logical groups, respectively, and the business rules should not be left to the discretion or competence of the user, thus ensuring that the work is performed in accordance with the standards.

Document search

The most important function of the ERMS should be quick access to the document. The ability to search all fields by keyword prevents loss of time. The list of results returned by the search should be presented according to the title, and the total number of documents listed should be shown to the user. Buttons for navigating through the pages shown for long lists should be easily clickable and should allow navigation to a particular page. In order to sort/differentiate documents created on the same date, time information should be presented along with date.

Cost of access to required/related information

Information should be delivered to the user in the minimum number of steps during document processing in ERMS, thus achieving information access cost efficiency. For example, it is unnecessary and confusing not to list the departments automatically when the department selection window is opened but to wait for the user to click on the "search" button.

Barriers to fast data entry design

Forms should be designed to facilitate data entry, and the use of shortcut keys should be enabled. Unnecessary/non-authorized UI elements should be hidden, and the page design should be as simple as possible. For example, the staff listed in the signature window should only be those who can sign a document. In this way, selecting a wrong person will be prevented from the beginning, and a shorter staff list can be seen instead of the long staff list. The help menu should be easily visible.

Feeling lost

Flexibility of navigation in the ERMS prevents the user from feeling lost. Each page must have place pointers to indicate the menu from which it was accessed, and users should be given the opportunity to return to the previous page. The items on the screen should be legible and clearly visible. The pictures on the icons used in the design should be designed to express the meaning of the function. Page elements that perform the same function should also have the same design. This will make it easier for users to remember to use it. The appearance of active and passive page elements should be designed to reflect the difference.

Error messages

A special error page should be used for unexpected, exceptional situations and errors, and the user should be guided how to solve them. To prevent data loss, such as deleting records or exiting the form without saving, the user should be informed about the result of his/her operation with a warning or information message. The user should be directly pointed at the incorrect field or the one missing the required data entry during the form validation process instead of giving general warning messages.

Following ERMS standard by design

The items on the pages should be arranged in a way to guide the user correctly. Precautions should be taken to prevent the user from performing transactions contrary to national or organisational standards. For example, the system should not allow the distribution/archiving of documents without filing them in the first place.

Heuristic evaluation is a cost-effective, detailed, and reliable method for assessing HCI usability. However, based on the study observations and results, the following recommendations for increasing efficiency of the HE method were formulated.

1   to have the experience of a new/novice user, it is necessary to start the heuristic evaluation without any training
2   after the first round of software review, the usability specialist should have as much information as possible about the organisation, users, and working conditions; ideally, the tests should be conducted using the organisation's network so that the effects of network conditions are included in the test
3   it is recommended that the heuristic evaluation is performed with more than one evaluator, if possible; however, if there is only one evaluator, this evaluator must be a "double expert," i.e. have both usability expertise and domain knowledge
4   it is important for the usability specialist to test the system from the following three perspectives to evaluate it from formal, semantic, and business rules standpoints

• compliance with web usability criteria
• data usability
• compliance with the national/organisational standards and business rules.

Conclusion

The heuristic evaluation method is a practical method that organisations can use to detect many usability issues at minimum cost. For this test, it is sufficient to have (preferably) two usability specialists and a list of usability criteria (heuristics), such as the one developed in this study. According to the findings of the heuristic evaluation method, improvements can be made in interface design, workflow design, data presentation style, content of system messages, content of help documents, navigation design, and compliance with standards. If the findings of the test cannot be understood or if the perception/interaction of the user with a problematic interface needs to be investigated, a problem-oriented or page-oriented user test should be organized. In that case, instead of a comprehensive ERMS user test, only the problematic user interfaces and functions will be identified using HE. This will reduce the user test time and overall evaluation costs.

The usability tests described in this study can be used by software developers, by organisations evaluating ERMS solutions before purchasing, or by ERMS certification authorities.

Developing multiple prototypes during the design phase is one of the least preferred practices in IT sector because of its cost (Koyuncu Tunç, 2014). Yet prototype development is a very effective way to avoid poor designs. Prototypes prepared before software development can be tested using the heuristic evaluation method explained in this study and improved before the final product reaches the market.

By evaluating ERMS using HE before purchasing, organisations can achieve the following benefits

- the organisation can test whether the product performs as described in the promotional video/document(s)
- compliance of the product with the operation of the institution and its workflow can be tested
- compatibility of product design and computer skills of institutional staff can be checked
- elements that do not meet the expected standards can be detected before the product is purchased, and product refinement could be requested
- features found to be missing from the product can be identified before the product is purchased, thus reducing the risk of increased cost after purchase
- if usability of the product is determined to be under expectations, purchase can be cancelled.

Finally, the ERMS certification authorities who evaluate the functionality, security, and interoperability features of the ERMS can and should also check the usability level of the ERMS using the HE method described in this chapter. They can reveal design problems, processes designed contrary to the workflow of the ERMS standards, the appropriateness of error messages, efficiency, data usability, and presentation problems, legibility problems, and problems in consistency between visual and text elements.

To conclude, this chapter showed the importance of human-computer interface analysis using the heuristic evaluation method to improve the user experience with the electronic records management systems, efficiency of interaction, and overall experience of a user, either the state side or the citizen side, in connection with the documentary form.

References

Blandford, A., Keith, S., Connell, I., & Edwards, H. (2004). Analytical usability evaluation for digital libraries: A case study. In *Proceedings of the 4th ACM/IEEE-CS Joint Conference on Digital Libraries 2004* (pp. 27–36). Tucson: ACM Press.

Chui, M., Manyika, J., Bughin, J., Dobbs, R., Roxburgh, C., & Sarrazin, H. (2012). *The social economy: Unlocking value and productivity through social technologies*. Retrieved from https://www.mckinsey.com/industries/high-tech/our-insights/the-social-economy

Dix, A. J., Finlay, J. E., Abowd, G. D., & Beale, R. (2004). *Human-computer interaction* (3rd ed.). Harlow, Essex: Pearson Education Limited.

Geng, R., & Tian, J. (2015). Improving web navigation usability by comparing actual and anticipated usage. *IEEE Transactions on Human-Machine Systems 45*(1), 84–94.

Gray, W. D., & Salzman, M. C. (1998). Damaged merchandise? A review of experiments that compare usability evaluation methods. *Human-Computer Interaction*, *13*(3), 203–261.

Karoulis, A., & Pombortsis, A. (2003). Heuristic evaluation of web-based ODL programs. In C. Ghaoui (Ed.), *Usability evaluation of online learning programs*. Hershey, PA: Information Science Publishing.

Koyuncu Tunç, S. (2014). *Türkiye BT Sektöründe İnsan Bilgisayar Etkileşimi Bilgisi ve Farkındalığı – Eğitim Yeterliliği* [HCI knowledge and awareness in the Turkish IT industry – HCI education adequacy], IMCW 2014.

Külcü, Ö., & Koyuncu Tunç, S. (2015). *Usability and human-computer interaction of electronic records management systems* (EU34). InterPARES Trust. Retrieved from https://interparestrust.org/assets/public/dissemination/2_ITrust_EDMS_Usability_NewTask_Proposal_ok2.pdf

Nielsen, J. (1993). *Usability engineering*. San Diego, CA: Academic Press.

Nintex. (2018). *Definitive guide to America's most broken processes*. Retrieved from https://info.nintex.com/rs/272-JVS-996/images/Nintex%20AMBP%20Ebook%20Final.pdf

Preece, J. (1993). *A guide to usability: Human factors in computing*. Boston, MA: Addison-Wesley Longman Publishing; The Open University.

15 Education of records managers and archivists

Liudmila Varlamova with Liudmila Fionova, Julia Kukarina, Grigory Lanskoy, and Elena Latysheva

Introduction

At present, we can observe a transformation of the professions of record-keepers and archivists. This is connected with the changing role of documents in modern society due to several factors such as the introduction of information technologies, the emergence of electronic/digital documents, and the increase in the value of documents for the society as a whole and for the individual in particular.

Professional training for recordkeepers and archivists to be employed at government institutions has existed in Russia for many centuries. This professional training has always been closely connected with development of the regulatory base used first in recordkeeping, then in the documentation support of management, and presently in records management. Thus, the process of specialists' training cannot be analyzed separately from the history of official state recordkeeping (modern records management), state archives' policy, and institutions. The information for this analysis came from the ten most successful Russian universities, four of which participated in the ITrust project.

History of training archivists

The first higher education institution in Russia created specifically for training archivists was the Archival Institute (presently the History and Archives Institute, part of the Russian State University for the Humanities, or RSUH). It was established in 1930 to provide qualified specialists for the state, departmental, and municipal archives. In 1952, the subdepartment of the History of State Institutions and Recordkeeping was founded at the Institute. The curriculum of the Institute included regular professional practice and special recordkeeping courses. In 1960, the Department of State Recordkeeping was set up within the Institute. This department was the first to award degrees in recordkeeping in Russia. Since that time, there have been two independent areas of training – one for archivists, the other for records managers.

At the same time, two special State Educational Standards for record-keepers and archivists were created: "document science and recordkeeping" and "history and archives." All universities' and colleges' curricula and educational programmes were based on those State Educational Standards approved by the Russian Ministry of Education, which ensured stability and uniformity of educational practice all over the country.

All of that was supported by the creation of All-Russia Educational and Methodical Association for recordkeepers and archivists, headed by the RSUH as the leader in the professional area of education. This Association has included all Russian universities and colleges awarding degrees in documentation support of management and archives.

The Association's objectives are

- appraisal of course books and manuals
- curricula development and coordination of educational programmes between universities
- methodical assistance and support of departments and subdepartments in their educational work
- interaction with the All-Russian Scientific and Research Institute for Records and Archives (VNIIDAD) and introduction of its latest results into the educational programmes.

Introduction of the Bologna system

At the beginning of the 2000s, the Russian higher education system was forced to switch from the traditional specialist programmes (a five-year programme) to the Bologna system (a four-year bachelor's programme and a two-year master's programme). It is very important to note that two professional areas which had always been separate ("document science" and "archival science") were united in one joint bachelor's programme "document and archival science," which led to the transformation of the state educational standard and programme.

This practice is not completely unknown. For example, University College London (UCL) has the same combined approach to the study of recordkeeping and archival research, but at the graduate level. Its MA programme has five core modules: 1) concepts and contexts; 2) creation and capture; 3) curation and stewardship; 4) the recordkeeping professional; and 5) access and use of archives and records.

> Whilst these modules aim to provide a solid information of conceptual knowledge and practical skills, students' individual interests can be explored in depth through two optional modules chosen from the following subject areas: Collection care, Database systems analysis, Digital resources in the humanities, Information governance, Manuscript studies, Reading and interpretation of archives from 1500.
>
> (Rhys-Lewis, 2017, p. 211)

Rhys-Lewis (2017) notes that "archives and records management at UCL is one of the longest-established archival education programs in the English-speaking world" (p. 210).

Another important step of the last decade in Russia was integration of separate Educational and Methodical Associations into enlarged groups, which resulted in combining history and archaeology with document science and archival science. That was quite logical for archivists but absolutely inappropriate for records managers. That decision decreased the popularity of the profession, as well as the quality of professional education, because many history-oriented courses needed to be included in the curriculum.

However, even the universities with sufficient educational material and personnel resources claimed that a four-year bachelor's cycle was too short. Given the large amount of newly introduced material, it became evident that it is practically impossible to carry out training of document science and archival science specialists within one educational programme. These trends have resulted in worsening of the quality of education in both areas and in closing special records management departments in provincial universities due to a decrease in the number of applicants. It must be noted that all Russian universities involved in the ITrust project insist on the negative effects of introduction of the Bologna system in our professional area.

Before 1991 (i.e. in the USSR), there were three cycles of higher education

- specialist's programmes (a five-year programme)
- postgraduate cycle (from 2–4 years depending on the area and the degree equivalent to a standard PhD dissertation)
- doctorate cycle (minimum one year to perform all necessary formalities to be admitted to the defence) – this is the highest scientific degree in Russia.

In modern Russia, there are four cycles of higher education

- bachelor's programme (can be academic or applied with a four-year programme)
- master's programme (academic two-year programme)
- postgraduate cycle (two-year programme and the degree equivalent to a standard PhD dissertation)
- doctorate cycle (minimum one year to perform all necessary formalities to be admitted to the defence).

In this way, Russia was able to keep the top academic levels but at the expense of the first, fundamental level of higher education, whose quality decreased. However, the RSUH has all four cycles, and it is the only educational institution in Russia which is authorized to hold the defences (PhD and full doctorate degree) in document science and archival science.

After the 2000s, most Russian universities started to award degrees in document science and in archival science, but only a few can fully carry out the programme due to the lack of professional staff with enough practical experience in the area and the required scholarly degrees (PhD). While the core part of the university programmes is based on the state educational standards, the elective part of those programmes depends on the university resources, the availability of staff, and the regional job market.

The VNIIDAD Institute

Transformation of the Russian educational system has also had a negative impact on the VNIIDAD. Before 1991, the Institute had two records management departments and two archives departments. Now, the University has only two departments (one in each of these areas). After this unification, the Institute was transformed and updated the educational programmes at all cycles. Presently, VNIIDAD has five main educational programmes

1 applied bachelor's programme "Office work in the organization" (with emphasis on the functions of an assistant to the head of the organization and on personnel records management)
2 academic bachelor's programme "Information and documentation support of management" (with emphasis on preparation of records managers, experts in information technologies used in documentation support of management)
3 academic bachelor's programme "Audio-visual, scientific, technical, and economic archives" (with emphasis on special technology-supported documentation systems, including digital documents and their storage in archives)
4 academic bachelor's programme "State and municipal archives" (with emphasis on traditional archival work)
5 master's programme "Theory and practice of working with digital records in management and archives" (with emphasis on the technologies of work with digital records, interdepartmental digital records management, and archives holding digital records).

All these programmes have their own curricula, which consist of core and elective parts. The core part of the undergraduate curriculum includes the following blocks of subjects

1 history and organization of state and commercial sectors of all levels in Russia
2 legal subjects with emphasis on administrative, informational, and archival laws

3   creation and use of the traditional systems of documentation support of management and personnel records, as well as the history of record-keeping in Russia

4   specifics of creation and use of audio-visual, scientific, technical, and economic documentation, both in traditional forms and in digital form

5   modern information technologies used in records management and archives

6   foreign experience in management of informational resources and records, international standards used in this field

7   the main issues of archives management in Russia and abroad.

The students learn foreign languages throughout all training period, which enables them to work with original texts and communicate in the professional environment.

The elective part of the curriculum includes specialised disciplines. For example, in the programme *Information and documentation support of management*, special attention is paid to information technologies used in management in general (including issues of e-government, organization of interdepartmental electronic interaction, etc.), as well as to issues in document management (including electronic document management systems (EDMS), formats of electronic documents, methods of digitisation, storage, etc.).

The core subjects of any state curriculum for records managers and archivists are Russian history, world history, philosophy, informatics, management, administrative law, informational law, civil law, records and archives management standardisation, document science, information technologies used in documentation support of management, archival science, information technologies in archives, etc.

While the approach to university teaching may be different, the types of scientific activities are the same almost everywhere. The structure of a typical Russian educational programme for any subject consists of four elements: lectures, tutorials, practical or laboratory work, and individual work (research, projects, etc.).

Professional standards

The drawbacks of the integrated educational programme became evident after the first students' graduation. This brought the professional records management associations, universities, and experts to begin developing qualification standards which are to form the basis of state educational standards in document science and archival science. The Institute and all other universities involved in the ITrust project took an active part in this work. Today, Russia has two qualification standards in records management

- "specialist in organizational and documentation support of management" (qualification levels 5, 6)

  - level 5: recordkeeper (pre-university education and work experience or applied bachelor's degree)
  - level 6: specialist in the documentation support of management (applied bachelor's degree and work experience or academic bachelor's degree).

- "records management specialist" (qualification levels 7, 8)

  - level 7: head of the department of documentation support of management (academic bachelor's degree and work experience or master's degree)
  - level 8: manager – supervises all the systems of managerial documentation in the organization (master's degree and work experience or PhD).

A qualification standard for archivists is being developed.

In Russia, there is a principle of considering the organizational and administrative documentation system as an independent system used in management. Recordkeeping as a concept is used in management. Other documentation systems (e.g. accounting documentation) are not included in the concept of traditional recordkeeping and are not studied by recordkeepers. Yet with introduction of information technologies in management and the implementation of electronic corporate records management systems, this approach has become outdated and is to be reconsidered.

There are three levels of experts engaged in records management in Russia (Varlamova, 2016, p. 106)

- recordkeepers
- experts in documentation support of management
- records managers.

Requirements imposed to these experts are different in terms of their education level, as well as competence and responsibility. On the first level are recordkeepers who are responsible for registering the incoming and outgoing documents and controlling if the responses are made in time. They study four years to achieve academic bachelor's degree in records management. On the second level are experts in documentation support of management who are responsible for providing documents and documented information for the management processes of a company. They create regulatory acts on records management for the company and control their execution. They also study four years to achieve academic bachelor's degree in records management. On the highest, third level are records managers who are a company's top managers responsible for organizing and implementing work with all documentation systems of the company. These specialists must have a master's degree in records management. It is essential to note that in Russia there are nine levels of qualification, and records managers are at level eight, which is very high.

In order to perform, records management experts need relevant knowledge, competences, and skills, especially around digital records. This requires a reorganization of the system of records management experts' professional education at the universities of many countries, including Russia. Indication of the job functions are usually included in the job descriptions, and the Russian students should have relevant knowledge and experience for their realization. The demands of the job market are presented in the occupational standards. Universities use their elements to update the academic curricula according to the current needs of the country. As a result of this flexible approach, the students are always in demand on the job market. Figure 15.1

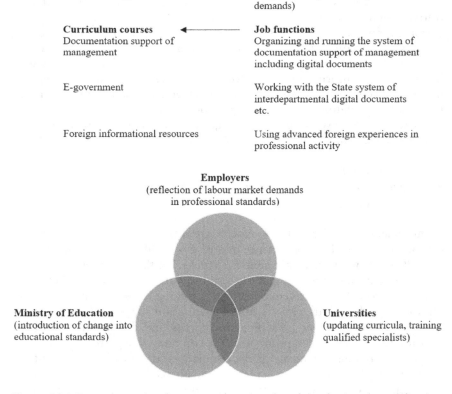

Educational standard ◄─────── **Professional (occupational) standard**
(meets the demand of the modern society)
(contains a list of job functions and competences based on the job market's demands)

Curriculum courses ◄─────── **Job functions**
Documentation support of management
Organizing and running the system of documentation support of management including digital documents

E-government
Working with the State system of interdepartmental digital documents etc.

Foreign informational resources
Using advanced foreign experiences in professional activity

Employers
(reflection of labour market demands in professional standards)

Ministry of Education
(introduction of change into educational standards)

Universities
(updating curricula, training qualified specialists)

Figure 15.1 Interconnection between educational and professional qualification standards in Russia

shows connections between educational and professional standards and the key players in their development.

The discussion so far has shown that in the modern Russia there is a coordinated system of professional education in records management which includes recordkeeping and documentation support of management. With rich experience and traditions in this area, there is a clear idea of future perspectives. The demand for experts in this area is steadily growing, and a rise in their status will attract more motivated young people to the professional sphere.

All Russian universities awarding the state-recognized degrees must adjust their academic programmes to the state educational standards and professional (occupational) standards, which will ensure a high level of professional training with a focus on the job market. At the same time, the elective part of the state educational programme will enable universities to develop their original academic programmes in view of the local demands, the availability of staff, and the universities' priorities. It must be noted that the consolidated position of all Russian universities participating in the ITrust project has made it possible to dramatically change the former situation of decline in the professional level of recordkeepers and records managers, and regain prestige of the profession and quality of university education. A transformation of the records managers' profession can be seen from the changing role of documents. This is due to:

1 implementation of information technologies and introduction of digital records
2 increase in the role the documents play both for the society and for the individual.

The first point tells us that the students need to know how to properly apply information technologies in their work as professionals. The second point needs special attention because it determines the vector (programme) of students' education, i.e. it requires the development of specialised knowledge about the specific characteristics of both working with (digital) documents and of (digital) documents themselves. For example, it might be expected that university programmes include a set of courses related to the work with open data in the cloud, i.e. to educate on the complexity of information resources including raw data, documented information, documents, and records.

Archival science education and (re)training

A brief overview of several European and Commonwealth of Independent States (CIS) countries shows lack of separate "archival science" specialization. It exists as a university specialization in some CIS countries (e.g. Belarus, Kazakhstan), and at the University of Zagreb, Croatia, while several other countries offer it as an applied programme. In most countries "archival science" is a part of a specialization in history or as a special course at the postgraduate level. For example, Schoggl-Ernst (2017) points out that the Institute for Austrian Historical Research provided postgraduate studies for Austrian archivists, which was the only archival science education possible up to 2006. In Hungary, Reisz (2017) points out, archiving was studied in the framework of history, as a block situated amongst general courses. In 2009, the "Master's Education of Archivists" programme was introduced, which is open to the students with a BA degree in history, law, sociology, or economics. This programme consists of compulsory courses covering archival systems and organization, basic legal archival knowledge, archival IT knowledge, document studies, document handling systems, document handling and archival standards, organization, preparation of finding aids, data safety, Hungarian administration, and field training. Later, the curriculum is specialized according to the directions "archival IT studies," "communication knowledge for archivists," and "archival and records managers standards."

In general, there are two approaches to records management curricula. They are grouped either as: 1) library science, archival science, and information sciences; or 2) document management, information technology, and management. The first approach perceives the document as a source, and everything that may contain information is considered as a document. For example, publications in a tabloid or in a book about an event are believed to be documents. Hence, this approach tends to include internet resources into collections of documents. From the point of view of the history framework, this is the right approach because these resources will complement those containing official information. The second approach to teaching document management is inextricably linked with management and the information technologies used in management. From its point of view, the document is perceived as the starting point of management on the one hand, and as its result on the other hand. In this regard, the creation and use of the document (both traditional and digital), the legal force of the document, and its long term storage and use, are presented within the framework of management tasks. For example, in Switzerland, document managers study at universities to become records information officers (Bianchi, 2017).

The most common practice of training archivists in the field of preservation and conservation is in research centres offering programmes for qualification upgrade, which operate at research institutes and archives. Grabnar (2017) provides example of the Book and Paper Conservation Centre of the Archives of the Republic of Slovenia. As part of the activities of these centres, short term and long term retraining or advanced training programmes are formed, which are especially popular.

An important role in this process is played by professional associations of archivists and document managers. For example, the Swiss Association of Archivists and the Association of Austrian Archivists organize professional development courses.

In Russia, a number of organizations are engaged in the issues of retraining and advanced training of specialists, but only VNIIDAD and the RSUH have permanent state accreditation of this type of educational activity. At the same time, VNIIDAD is the basic organization engaged in professional development of records managers and archivists of the CIS countries.

According to the state standard, retraining programmes cannot be less than 320 hours and should include all the core fields from the university curriculum. Continuing education programmes can be from 16–72 hours. Retraining and advanced training can be carried out remotely, including final certification. Looking at the size and geography of Russia, this is very convenient.

Conclusion

This chapter discussed the transformation of the professions of recordkeepers and archivists, taking the example of Russia. It was shown that the university education, professional training, and continuing education in records and archives management have very diverse solutions in different countries. Although different in approach, they are covering almost the same set of core courses, among which IT rightfully so plays an important part. Therefore, the development of future educational profiles in records and archives management qualifications should include aspects of creation of open digital environments supporting transparency and accountability of digital records.

References

Bianchi, C. (2017). Swiss competence model for the archivist of the 21st century. *Atlanti*, 27(2), 33–42.

Grabnar, M. (2017). Education in the field of preservation and conservation of archival heritage in Slovenia. *Atlanti*, 27(2), 97–105.

Reisz, T. C. (2017). Education of archivists in Hungary at the beginning of the 21st century. *Atlanti*, 27(2), 199–214.

Rhys-Lewis, J. (2017). Teaching preservation to students archivists at University College London. *Atlanti*, 27(2), 209–214.

Schoggl-Ernst, E. (2017). The non-university education of archival staff in Austria. *Atlanti*, 27(2), 53–61.

Varlamova, L. N. (2016). Different aspects of training records management experts in modern Russia. In *Global science and Innovation* (pp. 104–108). Chicago, IL: Accent Graphics communication.

16 Conclusion to Part II

Part II of the book took the citizens' view on trust and records in an open digital environment and looked at privacy "from above" and "from below." The former examined the central government's regulations and policies, while the latter examined civil society's information activism. It was argued that promotion of openness necessarily entails a loss of control. This is the reason why governments are finding it difficult to resolve the fundamental tensions between privacy and openness. The drive to achieve data-fuelled economic growth, based on government transparency on one side and participatory governance on the other, is behind the open government data laws, regulations, and policies entangling together privacy and government openness. (Pseudo)anonymisation procedures allow data, information, documents, and records to be made publicly available without identifying individuals and opening their personal identifiable information to the public. However, it was shown in the case of the UK's *care.data* programme that a lack of transparency about the usage of identifiable patient data (e.g. what data is used, who is using it, and for what purposes) in one governmental e-service lead to overall decrease in public trust in government, despite the community benefits. That example clearly showed that if the benefits of the big data are to be realized, "transparency by default" in research methodology and visibility of data use, accompanied by detailed explanations of the process, should be achieved. It was argued that the citizens themselves should have a more granular level of control over their data. If we take this idea even further, we can observe a movement towards incentivizing personal data, i.e. allowing citizens to earn from their personal data every time someone uses it. However, there is a fundamental question – if individuals are no longer identifiable, is the data still "theirs"?

Going from the *citizen-state* relationship, in which the focus was on the citizens' expectations of the role the state should play in regulating the use of data collected about them, to the *citizen-document form* relationship, this part further explored the way in which citizens perceive a document to be a thing (having physical presence) and the way they perceive it as authentic. This was motivated by the fact that recordkeepers are increasingly providing access to digital records from electronic records management systems

(ERMS), which represents a change from the traditional form of records and the way they used to be delivered. To be used as intended and trusted as authentic and reliable, the usability of the ERMS should be assessed. Part II argued for a heuristic evaluation method, as demonstrated in the example of the Hacettepe University's ERMS. The human-computer interface analysis using this heuristic evaluation method to improve the user experience with ERMS showed that the more efficient the interaction, the more motivated users will be. Nevertheless, the users, in this case recordkeepers, records managers, and archivists, should be properly educated in order to provide the expected level of service in relation to both the traditional, paper-based records and digital records, whether in an on-premise ERMS or, increasingly, entrusted to the cloud. The Russian experience in development of occupational and educational standards show that relationships between government, records professions, and universities should be established in order to develop professionals with the needed mix of traditional and digital skills whom the citizens can trust in managing open digital environments.

Part III
Documentary form

17 Introduction to Part III

Part III focuses on the documentary form. It starts by investigating the appraisal of websites. Although websites can be crawled and their snapshots archived, just as the Internet Archive's Wayback Machine does, the retention and disposition periods of different parts of a website may be different. If the information from different parts of a website can be considered records, should the number of section visitors, the time spent in the section, and geographical distribution of visits influence appraisal of a website? Would it be possible to create a formula to guide the appraisal of different website sections? What would be the metadata elements relevant for retention and disposition of websites? After investigating structure, metadata, and appraisal strategies using the example of one website, part III takes a broader approach and examines the presentation of cultural heritage objects online through the web-based systems of cultural institutions – museums, libraries, and archives (MLA). The metadata about the online cultural heritage resources are identified and analyzed with accessibility, interoperability, and interconnection possibilities in mind. Part III proceeds to investigate yet another type of digital resource – the print masters. It would make sense to archive a digital print master of a publication, e.g. of a newspaper edition, instead of publishing it, submitting the legal deposit copy, and then digitizing it. Therefore, the European legal deposit practices are studied in view of the ingest automation of digital print masters, ensuring quality control, provision of bibliographic metadata for storage and retrieval, and preservation. Finally, part III focuses on long term preservation of digitally signed records and discusses the challenges of expiring validity of digital signatures. Could blockchain provide a viable solution and be integrated into everyday record-keeping and archival processes?

Part III brings together experiences and research results from the countries geographically belonging to Europe with concrete examples from Croatia, France, Germany, Israel, Norway, and Turkey.

18 Preservation of website records

Silvia Schenkolewski-Kroll with
Assaf Tractinsky

Introduction

The objective of the research presented here was to examine the process of archival retention and disposition applied to a website. Disposition, or transfer to another repository or suitable archival institution, relies on a set of procedures and guidelines which organisations can use to choose which documents are to be permanently preserved, and which are to be disposed of. The aim was to create a suitable system of methodologies and procedures for retention and disposition of records on a website, whether by application of macro appraisal principles, using the existing procedures in accordance with the regulations and guidelines from the Israel Archives Law (1955), or by using any other suitable method. This chapter brings research results of three ITrust studies (Schenkolewski-Kroll & Tractinsky, 2015a, 2016, 2017).

The research used the website of the Ministry of Foreign Affairs, Government of Israel as a case study example. Schenkolewski-Kroll and Tractinsky (2015a) argue that the Ministry's site was chosen because its content is in English, its data is updated, earlier versions are available at the website, it receives inquiries and comments from the public, and it develops consular services online.

In general,

> on a website three main types of records can be identified, as to their completeness and authenticity: 1) the records created for the purposes of the website itself, which are considered original to it, and therefore all the rules of contemporary diplomatics apply to them, 2) records copied from other frameworks, but which retain all their original characteristics, and 3) records that retain their contents, but not their form.
> (Schenkolewski-Kroll & Tractinsky, 2015a, p. 6)

Attempts to find a basis for appraisal in existing retention schedules

Schenkolewski-Kroll and Tractinsky (2015a, pp. 19–21) attempted to apply the existing model of appraisal to the website of the Ministry of Foreign

Affairs, but it soon became apparent that such application is not possible. The characteristics of the website records are fundamentally different from those of traditional and other digital records. Therefore, the existing method needs to be adapted to the special characteristics of a website. Just as appraisal of archival material in operational records is conducted according to the Ministry's administrative units, the various sections of the website are taken into consideration, as well.

It is important to mention the relationship between the various website sections and the fact that records are regularly moved between them. Also, there are examples where content has been taken from the traditional and digital records, but the format, wording, and original content have been changed. Special sections, such as Consular Services and Israel's Agency for International Development Cooperation (MASHAV) that are not only informative but also operational, provide empty forms to be used by the public for various purposes. These forms are of value in terms of their format as they point to governance practices, yet they lack content that can help in determining their retention schedule classification (Schenkolewski-Kroll & Tractinsky, 2015a, p. 20). Due to the nature of the service and its operation, a website is defined as social media.

One of the special characteristics of a website is the constant updating of the records appearing on it, with the goal of providing current information in all the fields of concern (Schenkolewski-Kroll & Tractinsky, 2015a). Updates may be made as often as several times a day during critical periods, and up to every few weeks or more when dealing with permanent administrative material. This makes it possible to adapt harvesting of the material to the structure of the site, its content, the time, and a specific situation (Schenkolewski-Kroll & Tractinsky, 2015a). For example, on the Ministry of Foreign Affairs site, during times of war, material is harvested at very short intervals, compared with harvesting information during periods of peace. Retention by harvesting parameters is the accepted practice and is mentioned in the literature (Schenkolewski-Kroll & Tractinsky, 2015a).

In the research, an analysis of the structure and content of the Ministry of Foreign Affairs website in English was conducted, focusing on the MASHAV and Foreign Policy sections in order to demonstrate two different types of records and information available from each section, on the assumption that they can constitute a basis for appraisal of additional sections (Schenkolewski-Kroll & Tractinsky, 2015a). Although a section, MASHAV can be defined as a subsite, since it is operated by an administrative unit having a certain amount of autonomy when compared to other administrative units of the Ministry of Foreign Affairs. It is mainly operationally oriented and serves as a means of fulfilling the functions of the unit responsible for it, such as presenting courses and related information, MASHAV's activities on four continents, etc. The function of the Foreign Policy section is to present the past and current policy and activities of the Ministry through past information and current news. The format of the material is similar to traditional publications in written and electronic media (Schenkolewski-Kroll & Tractinsky, 2015b, p. 99).

Due to the special characteristics of the sections, the method of their analysis needed to be adjusted for each of them (Schenkolewski-Kroll & Tractinsky, 2015a). In the case of MASHAV, the retention periods that are determined for the administrative unit by the Israel Archives Law (1955) may apply. In the case of the Foreign Policy section, it may well be that there is an intrinsic value to statistical data – quantity of users, and the time they spend in a section – so that they can be considered as parameters for appraisal, beyond the content itself. With regards to this section, it is not possible to rely on previous appraisal because it does not exist.

The Israel Archives Law (1955) does not recognize appraisal of archival materials of websites, and as a result, there are no parameters for appraisal. On the other hand, it is perhaps possible to use the appraisal method recommended by the UK's National Archives, which harvests the entire website based on the self-determined parameters (The National Archives, 2014, 2017). However, this method is not applicable at the lower levels of the website. Therefore, it is preferable to apply other criteria if it is intended to perform appraisal at the level of subsites or subsections. The reason for this choice is an analysis of the internal distribution of the site (Schenkolewski-Kroll & Tractinsky, 2015a) in which various sections are different in nature, in accordance with their goals and the content they present.

Therefore, in accordance with the nature of the website, the harvesting periods need to be determined and tailored to each subsite or division according to its specific characteristics, as well as the location of retaining those parts intended to be saved on a permanent basis (Franks, 2019).

Behaviour of users as a category for appraisal

Behaviour of visitors was also examined as a factor in appraising the information and records from the Ministry of Foreign Affairs website, using the web analytics method. The reason for this approach lies in the fact that one of the objectives of the site is distribution of current information. Therefore, the number of users is considered as one of the criteria for determining the measure of the site's success, as opposed to other records which are not made available to the public until they become archival materials. This aspect, to the best of our knowledge, has not been taken into consideration in any website appraisal framework (Schenkolewski-Kroll & Tractinsky, 2016). In addition, the country of a section's visitors was used as one of the parameters.

The choice of metrics

In order to examine behaviour of users, Google Analytics (GA) metrics were used. These provide the following information: bounce rate, average time on page, page views, unique page views, and percentage of exit (Schenkolewski-Kroll & Tractinsky, 2016; Foscarini, 2019).

Table 18.1 (Schenkolewski-Kroll & Tractinsky, 2016) shows several main measurement categories from GA calculated for pages in various sections of the case study website. The first column shows names of sections. The following columns (page views, unique page views, average time on page, bounce rate, and % exit) show measurements of total data by section and their percentages. The categories Unique page views and Bounce rate were not used in the research. The section with the most page views (19.39%) is defined as "Pages." Due to the structure of the site, this category includes, among others, the home page, the home pages and display templates of the sections, search result pages, and "Contact us" pages, so that in many categories, this section shows higher results in relation to other sections (Schenkolewski-Kroll & Tractinsky, 2016).

The sections compared here, "Foreign Policy" (14.88%) and "MASHAV" (5.6%), and the control section "About Israel" (16.47%), together constitute 36.95% of the total views on the site. The three sections appear relatively high in the list of total views, with "About Israel" and "Foreign Policy" being in second and third places, respectively. The "MASHAV" section is in seventh place.

Table 18.1 shows that most of the new visitors entering the site exited it immediately on their entry. Of those entering the site, the focus was put on the returning visitors' population since they know the information that exists on the site. It is reasonable to assume that if they are returning to the site, it is because they had found information that interested them or because they know from experience of the site that they can find information there. The percentage of returning visitors in the total number of users on the site is low. Most of the sections on the site are of a public relations nature. As a result, most of the pages have the same nature and many entries have not so high an average time on page. In contrast, the sections of a more administrative nature have fewer entries of users to the pages, but the average time spent on the pages is higher.

In light of this, it is perhaps possible to arrive at a formula according to which it will be possible to determine a parameter for users (Schenkolewski-Kroll & Tractinsky, 2016), in which

Number of page views by returning visitors
× average time spent on a page by returning visitors
× (1 − [% Exit]) = appraisal metric

The formula differentiates between new and returning visitors. The formula uses the data of the returning visitors because they show more interest in the information found in a section. To calculate the result, the number of page views by returning visitors is multiplied by the average time spent on a page by returning visitors. The last part of the formula consists of the "% Exit," which represents those leaving the page; "1 − % Exit" equals those remaining on the page, and the formula gives the estimated total number

Table 18.1 Main measurement categories by website sections

	Page path level 2 ⑦	Page views ⑦ →	Unique page views ⑦	Avg. time on page ⑦	Bounce rate ⑦	% Exit ⑦
		2,088,237 % of Total: 54.31% (3,844,896)	1,679,903 % of Total: 56.57% (2,969,596)	00:02:13 Avg for View: 00:01:46 (26.03%)	73.97% Avg for View: 75.00% (-1.37%)	55.29% Avg for View: 52.63% (5.06%)
1	□ □ /pages/	404,831 (19.39%)	267,910 (15.95%)	00:02:17	54.45%	40.69%
2	□ □ /aboutisrael/	343,932 (16.47%)	284,322 (16.92%)	00:02:23	78.23%	60.62%
3	□ □ /foreignpolicy/	310,790 (14.88%)	266,413 (15.86%)	00:02:15	80.03%	58.80%
4	□ □ /consularservices/	306,682 (14.69%)	250,822 (14.93%)	00:02:04	68.53%	52.17%
5	□ □ /pressroom/	172,234 (8.25%)	145,595 (8.67%)	00:01:47	83.84%	56.45%
6	□ □ /israelexperience/	162,938 (7.80%)	142,610 (8.49%)	00:02:38	85.60%	73.55%
7	□ □ /mashav/	116,938 (5.60%)	92,583 (5.51%)	00:02:14	62.49%	47.95%
8	□ □ /mfa-archive/	84,141 (4.03%)	73,287 (4.36%)	00:02:52	82.84%	70.44%
9	□ □ /abouttheministry/	59,342 (2.84%)	48,082 (2.86%)	00:01:36	70.25%	42.55%
10	□ □ /innovativeisrael/	48,340 (2.31%)	41,703 (2.48%)	00:02:23	83.60%	67.01%

Source: (Schenkolewski-Kroll & Tractinsky, 2016)

of hours spent by returning visitors on a specific section during a specific period. The higher the resulting value, the higher the level of interest. Thus, it may perhaps serve as a parameter for appraisal. It may then be possible to determine a minimum threshold of the metric, and if it is not passed, the material will not be destined for permanent retention. The results of the analysis should be taken into account in appraising each section separately, and no overall appraisal of the site should be made because each section has a different nature – from the aspect of its content, goals, method of presenting the materials, and periods of change.

Google Analytics data: visitors returning to the section

The Google Analytics data used in the appraisal formula was collected over 11 months, between September 2015 and August 2016, and as a result, a list of time spent in the various sections for each month was obtained (Schenkolewski-Kroll & Tractinsky, 2016). These results were ranked in descending order for each section, with the highest result ranked as 1, the next as 2, etc. The average result was then calculated for the entire period – it was 4.4435211709. For the rest of the research, only the sections above that average were taken into consideration (Schenkolewski-Kroll & Tractinsky, 2016).

Table 18.2 (Schenkolewski-Kroll & Tractinsky, 2016) shows results of the ranking for various sections by month. The sections that have no consistency of data for the entire period were deleted from the list of sections that were examined.

The "Foreign Policy" section achieved the highest ranking six times, and was followed by the "Consular Services" section, which achieved the highest ranking five times. The "MASHAV" section consistently had the lowest rank. The results show fluctuations of the sections during the months. Therefore, it is possible to estimate the importance of sections in each month, which may point to a specific event worth considering.

Google Analytics' geographical data does not provide information on returning visitors, only the total number of visitors who visited the section. The average number of countries was calculated, and the results were again ranked in descending order with the highest result of time spent receiving the highest ranking of 1, the next as 2, etc. (Schenkolewski-Kroll & Tractinsky, 2016). Later, a number of additional countries that are considered to be developing countries – Uganda, Ghana, Kenya, Nigeria, South Africa, and Zambia – were added to examine their influence on the results of the MASHAV section. In total, the data of ten countries was examined.

Table 18.3 (Schenkolewski-Kroll & Tractinsky, 2016) shows the section data for visitors originating from various countries. Certain sections did not rise above the monthly average, e.g. "Innovative Israel," "International Organizations," etc., which were later excluded from the research.

On average, the Consular Services section received the highest ranks, while About the Ministry section received the lowest. The most stable section in

Table 18.2 Results of the ranking of the sections by month

Section	Oct. 2015	Nov. 2015	Dec. 2015	Jan. 2016	Feb. 2016	March 2016	April 2016	May 2016	June 2016	July 2016	Aug. 2016
/aboutisrael/	3	3	4	4	4	4	3	3	5	5	6
/abouttheministry/								7	7		
/consularservices/	5	5	3	2	3	2	4	4	2	2	2
/foreignpolicy/	2	2	2	3	2	3	2	2	3	4	3
/israelexperience/	7	7	7	7	7	7	7			7	7
/mashav/	6	6	6	5	5	6	6	6	6	6	5
/mfa-archive/	7										
/pressroom/	4	4	5	6	6	5	5	5	4	3	4

Source: (Schenkolewski-Kroll & Tractinsky, 2016)

Table 18.3 Visitors from various countries by section

Section	Germany	Ghana	Indonesia	Kenya	Nigeria	South Africa	Uganda	United Kingdom	United States	Zambia
/aboutisrael/	4	10	3	2	4	3	6	4	1	3
/abouttheministry/	8	9	8	9	10	9	7	6	8	8
/consularservices/	3	2	5	4	2	2	2	1	2	1
/foreignpolicy/	2	7	4	6	7	7	9	2	3	10
/innovativeisrael/		5	9	10	6	8	10	10	9	
/internatlorgs/										
/israelexperience/	6	4	6	8	5	6	8	8	5	9
/mashav/	10	1	10	1	1	5	1	9	10	6
/mfa-archive/	7	6	7	7	8	10	4	7	7	2
/mfade/	9									7
/pages/	1	3	1	3	3	1	3	3	4	4
/pressroom/	5	8	2	5	9	4	5	5	6	5

Source: (Schenkolewski-Kroll & Tractinsky, 2016)

terms of visitors from various countries was "About the Ministry," while the "MASHAV" section had the greatest fluctuations.

Findings

It was found that the number of section visitors greatly influences the overall result of the formula, and that the time spent in the section influences it less. That is, the high number of visits ranked the section higher despite the fact that the time spent there was less than in other sections – i.e. those in which the number of visitors was lower and time spent was greater. This situation was caused by great differences between the quantity of returning visitors to the information-providing sections, and the number of returning visitors in the sections with a partly administrative nature. This gap in the quantity of visitors between the two types of sections could not be bridged by longer periods of time spent in the sections of the second type. Therefore, these results did not confirm the assumption that the more time spent in a section, the greater the interest in it.

The results of visits from geographical locations are also not unequivocal. The developing countries sometimes received low results in sections that should have received high results, whereas the developed countries received higher results. Therefore, visits from several developing countries that are supposed to need services from MASHAV were included in the research to see how this affects the results. Since this experiment did not influence the results, human involvement is needed to interpret them, e.g. to determine the nature of the relations between a specific country and Israel, etc.

To sum up, the mathematical-statistical calculations still cannot be used as the only parameter for appraising archival material from a website. Therefore, humans should be included since they meaningfully contribute to successful appraisal. Nevertheless, the mathematical-statistical approach can help them in understanding the complexity of the website and its dynamics.

The use of other elements as parameters for appraisal

Another element that has not yet been studied, and that may serve as an additional parameter, is the period of time a page remains part of a section or subsection (Schenkolewski-Kroll & Tractinsky, 2017). This is determined by the reasons for introducing changes to pages, and whether the frequency of change is a result of a permanent rule determined by the preordained circumstances or the result of the ad-hoc decisions that change in accordance with the circumstances. An example of the first case (the need to introduce changes) is the "Consular Services" section in which, according to the rules, if the slightest change occurs in the text appearing in the section, the page must be changed. This is due to the legal nature of this section's content. Permanent sections, such as "MASHAV," which publish programmes of courses at set times, is another example. The "About Israel" section can serve as one example of the second case (preordained or changing circumstances) because it changes according to the events occurring within Israel. This is similar for the "Foreign Affairs" section. For example, it coordinated information about the operation Protective Edge as a special subsection of material. Theoretically, it could be now removed from the site since there has not been any new material for the last two years. All these may affect appraisal and determine periods of retention of a section or a subsection. It does not seem that, regarding the appraisal itself, there are any additional parameters specific to websites. All the other parameters do not deviate from the norm in appraising physical and electronic records. As for the four values driving this appraisal – legal, administrative, research, and social – it seems that according to the characteristics of the material, the last two are those that stand out. The legal value appears in the original record, which is found in the organisation's archive, while the administrative value exists if the site serves an administrative purpose of any sort, such as in the case of the "Consular Services" and "MASHAV" sections.

With regards to retaining samples and examples, there also does not seem to be a need to implement special methods, but rather to use the existing ones for records that repeat themselves. In any case, considering the nature of the material, this subject requires further study. In the earlier stages of the research, it was already determined that the retention periods that were set for the administrative records of the Ministry of Foreign Affairs are not suitable for the website records. The question arises whether to implement the same procedure, and by the same people, for the website records, despite their special characteristics or not. It seems that, in principle, the same composition of factors that determine appraisal of the ministry's records can determine appraisal of the various parts of the website.

Determining retention schedules in Israel

The administrative process of determining retention schedules for website records (Schenkolewski-Kroll & Tractinsky, 2017) should not be much different from that used for regular records. The people or position-holders participating in the process do not have to be different from those participating in appraisal procedures of office systems, i.e. records creators, records managers, technical personnel, legal personnel, and archivists. In addition, the various types of records relating to raising publicity, e.g. informative records, are in essence no different than other "special" records, e.g. audio-visual records.

Metadata elements required for appraisal and disposition of websites

The basic metadata fields required for appraisal and disposition of the website of the Ministry of Foreign Affairs, and the processes required to fill them, were examined. From a study of the main regulations and sites of several archives in the world, it was found that other than in the US Department of Defense (DoD) regulations, and the instructions and procedures for creating metadata for managing records on the websites of the

Canadian government, there are no specific references to metadata fields on websites.

Therefore, the research concentrated on the stages from appraisal up to the stage of transfer of records in accordance with the appraisal decision, and investigated both the process and its metadata. It should be mentioned that the records arrive at these stages accompanied with metadata for content and records management.

Regarding the process, the InterPARES 2 project, which dealt with appraisal and disposition, was considered. However, since it did not deal with retention schedules in practice, the process of setting retention schedules was taken from the Israel Archives Law (1955) and/or the procedures of The National Archives, UK (2014, 2017).

Methodology of determining metadata fields

The research for determining metadata fields (Schenkolewski-Kroll & Tractinsky, 2017) was based on an examination of three records management standards

1   ICA Module 2 (ICA, 2018)
2   DoD 5015.02 (DoD, 2007)
3   MoReq 2010 (DLM Forum, 2010)

and the Rogers and Tennis (2016) metadata schema research.

The standards surveyed are common in the field of records management, and present requirements for metadata are in accordance with their needs (Schenkolewski-Kroll & Tractinsky, 2017). The difficulty in comparing them stems from the fact that each details the functional requirements at different levels, emphasizes certain components, and calls identical or almost identical components by different names.

The research conducted by Rogers and Tennis (2016), part of the Inter-PARES 3 project, expands the metadata fields and presents those required to reinforce presumption of authenticity of records according to the Inter-PARES model. Two subsections from that report, directly related to this research, were used – "Managing Records in a Record-making System" (A2) and "Managing Records in a Recordkeeping System" (A3).

In conclusion, all the standards and the InterPARES 3 scheme refer in different amounts of detail to all the processes in the research of appraisal, disposition, and destruction. However, MoReq 2010 differs in an essential matter – it emphasizes that in the destruction process metadata of the record is preserved, even after the record is destroyed.

Metadata fields

From the survey conducted, a table was created containing metadata elements relevant for retention and disposition of websites (see Appendix 5).

The table presents, at first, general metadata features of the site that are required for a technological appraisal. These define the digital platform used on the site, what hardware and software are used by those operating the site, and the date they were installed, as well as any changes of the platform and the dates of the changes. In addition to the hardware and software that operate the site, information is needed on the website address, its name, and the content management system used. Additional information listed is the structure of the website regarding its content and whether any changes to the site were made. After that, a cluster of metadata fields related to the lifecycle of the folder/section appears, which includes a minimum of metadata collected from the folder for record management requirements. At the end, there are appraisal- and disposition-related metadata. It should be noted that three new elements, non-existent in any other standard, have been added.

Conclusion

The main conclusion of the three-stage case study (Schenkolewski-Kroll & Tractinsky, 2015a, 2016, 2017) using the English website of the Ministry of Foreign Affairs, Government of Israel, as the example, is that the website sections should be used as the units upon which decisions regarding appraisal, retention, and disposition are to be made. The reason for that lies in the fact that the difference between the sections justifies this approach, which is the opposite of the accepted method of harvesting the entire site. On the other hand, it can be concluded that going down to the level of single records would unnecessarily complicate appraisal, especially when the records relate to attracting publicity, i.e. those that are of an informative nature. In the processes related to appraisal and determining retention schedules, the classic parameters (administrative, legal, research, and social) should be taken into account, along with the aspect of users and the characteristics and content of records that constitute the section (events, topics, technological changes, etc.). The appraisal process itself, and determination of the retention schedules, are not different from common practice in the management of physical and digital records that are related to the administrative function of the ministry. There are additional aspects that must be taken into consideration, along with the classic appraisal process – investigation of the possibility of preservation of the records, and preservation of their authenticity. As for the metadata that accompanies the entire process, it was found that there is almost no reference in the standards and procedures in the world to the metadata of websites in general, and their appraisal. There is also no reference to a granular approach, i.e. to the section level. Therefore, metadata that was designated to the level of records was adapted to the level of the sections. The sources of this metadata are standards and procedures from various organisations and countries, with an addition of three new items resulting from this research.

References

DLM Forum. (2010). *Model requirements for records systems (MoReq). Core services and plug-in modules.* Volume 1. Retrieved from https://www.moreq.info/

DoD. (2007). *Electronic records management software applications design criteria standard* (DoD 5015.02-STD). Retrieved from https://www.esd.whs.mil/Portals/54/Documents/DD/issuances/dodm/501502std.pdf

Foscarini, F. (2019). Citizen engagement. In L. Duranti & C. Rogers (Eds.), *Trusting records in the cloud: The creation, management, and preservation of trustworthy digital content* (pp. 65–96). London: Facet Publishing.

Franks, P. C. (2019). Retention and disposition. In L. Duranti & C. Rogers (Eds.), *Trusting records in the cloud: The creation, management, and preservation of trustworthy digital content* (pp. 117–133). London: Facet Publishing.

ICA. (2018). *Principles and functional requirements for records in electronic office environments. Module 2 – Guidelines and functional requirements for records in electronic office environments.* Retrieved from https://www.ica.org/en/ica-tools

Israel Archives Law. (1955). [Hebrew]. Retrieved from https://www.nevo.co.il/law_html/Law01/028_001.htm

The National Archives. (2014). *Operational Selection Policy OPS 27, UK central Government web estate.* Retrieved from https://www.nationalarchives.gov.uk/documents/information-management/osp27.pdf

The National Archives. (2017). *The UK Government Web Archive: Guidance for digital and records management teams.* Retrieved from https://www.nationalarchives.gov.uk/documents/web-archiving-technical-guidance.pdf

Rogers, C., & Tennis, J. T. (2016). *General study 15. Application profile for authenticity metadata: General study report.* InterPARES 3 Project. Retrieved from http://www.interpares.org/ip3/display_file.cfm?doc=ip3_canada_gs15_final_report.pdf

Schenkolewski-Kroll, S., & Tractinsky, A. (2015a). *Research on retention and disposition processes in an internet website of the Government of Israel: The Ministry of Foreign Affairs case study* (EU01). InterPARES Trust. Retrieved from https://interparestrust.org/assets/public/dissemination/EU01_20150909_RetentionDisposition ProcessesIsraeliForeignAffairs_FinalReport_Final.pdf

Schenkolewski-Kroll, S., & Tractinsky, A. (2015b). A comparison of users' data in retention and disposition processes in an Internet website: The Ministry of Foreign Affairs of Israel as a case study. In K. Anderson, L. Duranti, R. Jaworski, H. Stančić, S. Seljan, & V. Mateljan (Eds.), *e-Institutions: Openness, accessibility, and preservation* (pp. 95–108). Zagreb: Department of Information and Communication Sciences, Faculty of Humanities and Social Sciences, University of Zagreb, Croatia. Retrieved from https://infoz.ffzg.hr/infuture/2015/images/papers/3-01%20Schenkolewski-Kroll,%20Tractinsky,%20Retention%20and%20Disposition%20Processes.pdf

Schenkolewski-Kroll, S., & Tractinsky, A. (2016). *Research on users of the English website of the Israel Ministry of Foreign Affairs as a criterion for appraising records* (EU25 Final report). InterPARES Trust. Retrieved from https://interparestrust.org/assets/public/dissemination/EU25_20161001_WebAnalyticsAndAppraisalMinistry ForeignAffairsIsrael_FinalReport_Final.pdf

Schenkolewski-Kroll, S., & Tractinsky, A. (2017). *Archival appraisal, retention schedules and metadata in web sites – The case study of the Ministry of Foreign Affairs, Israel* (EU36 Final report). InterPARES Trust. Retrieved from https://interparestrust.org/assets/public/dissemination/EU036_20171120_AppraisalWebsites_Final Report.pdf

19 Metadata description schemas of cultural heritage institutions in the context of interoperability

Özgür Külcü with Tolga Çakmak and Şahika Eroğlu

Introduction

Producing their own cultural values and products, societies continue their existence through information resources related to their products and values in line with their social, cultural, political, and technological development. Management of these products (such as identification, preservation, accessibility, and sustainability) is becoming an important process, since they have symbolic power reflecting not only social memory but also the history of a given society. Accordingly, national and international regulations regarding the preservation of cultural heritage were enacted and from the year 2000 onwards, institutions such as the Council of Europe and the European Union have concentrated their agenda on this issue (Dağıstan Özdemir, 2005 as cited in Çakmak & Yılmaz, 2017, p. 50).

Cultural heritage resources are information-based content that include historical records, manuscripts, historical books, ephemeral documents, audio-visual materials, and every type of printed or electronic content which provide evidence about the past and are kept in museums, libraries, archives, and research centres. While traditionally all cultural heritage resources, as information content, were created in the printed environment, now some resources are created in digital form (Külcü, 2016, p. 640). Digitisation and developing digital systems for printed resources are still major challenges for cultural heritage organisations.

Museums, libraries, and archives (MLA), which can be referred to as cultural memory institutions, have begun to take steps to enhance their capacity for digitisation, digital preservation, and technological infrastructure in order to manage the cultural heritage objects in their collections and respond to the expectations of users, especially since the late 1990s (Astle & Muir, 2002). At the beginning of the 21st century, good examples of digital museums, libraries, and archives have appeared around the world. In the past decade, studies on new kinds of digital content management focused on good examples, preparing international standards and integration. In addition, national and international studies started to aim for standardisation, creation of guidelines, and examples of good practice to solve the problem of accessing and managing all content kept in different organisations. Organisational approaches to the management of cultural resources, as well as the types of cultural resources, differ greatly. For example, for description and classification of content, while libraries use the Dewey Decimal Classification or Library of Congress Classification (LCC) systems, archives use Encoded Archival Description (EAD) or Standard Filing System (SFS) in Turkey, and museums Spectrum,[1] or local systems for cultural materials such as manuscripts, historic books or records, museum objects, etc. (Külcü, 2015). The development of a common metadata set continues to aim to create usable resources in a manageable form(s) on one information retrieval platform. Some good examples are the Online Archive of California (OAC, https://oac.cdlib.org/), the Electronic Cultural Atlas Initiative (ECAI, http://www.ecai.org/), and Europeana (https://www.europeana.eu/en). A wide variety of the content coming from more than 300 culture organisations, MLAs, and research centres is accessible via the OAC interface. Using ECAI, a modern kind of atlas and gazetteer, it is possible to discover the content powered by temporal and geospatial tools from all around the world as part of cultural heritage. Europeana is a platform for 40 million cultural resources from 32 countries. However, digital museums, libraries, and archives are mostly not ready for integration such platforms or with union catalogues to make their collections more visible because of differences in software architecture. International standards for describing, creating, and managing digital cultural resources are readily available, for example EAD, Metadata Object Description Schema (MODS), Metadata Encoding and Transmission Standard (METS), Dublin Core (DC), Lightweight Information Describing Objects (LIDO), and Connecting ARchaeology and ARchitecture in Europeana (CARARE) (Külcü, 2015).

As in every stage of technological development, services are delivered according to the current technological solutions in the field of cultural heritage management, as well. The study presented in this chapter investigates the presentation of cultural heritage objects and web-based systems of cultural institutions in Turkey in terms of their web platforms. Based on the research results, recommendations and necessary improvements related to the visibility of Turkish cultural heritage objects are defined.

Metadata models for digital cultural heritage resources

One of the most important parts of the studies on the development of integrated digital information systems for cultural heritage resources originating from the MLA institutions are metadata models. According to Haynes (2004), metadata is structured information that is formed to facilitate description, explanation, discovery, and access to information resources. Generally, three main types of metadata are used

1   *descriptive metadata*: describes a resource for purposes such as discovery and identification. It can include elements such as title, abstract, author, and keywords

2   *structural metadata*: indicates how compound objects are put together, e.g. how pages are ordered to form chapters

3   *administrative metadata*: provides information to help manage a resource, e.g. when and how it was created, information on file type and other technical information, and access rights. There are several subsets of administrative metadata – two are sometimes listed as separate metadata types. They are *Rights management metadata*, which deals with intellectual property rights, and *Preservation metadata*, which contains information needed to archive and preserve a resource.

(Müller, 2010, p. 56 as cited in Külcü, 2016, p. 650, italics in original)

As a metadata model of cultural heritage resource, the Preservation Metadata: Implementation Strategies (PREMIS), launched by the Online Computer Library Center (OCLC) in 2003, is one of the important examples (PREMIS Editorial Committee, 2008). A PREMIS data dictionary describes long term preservation metadata tags supported by XML schemas. It is expected that PREMIS will be used as a basic standard and automatically assigned by digital systems for documentary content in the near future. PREMIS is supported by the Library of Congress, and the METS Editorial Committee has started to support PREMIS schemas for use with METS schemas (DigCurV, 2013; Higgins, 2007 as cited in Külcü, 2016, p. 649).

The International Council on Archives (ICA), as a general council of archival organisations all around the world, has also initiated studies on developing metadata models for cultural resources, for example the ICA Committee on Electronic and Other Records (ICA-CER) studies. The ICA-CER declared that in the process of describing cultural resources not only the catalogue information but also environmental and relational information should be taken into account (Hofman, 2000).

From an archival management perspective, the General International Standard Archival Description (ISAD[G]) and International Standard Archival Authority Record for Corporate Bodies, Persons and Families (ISAAR[CPF]) developed by the ICA (2011a, 2011b) provide models for the description of printed resources, whereas EAD has clear metadata tags that include XML schemas and can be used with both digital and printed resources. For current records in the records management area, ISO 23081–1 (International Organization for Standardization, 2017) provides clear metadata description tags, and ISO 15489–1 (International Organization for Standardization, 2016) covers records management system structures (Asproth, 2005; Niu, 2013; Zhang and Mauney, 2013).

In addition, from 1992–1995, the International Federation of Library Associations (IFLA) Study Group on Functional Requirements for Bibliographic Records (FRBR) developed a conceptual model for bibliographic description that covers not only library materials but also some other types of contents from museums or archives. In 1996, the International Council of Museums (ICOM) International Committee for Documentation (CIDOC) began the development of a conceptual model for the description of museum objects. It was the first attempt to describe museum objects. The Conceptual Reference Model (CRM), though initially focused on museums, came to be conceived as a reference model that could serve the broader ambition of enabling integrated access to cultural heritage, thus encompassing MLA access. In this regard, the International Working Group on FRBR–CIDOC–CRM harmonisation was formed in 2003 (Gueguen, da Fonseca, Pitti, & Grimoüard, 2013; IFLA, 1998 as cited in Külcü, 2016, p. 651). The working group has focused on mapping FRBR concepts to CRM concepts and, when necessary, enhancing and refining CRM concepts to facilitate the mapping, thereby making the CRM a single, overarching semantic model. The model was published as an object-oriented FRBR (FRBRoo). The archivists and museum specialists involved in the development of the CRM and the FRBRoo extension have expressed interest in working with the archival community to accommodate archival description and enable the model to fully incorporate the MLA communities. Resource Description and Access (RDA http://rda-rsc.org) is a library standard based on FRBR and thus, by extension, is related also to FRBRoo and, by further extension, to CRM. The early draft of the Finnish model thus reflects the influence of RDA, FRBR, FRBRoo, and CRM. The ICA Programme Commission formed the Experts Group on Archival Description (EGAD) late in 2012. EGAD is charged with the harmonisation of the four existing ICA standards – ISAD(G), ISAAR(CPF), International Standard for Describing Functions (ISDF), and International Standard for Describing Institutions with Archival Holdings (ISDIAH) (ICA, 2011a, 2011b, 2011c, 2011d) – based on a formal archival description conceptual model. The EGAD's members are drawn from the international professional community and have demonstrated expertise in archival description and standards.

Metadata descriptions of the cultural resources in MLAs in Turkey

In this section, metadata structures used for cultural resources in Turkish cultural heritage institutions are evaluated. The research used three general types of resources. In this context, the first resource type consisted of the records. The records were selected from the State Archives of Turkey (SAT) (https://www.devletarsivleri.gov.tr/) that are represented in the SAT electronic catalogue and individual pages on SAT webpage. The second resource type consisted of manuscripts. As the main access point to the manuscripts, the Turkish Manuscripts of the Ministry of Culture and Tourism platform (https://www.yek.gov.tr/) was used. The third resource type consisted of museum and archaeological objects. Content from the publicly open catalogues of the Inventories of Turkey and of the Hatay Archaeology Museum was selected as the example of museum materials in Turkey. Finally, the metadata descriptions of the city archives representing local cultural heritage were considered in the study.

Ottoman Archives catalogue of the State Archives of Turkey

Figure 19.1 shows the user interface of the Ottoman Archives catalogue that is made available online by SAT.

As shown in the Figure 19.1, the catalogue search is possible by group name, organisation, year interval, time span, or phrase. The results are listed with the date, file number, folder number, group code, and summary information. The webpage provides the service both in English and Turkish.

Turkish Republic catalogue of State Archives of Turkey

Figure 19.2 shows the search interface of the Turkish Republic catalogue of SAT.

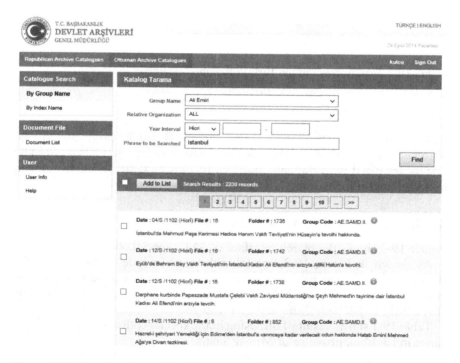

Figure 19.1 User interface of the Ottoman Archives catalogue

Sources: (Devlet Arşivleri Genel Müdürlüğü, 2016; Külcü, 2017, p. 29)

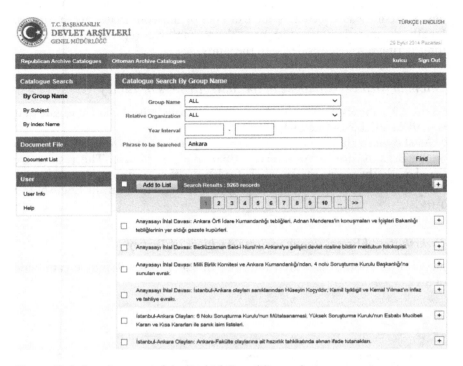

Figure 19.2 Search screen of the Turkish Republic catalogue

Sources: (Devlet Arşivleri Genel Müdürlüğü, 2016; Külcü, 2017, p. 29)

As shown in the Figure 19.2, the Turkish Republic catalogue can be searched by group name, organisation, time interval, and keyword. The results are listed with the date, number, file, group code, location number, and summary information.

Special collections of the State Archives of Turkey

Figure 19.3 shows the search interface of SAT's special collections.

As shown in Figure 19.3, special collections include firmans,[2] and the documents that have historic value can be accessed. The service and the web interface are only in Turkish and limited to keyword searches (kelime [keyword], başlık [title], and kategori [category]).

Table 19.1 shows result of browsing in the special collection for an inheritance in Istanbul, province of Mimar Sinan.

As in the preceding catalogue, datasets of firmans and special historical records collections consist of record type, reign, date, style of script, dimensions, description, annotation, reason issued, repository, and classification number.

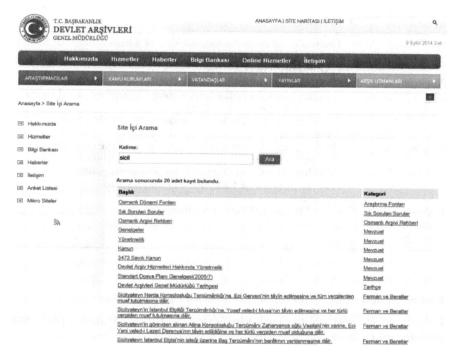

Figure 19.3 Search interface of the special collections of the State Archives of Turkey

Sources: (Devlet Arşivleri Genel Müdürlüğü, 2016; Külcü, 2017, p. 30)

Table 19.1 Detailed bibliographic description of the cultural resource

Record type	Firman
Reign	Mehmed IV.
Date	A.H. First decade of Rabi'-al-awwal 1059/March 1649 C.E.
Style of script	Cursive dîwânî. Text: 20 lines.
Dimensions	32.5 × 73 cm.
Description	Unembellished sultanic cipher drawn in gold ink.
	The scalloped cartouche of the sultan's inscription to the upper left of the cipher is surrounded by a floral composition in freehand on a ground of gold wash. His inscription reading "Mûcebince amel oluna" ("Let it be thus executed") is sprinkled with ornamental blotting sand.
	A freehand floral composition also adorns the crest figure above the inscription and above which carnation motifs in freehand constitute delicate vertical accents.

(*Continued*)

Table 19.1 (Continued)

Record type	Firman
	The frame, open at the top, consists of a heavy marginal line in lapis lazuli, edged in gold.
	Text inscribed in black ink.
Annotation	1 In the upper portion of the document is inscribed in the sultan's own hand the formulation "Mûcebince amel oluna" ("Let it be thus executed").
	2 In the lower left corner, the name of the locale where inscribed.
Reason issued	On the death of Hamza, the chief officer of the janissary battalion called the keeper of the Sultan's hounds, his house in the quarter of Mimar Sinan is placed at the disposal of Bâdıseher Hanım, a Palace servant.
Repository and classification number	BOA, Illuminated Firman Collection no. 3.

Metadata description and dataset of manuscripts in Turkey

Figure 19.4 shows the interface for browsing the Turkish Manuscripts of the Ministry of Culture and Tourism.

The metadata elements are

- Title
- Author name
- Collection

- Date of copyright
- Date of reproduction
- Archive number

- Location
- Paper type
- Type article
- Subject
- Reproducer
- Location of reproduction

- Notes
- Dimensions
- Row
- Sheet
- DVD number
- Language

The resources can be browsed by author name, resource name, archive number, dimension, line, page, and image.

Metadata sets of the Inventories of Turkey

The online catalogue of the Inventories of Turkey[3] (Envanter, n.d.) covers different kinds of cultural resources organized in categories: cultural entities, monuments, records, bibliographies, maps, and public culture. The catalogue has special features like map-based access, Facebook and Twitter links, most viewed resources, etc. (Figure 19.5).

Figure 19.4 Search interface of the system developed by the Ministry of Culture and Tourism for Manuscripts

Source: (Yazmalar, 2020)

The Turkish Inventory System gives detailed information about the objects based on archaeological inventories description areas that are used by Turkish archaeologists. The objects are described using the following metadata elements

Basic Information	*ID Information*
Village	Type
Registration condition	City
Registration date	Province

(*Continued*)

(Continued)

Basic Information	ID Information
Registration degree	Modern name
Period	Museum inventory number
Description	Excavation type
Dimension	
Special Information	
Related publication	
Finding	
Storage area	
Archive type	
Total piece	
Raw material	
Finds type	
Where it was found	
Location in museum	
Excavation number	

Figure 19.6 shows description of the Süleymaniye Mosque from the Monuments category. The building and location information are described in detail with social media links, inventory anthologies, and geospatial support.

The metadata elements used for monuments in the Turkish Inventory System are

Basic information	ID information
Current function	Type
Culture period	City
District	Province
Address	Block
Architectural style	Parcel
Contractor	
Registration condition	
Period	
Detailed information	
Repair date	
Carrier system	
Cover type	
Cover material	
Plan features	
Front features	
Construction materials	
Physical originality	
Functional originality	
Observation and explanations	
Primary resources	

Figure 19.5 Object description in the Turkish Inventory System

Source: (Bitik Höyük, n.d.)

Figure 19.6 Description of the Süleymaniye Mosque

Source: (Süleymaniye Mosque, n.d.)

Figure 19.7 shows an entry of the archaeological monument from the records category.

The metadata elements used for archaeological monuments in the Turkish Inventory System are

Basic information	ID information
Author	Inventory anthologies
Publication of the article	
Publication date	
City	
Tags	

Figure 19.7 Description of the archaeological monument
Source: (Osman Bey'in, 2020)

Since the records category has a very short description list consisting of only three tags about the resource, it seems that the description area was not designed by professionals.

Metadata sets of the resources from the Anatolian Civilization Museum

The Anatolian Civilization Museum (ACM) is the biggest and a very special museum holding content on the Anatolian region and its vicinity. ACM was selected as the best museum in Europe in 1997. Although it has a digital

Table 19.2 Description of a cultural object in the Anatolian Civilization Museum

Resource inventory records	Figure of the cultural object
Village Registration condition Registration date Registration degree	
Period Description Dimension	Province Finding location
Special information related to publication finding	
Storage area Archive type Total piece Raw material Finds type Where it was found Location in museum	Excavation date Publications City Back face

Source: (Külcü, 2017, p. 36)

records collection, ACM does not yet have a public catalogue on the internet. The collection seems to be based on the registry records of the archaeological objects, which includes detailed information about the object and location but not metadata as the international examples have (Table 19.2).

Metadata sets of the Hatay Archeology Museum

Although the Hatay Archeology Museum (HAM) is a state museum like the Anatolian Civilization Museum and the content of both museums are similar, the bibliographic records of the museums are rather different from each other. The entries of HAM are limited to only the inventory number, title, collection name, era, and period (Figure 19.8). In addition, the same tags are described with different names. For example, "Name/Type" in ACM is equivalent to "Resource Name" in HAM. The difference between era and period is not clear in the HAM entries.

City archives in Turkey

Next, the results of the ITrust study *Enhancing Visibility of Local Cultural Heritage: Analysis of Web Interaction Platforms of Turkish City Archives* (Çakmak, Eroğlu, & Külcü, 2017) are presented. The study analyzed 15 city archives (Table 19.3). According to the gathered data, 12 archives are

HATAY ARKEOLOJİ MÜZESİ **ENVANTER SAYFASI**

HATAY ARKEOLOJİ MÜZESİNE GERİ DÖN

Envanter No :

Kazı No :

Eser Adı :

Sınıfı / Koleksiyonu : Seçiniz...

Devri : Seçiniz...

Dönemi :

Sonuçları Göster

Envanter No	Eser Adı	Sınıfı / Koleksiyon	Buluntu Yeri	Devri	Dönemi
56	Çakıl Taşı Mozaik	Mozaik Koleksiyonu	Mersin , Tarsus	Roma	M.Ö. 1. Yy
139	Opus Sectila	Mozaik Koleksiyonu	Hatay , Antakya	Roma	
815	Sevinç Mozaiği	Mozaik Koleksiyonu	Hatay , Harbiye	Roma	M.S. 4. Yy
820	Avlanan Amazon	Mozaik Koleksiyonu	Hatay , Harbiye	Roma	M.S. 2. Yy
821	Meander Mozaik	Mozaik Koleksiyonu	Hatay , Harbiye	Roma	M.S. 4. Yy
825	Gece Alemi Mozaiği	Mozaik Koleksiyonu	Hatay , Antakya	Roma	M.S. 4. Yy
826	Lakedemonia Evrotas Mozaiği	Mozaik Koleksiyonu	Hatay , Antakya	Roma	M.S. 4. Yy
829	Gece Alemi Mozaiği	Mozaik Koleksiyonu	Hatay , Antakya	Roma	M.S. 4. Yy
831	Hokkabazlar Mozaiği	Mozaik Koleksiyonu	Hatay , Antakya	Roma	M.S. 4. Yy
835	Koç Başlan Mozaiği	Mozaik Koleksiyonu	Hatay , Harbiye	Roma	M.S. 5. Yy
840	Hermaphroditos Mozaiği	Mozaik Koleksiyonu	Hatay , Harbiye	Roma	M.S. 3. Yy
843	Genç Satyros Mozaiği	Mozaik Koleksiyonu	Hatay , Harbiye	Roma	M.S. 2. Yy
844	Lykurgos Mozaiği	Mozaik Koleksiyonu	Hatay , Harbiye	Roma	M.S. 3. Yy
845	Apollo Dafne Mozaiği	Mozaik Koleksiyonu	Hatay , Harbiye	Roma	M.S. 3. Yy
846	Psykheler Kayığı Mozaiği	Mozaik Koleksiyonu	Hatay , Harbiye	Roma	M.S. 3. Yy

Figure 19.8 Description of cultural heritage objects in the Hatay Archeology Museum
Source: (Külcü, 2017, p. 37)

founded under the state institutions and three archives have private archive status. It is also important to mention that municipalities and universities are involved in the city archive initiatives in Turkey.

All analyzed city archives provide descriptive metadata about their collections. The metadata elements available from the browsing options of the city archives are shown in Table 19.4.

As shown in Table 19.4, eight city archives allow users to browse collections. It should be mentioned that one city archive in the study does not have a search interface, but it does have browsing options. The analysis revealed that all city archives which provide information via web platforms use "Creator," "Title," "Description," "Identifier," and "Date" fields metadata elements. Further, seven city archives provide "Collection Name," while six use the "Type" field in their description processes of cultural heritage objects. In terms of access, six city archives provide links to digital objects. The analysis

Table 19.3 Geographical distribution of participant city archives/museums

Code	City archive	City
P1	Balıkesir Kent Arşivi	Balıkesir
P2	Bursa Kent Müzesi	Bursa
P3	Tire Kent Müzesi	İzmir
P4	Ahmet Piriştine Kent Arşivi ve Müzesi	İzmir
P5	Kayseri Kent Müzesi	Kayseri
P6	Atılım Üniversitesi Ankara Dijital Kent Arşivi	Ankara
P7	Mudurnu Kent Arşivi	Bolu
P8	Erciyes Üniversitesi Kayseri Araştırma ve Uygulama Merkezi	Kayseri
P9	Eskişehir Kent Belleği	Eskişehir
P10	Çorum Belediyesi Kent Arşivi	Çorum
P11	Sakıp Sabancı Mardin Kent Müzesi	Mardin
P12	Uşak Kent Tarihi Müzesi	Uşak
P13	Ödemiş Yıldız Kent Arşivi ve Müzesi	İzmir
P14	Edirne Kent Belleği Müzesi	Edirne
P15	Koç Üniversitesi VEKAM	Ankara

Table 19.4 Descriptions and metadata elements displayed for browsing cultural heritage objects

Participating City Archive	P1	P2	P3	P4	P5	P6	P7	P8	P9	P10	P11	P12	P13	P14	P15
Creator	✓		✓	✓	✓		✓							✓	✓
Title	✓		✓	✓	✓		✓							✓	✓
Description	✓		✓	✓	✓		✓							✓	✓
Identifier	✓		✓	✓	✓		✓							✓	✓
Subject			✓	✓	✓									✓	✓
Coverage							✓								✓
Type		✓		✓	✓	✓		✓						✓	✓
Collection name	✓		✓	✓	✓									✓	✓
Links to digital object		✓		✓	✓	✓		✓						✓	✓
Exhibition notes							✓								✓
Rights							✓								✓
Date	✓		✓	✓	✓		✓							✓	
Citation information							✓								

also showed that fields such as "Coverage," "Rights," "Exhibition Notes," and "Citation" information are preferred by few city archives. On the other hand, two city archives (P7 and P15) describe their cultural heritage objects using all, or almost all, detected descriptions and metadata elements. The study detected that only five city archives use a metadata standard for their description processes.

Finally, it was investigated whether the city archives provide their description information of cultural heritage objects in open data formats. The results show that only one city archive allows users to download bibliographic descriptions of cultural heritage objects as open data.

Conclusion

Managing cultural heritage objects requires many decision-making steps that are related to each other. The research results show that local cultural heritage objects are not adequately presented in local cultural heritage institutions because of insufficient budgets and infrastructure. At this point, it is seen that medium and small-sized heritage institutions attempt to make their collections accessible with limited facilities. It is also reported that only a tiny portion of the local cultural heritage objects are available online via digitisation activities (Europeana, 2015). Nevertheless, usage of metadata standards enables the digital cultural heritage objects to be discoverable and accessible via search engines and discovery services. Thus, the description of cultural heritage objects with proper metadata supports the preservation of master copies and makes these objects accessible to wider communities. At this point, it is possible to say that these attempts contribute to promoting the cultural heritage institutions.

One of the most critical parts of developing electronic systems for cultural heritage resources is to support research and education. In these circumstances, observing practices and operations, getting information about the infrastructure and structure of the models, learning from good and bad experiences, developing information background with literature reviews, and investigating international best practices, guides, and standards are as important at the local level as doing the same things at the national level.

In the preparation phase of the collections, focusing on topics such as information discovery, integration with different resources, long term preservation, and digital rights management is significant for accessibility and preservation. The results obtained from analysis and evaluation of Turkish cultural heritage institutions reveal that there are local descriptions for cultural heritage objects. The data elements that are widely used in international examples are not implemented in some of the analyzed systems. For instance, the research showed that unique identifiers are not used for some museum records. It was also observed that the controlled vocabularies are not used in most of the systems, and that the subject indexing is insufficient. The analysis revealed that the collections are built on the object-oriented structures, that the logical hierarchy is fuzzy, and that the linkage with related resources are mostly overlooked.

The evaluations carried out in this study reveal that the description of cultural heritage objects is seen as a bureaucratic process rather than a technical procedure. Accordingly, it is recommended that the systems implemented for the accessibility of cultural heritage institutions should be managed based on the models developed for the digital environment. As a first step, system interoperability should be considered to enable or improve integration processes. Additionally, in the creation of local collections, the metadata should be mapped to international and local standards. In this regard, meeting local needs and expectations with proper metadata schemas should be prioritized by cultural heritage organisations instead of implementing a single metadata schema.

Finally, based on the metadata analysis and literature review, the metadata structures of the systems analyzed should be revised based on international metadata standards and schemas. The institutions should also implement their metadata policies and determine mandatory and optional fields that will be used to describe their collections. Thus, fields such as creator, title, date, description, language, subject, type, publication, excavation, unique identifiers, rights, and related resources should be implemented for accessibility of described objects. The administrative and technical metadata fields should also be created for each described object to increase its accessibility and trace its description history.

Notes

1 Spectrum is the UK Museums Collections Management Standard.
2 A firman, or ferman (Turkish), at the constitutional level, was a royal mandate or decree issued by a sovereign in an Islamic state, namely the Ottoman Empire. During various periods, they were collected and applied as traditional bodies of law (Wikipedia, 2020).
3 The Envanter online catalogue can be reached only from Turkey's web space.

References

Asproth, V. (2005). Information technology challenges for long-term preservation of electronic information. *International Journal of Public Information Systems, 1*, 27–37.

Astle, P. J., & Muir, A. (2002). Digitization and preservation in public libraries and archives. *Journal of Librarianship and Information Science, 34*, 67–79.

Bitik Höyük. (n.d.). Retrieved from http://envanter.gov.tr/anit/index/detay/35278

Çakmak, T., Eroğlu, S,., & Külcü, Ö. (2017). *Enhancing visibility of local cultural heritage: Analysis of web interaction platforms of Turkish City Archives* (EU34, Phase II). InterPARES Trust. Retrieved from https://interparestrust.org/assets/public/dissemination/EU34_20171120_AnalysisofWebInterationPlatformsofTurkishCityArchives_FinalReport.pdf

Çakmak, T., & Yılmaz, B. (2017). Bellek kurumlarında dijitalleştirme ve dijital koruma: Türkiye'deki uygulamaların analizi [Digitization and digital preservation in the memory institutions: Analysis of practices in Turkey]. *Bilgi Dünyası, 18*, 49–91. https://doi.org/10.15612/BD.2017.580

Dağıstan Özdemir, M. Z. (2005). Türkiye'de kültürel mirasın korunmasına kısa bir bakış [A brief overview of the protection of cultural heritage in Turkey]. *Planlama, 1,* 20–25.

Devlet Arşivleri Genel Müdürlüğü [General Directorate of State Archives]. (2016). *Catalogue.* Retrieved from https://katalog.devletarsivleri.gov.tr/

DigCurV. (2013). *Call for contributions.* Retrieved from https://web.archive.org/web/20130304102528/www.digcur-education.org/eng/International-Conference/Call-for-Contributions

Envanter. (n.d.). Retrieved from http://envanter.gov.tr/

Europeana. (2015). *We transform the World with culture: Europeana stratagy: 2015–2020.* Retrieved from http://pro.europeana.eu/files/Europeana_Professional/Publications/Europeana%20Strategy%202020.pdf

Gueguen, G., da Fonseca, V. M. M. F., Pitti, D., & Grimoüard, C. S. (2013). Toward an international conceptual model for archival description: A preliminary report from the International Council on Archives' Experts Group on Archival Description. *The American Archivist, 76,* 567–584.

Haynes, D. (2004). *Metadata for information management and retrieval.* London: Facet Publishing.

Higgins, S. (2007). *PREMIS Data Dictionary.* Retrieved from https://www.dcc.ac.uk/resources/briefing-papers/standards-watch-papers/premis-data-dictionary

Hofman, H. (2000). *Metadata and the management of current records in digital form. ICA Committee on Electronic and other Current Records* (draft). Retrieved from https://www.ica.org/sites/default/files/CER_2000_electronic-records_draft_EN.pdf

ICA. (2011a). *General international standard archival description (ISAD(G))* (2nd ed.). Paris, France: International Council on Archives.

ICA. (2011b). *ISAAR(CPF). International standard archival authority record for corporate codies, persons and families.* Paris, France: International Council on Archives.

ICA. (2011c). *International standard for describing functions (ISDF).* Paris, France: International Council on Archives.

ICA. (2011d). *International standard for describing institutions with archival holdings (ISDIAH).* Paris, France: International Council on Archives.

IFLA. (1998). *Study Group on the Functional Requirements for Bibliographic Records, Functional Requirements for Bibliographic Records: Final Report.* Munich: K.G. Saur.

International Organization for Standardization. (2016). Information and documentation. Records management. Concepts and principles. (ISO 15489-1). Retrieved from https://www.iso.org/standard/62542.html

International Organization for Standardization. (2017). Information and documentation. Records management processes. Metadata for records. Principles. (ISO 23081-1). Retrieved from https://www.iso.org/standard/73172.html

Külcü, Ö. (2015). *EU07: Evaluating metadata description schemas of the cultural heritage organizations in electronic environment for interoperability.* InterPARES Trust Project Research Report. Retrieved from https://interparestrust.org/assets/public/dissemination/EU07_20150420_EvaluatingMetadataDescriptionSchemas_Report_Final.pdf

Külcü, Ö. (2016). Bilgi içerikli kültürel mirasın yönetiminde yeni gelişmeler [New developments in management of informational cultural heritage]. *Türk Kütüphaneciliği, 30,* 640–663.

Külcü, Ö. (2017). Elektronik ortamda belgelerin uzun süre korunması, güvenliği ve erişim etkinliğinin arttırılmasında üstveri elemanlarının önemi: Sorunlar ve çözüm önerileri [The importance of metadata elements in electronic environment for long-term protection of documents, increasing security, and access efficiency: Problems and solutions]. *Arşiv Dünyası Dergisi, 17–18*, 11–45.

Müller, N. (2010). *Change management on semi-structured documents* (Unpublished PhD Dissertation). Bremen: Jacobs University Bremen School of Engineering and Science. Retrieved from https://www.researchgate.net/publication/216797110_Change_Management_on_Semi-Structured_Documents

Niu, J. (2013). Recordkeeping metadata and archival description: A revisit. *Archives and Manuscripts, 41*, 203–215.

Osman Bey'in. (2020). *Osman Bey'in ilk fethi: Karacahisar kalesi – yüzey araştirmasi 1999* [The first conquest of Osman Bey: Karacahisar Castle – surface survey 1999]. Retrieved from http://envanter.gov.tr/belge/index/detay/67926

PREMIS Editorial Committee. (2008). *Data dictionary for Preservation Metadata: PREMIS version 2.0*. Retrieved from http://www.loc.gov/standards/premis/v2/premis-2-0.pdf

Süleymaniye Mosque. (n.d.). Retrieved from http://envanter.gov.tr/anit/index/detay/50171

Wikipedia. (2020). *Firman*. Retrieved from https://en.wikipedia.org/wiki/Firman

Yazmalar. (2020). *Catalogue search*. Retrieved from http://www.yazmalar.gov.tr/katalog-tarama

Zhang, J., & Mauney, D. (2013). When archival description meets digital object metadata: A typological study of digital archival representation. *The American Archivist, 76*, 174–195.

20 Preservation of digital print masters

Tomislav Ivanjko

Introduction

In contemporary library and archival practice, legal deposit provides a basis for providing public access to the national collection and plays an important role in preserving national publishing production, as well as preserving cultural heritage and national identity as a whole. In this context, the coverage of a legal deposit is sought to be ensured by law or by agreement between libraries and publishers, in such a way that all material is regularly received, regardless of subject, form, or producer. The obligation to provide a legal deposit is also based on international documents. The UNESCO guidelines for legal deposit legislation define legal deposit as "a statutory obligation which requires that any organization, commercial or public, and any individual producing any type of documentation in multiple copies, be obliged to deposit one or more copies with a recognized national institution" (Larivière, 2000, p. 3). Legal deposit often exists in legislation; however, it can be a voluntary regime (International Federation of Library Associations and Institutions, 2011). According to the provisions of the Croatian Library Law (Zakon o knjižnicama i knjižničnoj djelatnosti, 2019), entities bound by the legal deposit legislation are publishers and manufacturers of audiovisual and electronic publications, i.e. legal entities and natural persons publishing or manufacturing materials for the public, whether these materials are intended for sale or free distribution. These include printed publications (books, brochures, study prints, separates, journals, newspapers, magazines, bulletins, geographical and other maps, reproductions of pictorial works of art, music, catalogues, calendars, theatre, and other programmes and their supplements in printed, audio-visual, and electronic form, posters, leaflets, short advertisements and notifications, postcards, official and commercial forms), audio-visual materials (phonograph records, audio and video tapes, cassette tapes, recorded microfilms, and compact discs), electronic materials (compact discs, DVDs, magnetic tapes, floppy disks), and online materials (books, periodicals, annual reports, websites of institutions, events, research projects). At the expense of the depositor, nine legal deposit copies have to be submitted to the National and University Library, while the information on online publications has to be submitted using the "Online Publication Registration Form" (National and University Library, 2012).

One special case of legal deposit is to collect, process, store, and make available digitized pages of daily newspapers. Currently, within Croatian practice, these newspapers are scanned from print copies, and the scanning and encoding processes used in the digitisation of newspapers vary, as do the repository structures and storage media in which they are held. Since most newspaper producers shifted their operations to digital production, there is an increasing practice that these born-digital print masters are being acquired by libraries and archives. Data on the repositories of such digital print masters, as well as information on their infrastructure, quality and quantity of metadata, format, and preservation method, are currently not available. Gaining insight into print masters' repositories and the related preservation policies (provided that there are any) would be the basis for developing an operational digital print masters submission system, as well as partnership necessary for the management of this type of digital content, and the development and implementation of the national policy and standards aimed at its archiving and preservation.

Methodology

The ITrust study *Long-term Preservation of Digital Print Masters of National Publishers* (Ivanjko, 2018) presented in this chapter looked into various possibilities for making the deposit of digital print masters a part of the standard legal deposit system or a system whereby national publishers would deliver their digital print masters on an entirely voluntary basis. It also addressed the issue of ensuring permanent access to all forms of the national digital publishing output.

During its first stage, the research focused on the analysis of existing deposit practices in EU countries, whether those that are part of national legal deposit systems or those operating on a voluntary basis, along with the examination of the related legal issues regarding the legal deposit in the 39 European countries (EU28+). A questionnaire was created and sent to contacts found on the websites of respective national libraries – 46 contacts for 39 countries were selected for the survey. Along with the survey results, The Digital Information Documentation Office of the Government of the Republic of Croatia (now Central State Office for Development of Digital Society) gathered all available relevant documents regarding the legal deposit in the 39 European countries (EU28+). By using the survey questionnaire, relevant documents were additionally identified and analyzed, and relevant data was extracted.

Comparative analysis of the legal deposit practices

In this section, the survey data is quantified and compared to provide additional insight into the legal deposit practices where possible. Since some information was missing, the data is presented only for the countries where the information was available.

One of the first questions explored the deposit institution of each country, i.e. where the copies of legal deposit should be delivered. It was shown that most of the countries have multiple legal deposit institutions alongside the national library (Figure 20.1). According to the available data, it is evident that in addition to the national library, there are also local libraries to which compulsory copies are submitted. For example, in Austria, in addition to the national library, the deposit institutions are the university library, the study library, the provincial libraries, and the Parliamentary and federal libraries, while the Czech Republic legally prescribes the national library, the Moravian Library, and other regional libraries as deposit institutions. An interesting example is Greece, where the deposit institution is the Hellenic Chamber of Technology, from which copies are then distributed to the national library, Parliamentary library, and regional libraries. The required copies in Russia are submitted to the Federal Press and Communications Agency, the Government News Office, and regional and municipal libraries. It is also interesting to note that Russia and Belgium are the only countries where the National Library is not a depository.

The study explored whether the legal deposit is regulated within the legal system of the country or by some documents of less importance (ordinance, guidelines, recommendations, etc.). It was shown that legal deposit in most of the countries is regulated by some kind of law, mostly connected to libraries, in general as a part of the library institutions' legislature

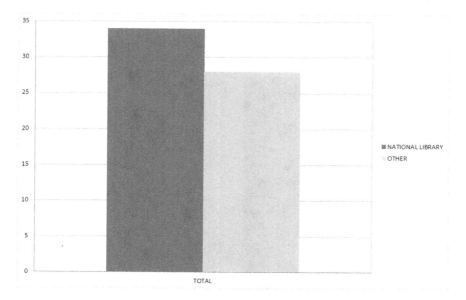

Figure 20.1 Deposit institution

(Figure 20.2). Some countries, such as Poland, have two laws that regulate legal deposit practices, while Slovenia has two separate ordinances that do the same. In Switzerland, there is no statutory requirement for delivering a legal deposit copy; however, to make sure the required copies arrive, the national deposit institution has signed a contract with two large national publishers.

Since different numbers of copies are in some cases prescribed for different materials and formats, the analysis included the minimum and maximum number of legal deposit copies. The analysis of relevant documents showed that there are significant differences between the countries, both in terms of minimum and maximum number of copies, ranging from 1–10 for the minimum number, and 1–16 for the maximum (Figure 20.3). The country with the highest number of legal deposit copies is Russia with 16 copies, while only the Netherlands requires one mandatory copy (both as minimum and maximum).

The prescribed deadlines for delivering legal deposit copies to the deposit institution were also explored. It was shown that the deadlines vary significantly, from four weeks before the publication is even made available to the public up to a year after publication (Figure 20.4). According to the data in Austria, Croatia, the Czech Republic, Hungary, Romania, Albania, and Russia, the minimum and maximum delivery deadlines are the same – four weeks after the publication is published. In the cases of France, Lithuania, and Serbia, the deadline is one week. Interesting cases are Bosnia and Herzegovina, and North Macedonia, where the statutory deadline for the submission of legal deposit copies is one week before the publication is even

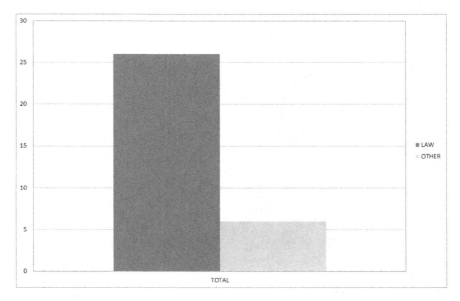

Figure 20.2 Level of documents regulating legal deposit

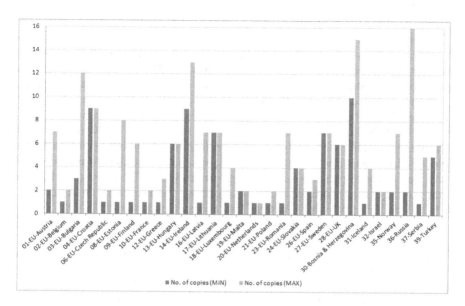

Figure 20.3 Minimum and maximum number of required legal deposit copies

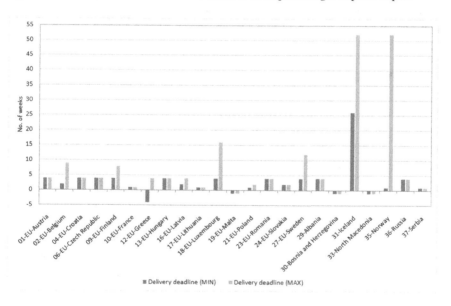

Figure 20.4 Deadline for delivering legal deposit copies

published; and Greece, where the deadline is set to four weeks before publishing, which is particularly interesting because the publication should be submitted before it is even available to the public. The largest gap between the minimum and maximum delivery deadlines was found in Norway, where the delivery ranges between one week and one year from the date that the publication was published.

Since the legal deposit is an obligation for publishers in most European countries, the study explored the prescribed financial sanctions for not delivering the copies of legal deposit within the defined deadlines. As can be seen from the data, most countries do not have any such sanctions, and those that do (Figure 20.5) vary significantly, with the range mostly between €1,000 and €5,000 for legal entities. The differences in the minimum prescribed fines are between €60 in Romania and €1,000 in Spain and Montenegro. The range between the maximum fine is between €1,000 in North Macedonia and €30,000 in Spain, which is the highest statutory penalty for failing to provide the legal deposit copy. North Macedonia, Bosnia and Herzegovina, Bulgaria, and Romania have a maximum fine of between €1,000 and €1,500 while Austria has a prescribed fine of €2,180. Montenegro, Serbia, Croatia, and Belgium have maximum fines ranging from €4,000–6,000. Although a number of countries have prescribed sanctions, according to the available survey data, no fines have ever been collected from the publishers.

Finally, the survey analyzed which types of materials are included in the legal deposit system. As expected, all the countries include printed materials, most of them also include audio-visual and electronic materials, while several also include some kind of web archive of their respective domains (Figure 20.6).

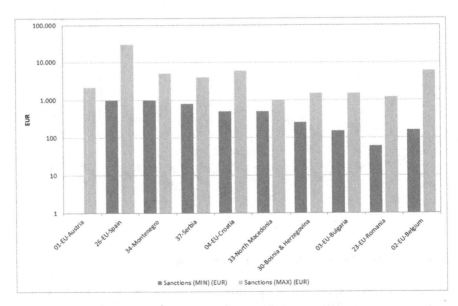

Figure 20.5 Financial sanctions for not meeting legal deposit deadlines

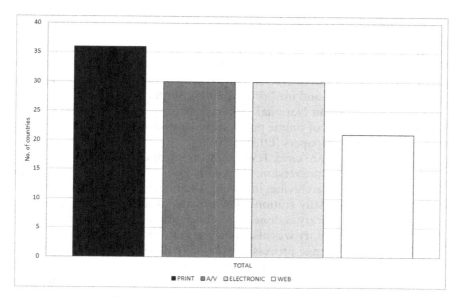

Figure 20.6 Types of materials included in the legal deposit

Archiving born-digital print masters: selected examples of the European legal deposit practice

The final question of the survey was also used to sample the countries that have already implemented solutions for archiving the legal deposit of the born-digital print masters. In order to examine good practices, technical solutions, and workflows associated with the legal deposit system of the national publishing output, three case studies of the developed and operational digital print masters' submission systems were analyzed in detail and are presented next.

Germany

The German National Library has been authorized to collect the legal deposit since 2006 under the provisions of the Law regarding the German National Library (DNBG, 2006) and the Ordinance on the Compulsory Delivery of Media Works to the German National Library. (PflAV, 2008), under which all publishers, commercial and non-commercial, are obliged to submit two copies of their material or one copy online, regardless of the medium in which they were published. Additionally, each federal state (Bundesland) requires one or two copies to be sent to their respective legal deposit institution (usually state university libraries). All the physical and non-physical media publications fall within the mandate of the collection, including all text-based, graphical, and audio presentations. Legal deposit should be given to the German National Library within one week from the date on which distribution began or the media work was made accessible to the public. However, the legal deposit regulations also state that the publisher "is not obliged to supply newspapers which, in accordance with the Library's regulations, have been submitted in an appropriate intangible form suitable for archiving and use" (PflAV, 2008). With the support of the 2006 legislation, the German National Library started in 2010, with the already established collection of online publications, a project of collecting e-paper editions of daily newspapers (PflAV, 2008).

In Germany, there are circa 1,500 daily newspapers, 1,200 of which are available in an electronic version. On a daily basis, 930 titles are included in the process of digital archiving, including 18 Sunday editions, which covers about 87% of total daily editions. The process of digital archiving for the German National Library is done by a service provider in cooperation with the library, and the library was also involved in the development of the automated ingest and storage process for the daily newspapers. The workflow uses PDF format since it is suitable for the delivery of large amounts of data. Three different interfaces are set up for the submission of online publications, depending of the quantity of data to be submitted: one for the submission of smaller quantities via a web form, and two machine-based interfaces for a larger number of (digital) objects. The service provider, an aggregator acting in the name of the library, accesses the restricted sections of newspapers' websites, using the login and password provided by the publishers, and harvests it. Due to its technical characteristics, the software needs to be configured for every single website separately. By logging into the subscribers' content, software selects the PDF download of a newspaper's issue, processes it, validates the title, date, number of pages, etc., and generates the metadata needed for ingest via the Open Archives Initiative Protocol for Metadata Harvesting (OAI-PMH, http://www.openarchives.org/pmh/) interface. Despite the automated process of ingest and storage, a part of the workflow will always be done by the library staff, e.g. contacting the publishers, requesting logging details, checking, defining criteria for quality checks for each title, creating bibliographic descriptions, etc. Each e-paper title is available within seven days from the day of harvesting on the library's premises. That way, by the end of 2014, 87% of total daily newspaper editions were covered.

Norway

Norway received a statutory requirement for a legal deposit copy of online publications much earlier than Germany, in 1989, according to which "electronic documents available through online transmission on telecommunications, television and data networks or the like shall be deposited in two copies at the specific request on the depository in each individual case" (WIPO,

2010, p. 3). The law applies from the moment the material is publicly available, which is why the Norwegian National Library does not have the right to request the submission of a mandatory copy of the digital (file) stencils used to produce the printed version of a publication. In order to collect digital print masters, the library had to enter into contracts with newspaper publishers to regulate the delivery of the mandatory copy, as well as cooperation on the digitisation of previous editions based on cost sharing and mutual benefit models (Solbakk, 2014).

The National Library of Norway aimed at establishing a system for ingest of digital legal deposit of daily newspapers, but out of 250 titles, only 35 publishers were included in the first phase of the project. By the year 2014, the digital deposit was implemented for 15 weekly and daily titles, while there are still negotiations with publishers of another 80 titles. The National Library has defined standards for the digital deposit of newspapers (file name, file format, image resolutions, delivery method), because of publishers' different digital production systems. All the files for a complete issue must be in the PDF/A format, while images should at least have the same quality as files used for the paper version. The process of collecting daily editions starts with the download from the publisher's FTP server, followed by PDF/A format quality check, extraction of the text from the pages, and formatting into XML/ALTO format. Files representing an issue are being archived into the Mavis database, which the library uses for storage of a variety of digital objects. Files intended for access are processed according to Metadata Encoding and Transmission Standard (METS https://www.loc.gov/standards/mets/) and created in XML format in order to be searchable and available through the library's digital service.

France

The National Library of France (Bibliothèque Nationale de France; BnF) is the main deposit institution in France. Legal deposit in France applies to printed material, prints, maps, plans, sheet music, photographs, posters, sound recordings, video recordings, multimedia documents, multimedia, software, databases, and the internet. The number of copies varies from a single copy, which applies to, for example, books, journals, magazines, sheet music, maps, atlases, photo albums, postcards, illustrated calendars, and posters; to two copies, which applies to, for example, sound recordings, CDs, video recordings, DVDs, multimedia documents, videogames, databases, software, electronic periodicals, and books with audio CDs. These numbers refer to the number of copies that are to be deposited to the BnF by publishers. Legal deposit also applies to e-books, which are automatically collected by the BnF, as is the case with the legal deposit of the internet. If an online e-book co-exists with a version in paper or electronic format (e.g. CD), it is still subject to legal deposit, i.e. one type of deposit does not replace the other.

The delivery of a digital compulsory copy is governed by the 2006 *Law on Copyright and Neighbouring Rights in the Information Society* (DADVSI, 2006), which intentionally provides a general definition of electronic material so that legal provisions do not apply to a particular technology that may soon become obsolete (Stirling & Illien, 2011). As in the early 2000s, the library sought to reduce the cost of digitizing print newspapers by deciding to obtain digital print masters directly from publishers, but it could only do so by contracting with them. The agreements allowed the library to accept digital files and use them in the library's reading rooms, within a time limited period. The 2006 law allowed the BnF to collect a digital version instead of a printed version if it is completely identical to the version distributed to the public.

The BnF has also attempted to find a solution for collecting online newspapers' content available through the subscriptions. A combination of web harvesting, which gathers all the publicly available websites of the newspapers that do not require consent from the publisher, and harvesting from the publishers, whereby the publishers provide the digital versions of the newspapers that are then imported and harvested by BnF – which requires prior consent and contracts with the publishers – has turned out to be the optimal solution and was implemented in 2012 within the "subscription-based project." By the end of 2013, 15 daily newspaper titles were collected on a regular basis, 13 of which represented regional editions (which, in fact, comprise 112 local editions) and two major daily national newspapers. Relying on harvesting web technologies, a crawler accesses and copies the protected content as a subscriber, using a login and password. This way, librarians have an important role in quality control, for example statistical (e.g. metrics and report of the crawls) and visual (comparison with online equivalent) quality control. Because of frequent URL changes, and with the maintenance of continuity of newspaper title in mind, a system of permalinks was set up and each title is given an archival resource key (ARK) identifier, which refers to all URLs on which the title has appeared through a period of time. Although there are certain disadvantages with this approach of newspaper harvesting (website technology, changes in website structure, non-timely manner of publisher's permission to free access to password-protected content), until mid-2014, it was used to collect more than 20 daily newspapers (mainly regional titles) with almost 200 different local editions. In the near future, the possibility of ingesting newspapers in PDF format via FTP protocol will be considered.

Conclusion

This chapter has focused on the analysis of existing legal deposit practices in EU countries, whether those that are part of national legal deposit systems or those operating on a voluntary basis, along with the examination of the related issues of archiving the legal deposit via born-digital print masters in the 39 European countries (EU28+). It was shown that most of the countries have multiple legal deposit institutions alongside their respective national libraries, have the legal deposit regulated via some kind of law, mostly connected to libraries in general as a part of the library institutions' legislature. The analysis of relevant documents showed that there are significant differences between the countries both in the minimum and maximum number of copies, delivery deadlines, and prescribed financial sanctions. As expected, all the countries include printed materials in their legal deposit, most of them also include audio-visual and electronic materials, and only a few include some kind of web archive of their respective domains.

The second part of the chapter focused on the countries that have already implemented solutions for archiving legally deposited born-digital print masters. Three case studies of the developed and operational digital print masters' submission systems were analyzed, namely those from Germany, Norway, and France, focusing on the legal deposit of daily newspapers. Selected examples showed that establishing a system for ingest of digital legal deposit can solve problems of on-time delivery of digital print masters and reduce the time and cost for the deposit institutions to collect, process, store, and make available digitized pages of daily newspapers. Despite the automated process of ingest and storage, each system's crucial part of the workflow is also ensuring quality control and providing bibliographic metadata for storage and retrieval. Apart from technology and staff, the third important part of the systems is the publishers. The importance of ensuring cooperation based on cost sharing and mutual benefit proved to be crucial. These three prerequisites are found to be the cornerstone for developing an operational digital print masters' submission system, partnership necessary for management of this type of digital content, and development and implementation of the national policies and standards aimed at digital content archiving and preservation.

Acknowledgements

I wish to acknowledge graduate research assistants Jana Borovčak, Lana Lončarić, Sara Semenski, and Martina Žugaj from the Department of Information and Communication Sciences, Faculty of Humanities and Social Sciences, University of Zagreb, as well as Danijela Getliher, Karolina Holub, Sofija Klarin Zadravec, Renata Petrušić, Sonja Pigac, and Ingeborg Rudomino from the National and University Library in Zagreb, and Tamara Horvat from the Central State Office for Development of Digital Society, Croatia, who participated in this research.

References

DADVSI – Droits d'auteur et droits voisins dans la société de l'information law [Law on copyright and neighbouring rights in the information society]. (2006).

Retrieved from https://www.legifrance.gouv.fr/affichTexte.do?cidTexte=JORFT EXT000000266350

DNBG – Gesetz über die Deutsche Nationalbibliothek [Law regarding the German National Library]. (2006). Retrieved from http://www.gesetze-im-internet.de/dnbg/BJNR133800006.html

International Federation of Library Associations and Institutions (IFLA). (2011). *Statement on legal deposit*. Retrieved from https://www.ifla.org/files/assets/clm/publications/ifla_statement_on_legal_deposit.pdf

Ivanjko, T. (2018). *Long-term preservation of digital print masters of national publishers* (EU24). InterPARES Trust. Retrieved from https://interparestrust.org/assets/public/dissemination/DigitalPrintMasters(EU24)_finalreport.pdf

Larivière, J. (2000). *Guidelines for legal deposit legislation*. Paris: UNESCO. Retrieved from https://unesdoc.unesco.org/ark:/48223/pf0000121413

National and University Library. (2012). *Legal deposit*. Retrieved from https://www.nsk.hr/en/legal-deposit/

PflAV – Verordnung über die Pflichtablieferung von Medienwerken an die Deutsche Nationalbibliothek [Ordinance on the compulsory delivery of media works to the German National Library]. (2008). Retrieved from http://www.gesetze-im-internet.de/pflav/BJNR201300008.html

Solbakk, S. A. (2014). *Implementation of digital deposit at the National Library of Norway*. Paper presented at IFLA WLIC 2014 on Libraries, Citizens, Societies: Confluence for Knowledge, Lyon, France.

Stirling, P., & Illien, G. (2011). *The state of e-legal deposit in France: Looking back at five years of putting new legislation into practice and envisioning the future*. Paper presented at World Library and Information Congress: 77th IFLA General Conference and Assembly, San Juan, Puerto Rico.

World Intellectual Property Organization (WIPO) Second Survey on Voluntary Registration and Deposit Systems. (2010). *Questionnaire part B: Answers from Norway*. Retrieved from https://www.wipo.int/export/sites/www/copyright/en/registration/replies/pdf/norway.pdf

Zakon o knjižnicama i knjižničnoj djelatnosti [Croatian library law]. (2019). Retrieved from http://digarhiv.gov.hr/arhiva/263/192306/narodne-novine.nn.hr/clanci/sluzbeni/full/2019_02_17_356.html

21 Blockchain in digital preservation

Hrvoje Stančić

Introduction

Digital records to be found in digital archives were either digitized or born digitally. Digital preservation, as opposed to preservation of analogue materials whereby preservation of a record depends on preservation of its medium, splits the notion of preservation into at least two parts – preservation of the content independently of the medium, and preservation of the physical carrier, i.e. the storage medium. There are authors who argue for a third aspect, as well. Thus, Thibodeau (2002, p. 6, italics in original) states that

> every digital object is a physical object, a logical object, and a conceptual object, and its properties at each of those levels can be significantly different. A *physical* object is simply an inscription of signs on some physical medium. A *logical* object is an object that is recognized and processed by software. The *conceptual* object is the object as it is recognized and understood by a person, or in some cases recognized and processed by a computer application capable of executing business transactions.

This should be considered when conversion, e.g. from an obsolete file format to a current one, or migration, e.g. from an obsolete medium to a current one, are performed, aiming to preserve digital records in the ever-changing technological space. However, while performing preservation actions it is important to have in mind that ISO 15489–1 (International Organization for Standardization, 2016) requires every digitally preserved record to have its characteristics of authenticity, reliability, integrity, and usability intact. This chapter adopts the ITrust's definition according to which trustworthiness of a record refers to its accuracy, reliability, and authenticity (InterPARES Trust Terminology Database, n.d.), and makes it an anchoring point in the research focused on long term preservation of digitally signed or sealed records. Those types of records have been chosen because of their specific technical requirements.

Digital signatures, digital seals, certificates, and timestamps

While technically the same, the difference between digital signatures[1] and digital seals is that a digital signature can be associated only with a *natural person* and the signing key must be under the sole control of the *signatory* with the aim of *signing*, while a digital seal can be associated only with a *legal person* and the signing key must be under the sole control of the *process* assigning the seal with the aim of *ensuring integrity and origin* (Cryptomathic, n.d.; eIDAS, 2014). A digital signature is a code created according to cryptographic principles using the Public Key Infrastructure (PKI) connected to a digital object, which serves as proof that the object has not been tampered with, and in some cases can be used to authenticate the sender's identity (Mihaljević, Mihaljević, & Stančić, 2015). Therefore, a scanned wet signature does not fall under the definition of a digital signature. It is merely an image placed at a certain place in a document which cannot confirm one's identity because anyone can place it there. However, if the partners in a process agree to trust it and if it becomes a basis for other business actions, it may be used. This chapter does not focus on digitized wet signatures but on advanced digital signatures. According to the eIDAS Regulation (2014), an *advanced electronic signature* (AdES) must meet the following requirements:

> a) it is uniquely linked to the signatory; b) it is capable of identifying the signatory; c) it is created using electronic signature creation data that the signatory can, with a high level of confidence, use under his sole control; and d) it is linked to the data signed therewith in such a way that any subsequent change in the data is detectable.

Therefore, such a signature has the qualities of *irrevocability* or *non-repudiation* because the signatory cannot deny that (s)he has indeed signed a document.

The PKI system, relying on the combination of public and private keys, provides the components necessary for managing (issuing, verifying, and revoking) public keys and certificates, as well as their storage and preservation. It also provides secure authentication of communication between participants, exchange of encrypted data, information, documents, and records, digital signing and co-signing, and a unique registry of public keys in the form of digital certificates.

Stančić (2018a, p. 9) explains that a *digital certificate* confirms the connection between a secret key owned by a person and the associated public key. It is a system whereby the identity of the person is stored together with the corresponding public key, and the entire structure is digitally signed by a trusted third party (certification service). A digital certificate is issued for a limited period (usually two to five years) during which the certificate, i.e. its validity, may be revoked. The validity can be verified by checking the digital signature, but there must be a direct trust or a trust chain to the Certification

Authority (CA) certifying the digital certificate. CA issues, manages, keeps, and revokes digital certificates and guarantees their validity. Thus, CA is a trust entity and a third party. The Registration Authority (RA) handles users' requests to issue digital certificates, registers users, and cooperates with the CA in certificate issuing. The RA ensures the correct physical identification of users, thus ensuring the non-repudiation characteristic of digital signatures. In addition to the RA and CA, there is a Certificate Repository (CR) where public keys, user certificates, and Certificate Revocation List (CRL) are stored. There are two ways of knowing whether a digital certificate is revoked – either to check whether the certificate revocation information has been published on the CRL, or by using the Online Certificate Status Protocol (OCSP), an internet protocol used for obtaining the revocation status of a certificate.

The *digital timestamp* plays an important role in the context of digital signatures. It represents a digitally signed certificate of a timestamp issuer – Timestamping Authority (TSA) – which confirms the existence of the data, information, document, or record to which the timestamp relates, at the time stated on the timestamp, thus ensuring reliable proof that, for example, a record originated earlier or just before the time indicated in the digital timestamp, but not after it was issued. Any subsequent changes to the record or timestamp are not allowed and can be easily detected. Therefore, the digital timestamp confirms that the record at hand existed in that form at the time indicated in the timestamp, and that it was not changed after the time indicated in the timestamp. The TSA digitally signs the hash value of the record, along with the time value (coming from a trusted source, e.g. Coordinated Universal Time), thus issuing the digital timestamp, which is subsequently combined with the record and the signatory's private key to create the digital signature with the indication of the time of signing.

The *archival timestamp* implements an onion-like approach. The ETSI (2016) standard defines four basic levels of baseline (B) digital signatures enabling interoperability and the lifecycle of records: 1) B-B – basic; 2) B-T – timestamp added to the B-level; 3) B-LT – long term validity verification information added to the T-level; and 4) B-LTA –enabling periodic addition of the archival timestamp to the LT-level (Figure 21.1).

Challenges to long term preservation of digitally signed, sealed, and/or timestamped records

The fact that digital signatures and seals are not designed with long or unlimited validity period in mind is a challenge for long term preservation in digital archives. Time-limited validity is necessary because the cryptographic algorithms used in PKI weaken with technology advancements and new, longer keys need to be used. A challenge for digital preservation is also the fact that digital signatures add another layer of complexity which needs to be addressed when preservation actions such as file conversion

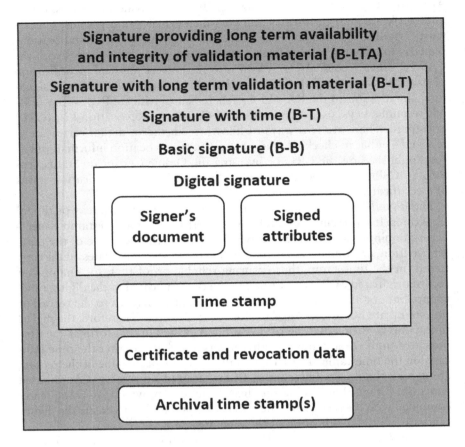

Figure 21.1 Archival timestamp

need to be performed. Broadly, we can distinguish between two different situations – one in which digital repositories are using digital signatures for their internal processes, and one in which digital repositories are preserving digitally signed records. In both situations, issues with expiration of digital signatures occur. Therefore, in all cases where digital signatures are used the signature itself and the information needed to validate the signature must be preserved (along with originals and supporting documentation – i.e. digital certificates, CRLs, OCSP responses, etc.). Revalidation of the signatures should be avoided whenever possible. According to Blanchette (2006), from the point of view of archives, there are three possible options

1   *preserve the digital signatures*: this solution supposes the deployment of considerable means to preserve the necessary mechanisms for validating

the signatures, and does not address the need to simultaneously preserve the intelligibility of documents

2 *eliminate the signatures*: this option requires the least adaptation from the archival institution, but impoverishes the description of the document, as it eliminates the signature as one technical element used to ensure the authenticity of the documents

3 *record the trace of the signatures as metadata*: this solution requires little technical means, and records both the existence of the signature and the result of its verification. However, digital signatures lose their special status as the primary form of evidence from which to infer the authenticity of the document. Moreover, this approach requires the existence of a trusted third party (CA) to authenticate the metadata.

The literature reveals other possible approaches, such as the one advocated by Dumortier and Van den Eynde (2002). The authors argue that the only option is to develop a Trusted Archival Service (TAS), which could guarantee that the signature of a record can still be validated years later, but this approach still has to see widespread implementation. Another option is to develop and implement official state registers of created/received records in combination with early archiving. On the other hand, results of the previous InterPARES projects recommend Blanchette's third option, i.e. to organize a digital archive in a way to check the validity of the digital signatures at the ingest phase (either by technical revalidation of signatures, or by obtaining assurances from the relevant authority), add the validity information to the records' metadata, and preserve the records without addressing the digital signatures' validity further. This is in line with ISO 16363 (2012b), the standard on trusted digital repository (TDR) audit and certification, because the issue of trust is shifted from the (digitally signed) record to the archive preserving digital records and the associated (validity) metadata.

The approaches explained so far follow the more traditional model of archival preservation, which stands in contrast to the fourth approach proposed in this chapter, which is to register a digital signature's validity information in a blockchain and eliminate the need for the trusted third party or preservation intermediary to confirm its validity during long term preservation.

Use of blockchain in digital preservation

The concept

To be able to fully understand the concept of blockchain and distributed ledger technology (DLT), their underlying principles need to be briefly explained. They are *hash*, *Merkle tree*, and *distributed consensus*. These concepts are explained – simplified, and with as little technical details as possible to avoid unnecessary complexity – to provide the necessary grounds for understanding the TrustChain model presented later in the chapter. An extensive blockchain bibliography (Stančić, 2018b) was compiled during the literature review phase of this research and could be consulted for more details on blockchain-related concepts. Also, the blockchain principles explained here should be clearly distinguished from cryptocurrencies as the more complex realisations. Those are based on blockchain, and if someone has exploited a cryptocurrency vulnerability, it would have been discovered because of the proofs in the blockchain.

Hash, or *message digest*, is a one-way function that calculates a unique fixed-length string from any plain text, data, information, document, or record of any size. The *one-way* characteristic means that it is not possible to recreate the original document by knowing its hash. This is important to keep in mind because classified records, or those not (yet) available to the public, can be processed by the hash function without revealing their content to anyone. A hash algorithm is *collision resistant* because it is practically impossible to create "collisions," i.e. to have two or more meaningful records with the same hash value. The resulting hash value is also referred to as its *digital fingerprint* because it uniquely identifies the input. A hash algorithm is *pseudorandom*. This means that the resulting value is unpredictable but also that even if, intentionally or unintentionally, only one digit in the binary stream is flipped, the resulting hash will be significantly different from the original one. This makes the hash function *deterministic*, i.e. the same input data will always result in the same calculated hash, thus proving the integrity (Drescher, 2017). Different hash algorithms result in different hash lengths, which can be seen in Table 21.1. showing the resulting values of the same input data – the title of this book. The longer the resulting value, the stronger the hash algorithm.

Table 21.2 shows a significant difference in the two resulting hash values if the input string changes slightly – the capitalisation of the word "Records" has changed.

Merkle (1980) was the first to introduce the concept of aggregation of hash values, which is used by blockchain today. The hash values can be aggregated (hashed) together to form an upside-down tree-like structure, or as it is called today – the *Merkle tree*. The hash resulting from all

Table 21.1 Hash values calculated by different hash algorithms

Original text	Trust and Records in an Open Digital Environment
MD5	0e8e86c085646651f33e91cb162688be
SHA-256	313a2ed7c159b22cc87f2f6a191f3dd95669c7d7f39 cd587690c2836c297abb3
SHA-512	f4686a1642bdc4acaff88961dcf3bf9a543a20b184203369b9b70d 2c5dd11168 5c9fac0ebb54dd47bd4705462520f65ac60ac822 29ac3321339e626db099c1d8

Table 21.2 Pseudorandom characteristic of hash function

Original text	Trust and Records in an Open Digital Environment
MD5	0e8e86c085646651f33e91cb162688be
Changed text	Trust and records in an Open Digital Environment
MD5	a30173575d3991f2473c0d4803d7515b

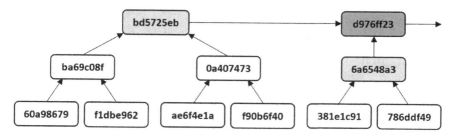

Figure 21.2 Top hashes of two Merkle trees linked to form a single chain

calculations from the lower levels is called the *top hash* or *root hash*. Two or more Merkle tree structures, each having a top hash, can be further joined by aggregating the top hashes to form a new, joint top hash. This results in a chain-resembling structure whereby each top hash is considered as a new link in the chain. If this approach is used to calculate hashes of the records, and to aggregate them, then if any record changes afterwards, for whatever reason, all calculations using that, and all subsequent values, will fail. This is illustrated in Figure 21.2, where the first two titles of each section of this book are used as examples – the first two sections creating one Merkle tree, the third section making another. Only the first eight characters of the calculated values using SHA-256 algorithm are shown (bottom values). Instead of the plain text of the titles used in this example, actual data, documents, or records might be used. This example was chosen so that anyone can recreate it.

Blockchain uses distributed (peer-to-peer) networks. This differs from centralised and decentralised networks in having no central node(s) and treating all interconnected computers/servers equally. A distributed type of network topology has no single point of control and therefore no single point of attack or failure. In the blockchain, every node stores its own copy of all transactions in the local *ledger*, which consequently becomes a *distributed ledger*. This enables blockchain to achieve *distributed consensus*, i.e. all collected hash values (e.g. of monetary transactions or registrations of records), combined with the previous top hash constitute a *block*, which becomes valid only if the qualified majority (50% + 1 node) agrees upon it,

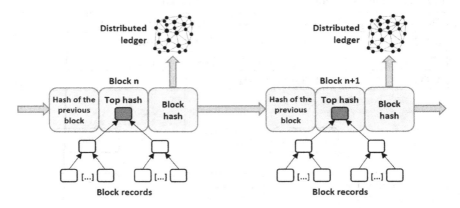

Figure 21.3 Blockchain creation

i.e. confirms that the Merkle tree calculations are correct. When confirmed, the block is *sealed*, and the new top hash is propagated throughout all nodes and registered in all copies of the distributed ledger (Figure 21.3).

It should be noted that cryptocurrencies implement the time-consuming computational tasks called *hash puzzles* in the process of top hash calculation, thus implementing the concept of *proof of work* and consequentially creating the value of the cryptocurrency, which originates from the combination of computational resources and time used. However, the explanation of that process is out of scope of this chapter. What is important to distinguish here is that the hash puzzle is the reason why cryptocurrencies consume a lot of electricity, while the blockchain itself without it, as explained here and used in the TrustChain model, is very efficient and does not require significant computational power.

The TrustChain model

The TrustChain model, as detailed by Stančić (2018a), emerged as a response to the challenges with expiring digital signatures. The research team first analyzed three real-life examples aiming to analyze the current use of and state of preservation of digitally signed records held by different institutions, to understand the perceived value of the need for archiving of the digitally signed records as well as preservation of the validity of the digital signatures, and to understand how could the expiration of certificates in digital signatures influences the admissibility of records as evidence in court. The three case studies investigated digitally signed retirement fund records in Croatia (Stančić, 2018c), digitally signed e-tax records in Croatia (Stančić, 2018d), and digitally signed medical records, procurement and supplier contracts, official political decisions, and minutes of meetings in Sweden (Stengård,

Almgren, & Stančić, 2018). Based on the insights from the case studies, the TrustChain model was formulated (Bralić, Kuleš, & Stančić, 2017).

The goal of the TrustChain is to enable archival institutions (or others with similar needs) to avoid having to periodically re-sign, or (re)timestamp (using an archival timestamp) all their archived, digitally signed records. The Trust-Chain is envisioned as a blockchain-based solution, being maintained by an international alliance of archival institutions. The system could also be implemented by a single institution, but then the degree of security in signature validity is significantly reduced because trustworthiness is directly related to the number of independent participating institutions. The TrustChain achieves the stated goal by checking a document's signature validity and, if it is valid, writing the signature's hash and a small set of metadata in the blockchain. Signature validity is checked by all or, if their number is sufficiently high, some of the participating institutions. Bralić et al. (2017) state that

> the voting system is based on a simplified version of the system used in the BigChainDB system (McConaghy et al., 2018). Once the originating node receives the responses from voting nodes (filled out vote fields in its block), it confirms the votes as valid by checking the voting node signatures.
>
> (p. 98)

When the signature is confirmed as valid, the information is permanently stored in the TrustChain blockchain. The high-level schema of the Trust-Chain model is shown in Figure 21.4.

Later, when the digital certificate confirming the digital signature has expired, a user checking it will get information that the signature is not valid. However, if the digitally signed record is checked against the TrustChain, and if the newly calculated hash matches the one from the digital signature (integrity of the record, and identity of the signatory are confirmed), and if the validity was confirmed at the time of the record's registration on the blockchain, the user will be able to obtain validity confirmation and use the record as if the digital signature were still valid.

The TrustChain is modelled to be tamper resistant. First, because each block contains the hash of the previous block, it is impossible to change a fragment of a previous block without rewriting all the subsequent blocks. Second, the voting information is also protected by a hash. This is achieved by hashing the previous block's hash together with the voting information, i.e. with the private keys of the voting nodes (Stančić, 2018b, p. 32).

The model explained so far relies on the idea that only the records with the still valid digital signatures are registered on the blockchain. Also, the records need to be made available to the international alliance of archival institutions, i.e. the blockchain nodes, for digital signature validity check. This is an adequate approach for current records, and the ones that are not sensitive in nature. However, it could be expected that a record with an already expired digital signature is ingested into a digital archive, or that

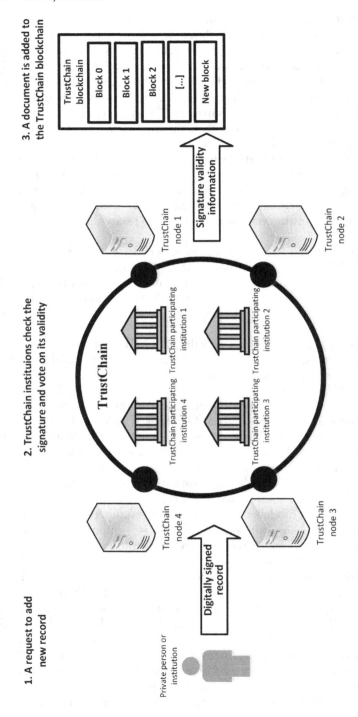

Figure 21.4 The TrustChain model
Source: (Stančić, 2018a, p. 30)

highly sensitive or classified records need to be registered on the blockchain. For these situations, Bralić, Stančić, and Stengård (2020) propose storing the certificate chains in the blockchain instead of, or in addition to, the information on the validity of the digital signatures and seals. By accommodating this approach, the TrustChain system is improved with the functionality to validate the records without gaining access to them – only the digital signatures' certificates are needed – and also to validate, in principle, the records whose certificates have already expired, and have not been previously processed by the TrustChain. In this case, one can argue that if someone's digital signature was valid at a certain point in time, and this was confirmed by the TrustChain, then the same person's already expired digital signature on a record not previously registered in the TrustChain should also be valid if the timestamp shows the signing time to be within the time period the TrustChain has marked the certificate as valid. In this case, the validity of an already expired digital signature can be confirmed.

Discussion

One misconception often surfacing in the discussions is that the large amount of records stored on the blockchain will eventually make it too big to handle. It is important to point out that the record is never stored on-chain – only its hash and metadata – making this concept safe even for sensitive or classified records. Therefore, a digital archive is still needed for storage and preservation of digital records whereby they will be as secure as the system itself is.

Any digital archive could easily be upgraded with the TrustChain solution. Adding a new layer of functionality would be required. In relation to the Open Archival Information System (OAIS) reference model (ISO, 2012a), the TrustChain functionalities could have connectors to the functional entities of ingest (for initial registration of digital signature validity or certificate in the blockchain), archival storage (for periodic integrity checks), and access (for confirming validity upon users' requests).

As it was pointed out earlier, the TrustChain model stores only hashes and metadata in the blockchain. The model uses ISAD(G)'s essential set of metadata elements to facilitate indexing, search, and retrieval, as well as to avoid putting personal information or other sensitive information in the immutable blockchain structure, thus achieving GDPR compliance. However, Lemieux and Sporny (2017) realize a shortcoming of blockchain and distributed ledger technologies in the context of the archival bond, i.e. their inability to link the process producing a record with the ledger entries, by stating that "even though the time-ordered nature of the transactional records is preserved, the link to their procedural context, and relationship to other transactional records relating to the same procedure, is not" (p. 1439). They argue that "through use of ontologies to represent the procedural context of ledger entries, it is possible to instantiate the archival bond between ledger entries as records of a variety of transactions" (p. 1442).

Conclusion

The proposed TrustChain model is a good example of how blockchain and DLT can be meaningfully used in processes involving documents and records. By implementing TrustChain, the process of the long term preservation of digitally signed records will benefit from not having to keep track of the certificate expiration date of every digitally signed record, possibly having more than one digital signature expiring on different dates, and constant re-timestamping just before they expire. In digital archives holding millions of records, the TrustChain validity information preservation (VIP) solution can make the digital preservation process more straightforward.

Taking into account all the characteristics of blockchain, and its underlying technologies and concepts, it could be concluded that blockchain can be used in public administration, businesses, and the archival profession to

- ensure that digital processes cannot be manipulated
- confirm integrity of a record
- confirm that a record existed or was created at a certain point in time (i.e. not after it was timestamped and registered in the blockchain)
- confirm the sequence of records
- support or enhance the non-repudiation characteristic of records
- improve validation possibilities of digitally signed records during long term preservation.

Acknowledgements

The author would like to acknowledge the research team members: Göran Almgren, Hans Almgren, and Mats Stengård (Enigio Time AB, Stockholm, Sweden); Natasha Khramtsovsky (Electronic Office Systems LLC, Moscow, Russia); Victoria Lemieux (University of British Columbia, Vancouver, Canada); Željko Mikić (TechEd Consulting Services, Zagreb, Croatia); and Elis Missoni (Financial Agency – FINA, Zagreb, Croatia). The author would also like to acknowledge the postgraduate students Vladimir Bralić, Hrvoje Brzica, Anabela Lendić, and Ivan Slade Šilović, and graduate research assistants Andro Babić, Nikola Bonić, Magdalena Kuleš, Ksenija Lončarić, Ana Stanković, and Ira Volarević from the Department of Information and Communication Sciences, Faculty of Humanities and Social Sciences, University of Zagreb, Croatia, who participated in this research.

Note

1 The terms *electronic signature* and *digital signature* are often used interchangeably to mean the same thing. However, in this chapter, the term *electronic signature* is used when referring to the signatures in which the identity of the signatory cannot be verified, while the term *digital signature* is used when referring to the signatures

when the Certificate Authority (CA) confirms the identity of the signatory (except in the citations where the original terminology is cited).

References

Blanchette, J.-F. (2006). The digital signature dilemma: To preserve or not to preserve. *Annales des Télécommunications*, 61, 908–923.

Bralić, V., Kuleš, M., & Stančić, H. (2017). A model for long-term preservation of digital signature validity: TrustChain. In I. Atanassova, W. Zaghouani, B. Kragić, K. Aas, H. Stančić, & S. Seljan (Eds.), *INFuture 2017: Integrating ICT in society* (pp. 89–113). Zagreb: Department of Information and Communication Sciences, Faculty of Humanities and Social Sciences, University of Zagreb. Retrieved from https://www.researchgate.net/publication/321171227_A_Model_for_Long-term_Preservation_of_Digital_Signature_Validity_TrustChain

Bralić, V., Stančić, H., & Stengård, M. (2020). A blockchain approach to digital archiving: Digital signature certification chain preservation. *Records Management Journal*, ahead-of-print. https://doi.org/10.1108/RMJ-08-2019-0043

Cryptomathic. (n.d.). *What is an electronic seal?* Retrieved from https://www.cryptomathic.com/products/authentication-signing/digital-signatures-faqs/what-is-an-electronic-seal

Drescher, D. (2017). *Blockchain basics: A non-technical introduction in 25 steps.* Frankfurt am Main: Apress.

Dumortier, J., & Van den Eynde, S. (2002). *Electronic signatures and trusted archival services.* Retrieved from http://www.expertisecentrumdavid.be/davidproject/teksten/DAVIDbijdragen/Tas.pdf

eIDAS. (2014). *Regulation (EU) No 910/2014 of the European Parliament and of the Council of 23 July 2014 on electronic identification and trust services for electronic transactions in the internal market and repealing Directive 1999/93/EC.* Retrieved from https://eur-lex.europa.eu/legal-content/EN/TXT/?uri=uriserv%3AOJ.L_.2014.257.01.0073.01.ENG

ETSI. (2016). *ETSI EN 319 102–1: Electronic signatures and infrastructures (ESI); Procedures for creation and validation of AdES digital signatures; Part 1: Creation and validation.* Retrieved from https://www.etsi.org/deliver/etsi_en/319100_319199/31910201/01.01.00_30/en_31910201v010100v.pdf

International Organization for Standardization. (2012a). *ISO 14721:2012 Space data and information transfer systems – Open archival information system (OAIS) – Reference model.* Retrieved from https://www.iso.org/standard/57284.html

International Organization for Standardization. (2012b). *ISO 16363:2012 Space data and information transfer systems – Audit and certification of trustworthy digital repositories.* Retrieved from https://www.iso.org/standard/56510.html

International Organization for Standardization. (2016). *ISO 15489–1:2016 Information and documentation – Records management – Part 1: Concepts and principles.* ISO. Retrieved from https://www.iso.org/standard/62542.html

InterPARES Trust Terminology Database. (n.d.). *Trustworthiness.* Retrieved from http://arstweb.clayton.edu/interlex/en/term.php?term=trustworthiness

Lemieux, V. L., & Sporny, M. (2017). Preserving the archival bond in distributed ledgers: A data model and syntax. *Proceedings of the 26th International Conference on World Wide Web Companion*, Perth, Australia (pp. 1437–1443). Retrieved from https://dl.acm.org/doi/10.1145/3041021.3053896

McConaghy, T., Rodolphe, M., Muller, A., De Jonghe, D., McConaghy, T. T., McMullen, G., . . . Granzotto, A. (2018). *BigchainDB: A scalable blockchain database.* Berlin: BigchainDB GmbH. Retrieved from https://www.bigchaindb.com/whitepaper/bigchaindb-whitepaper.pdf

Merkle, R. C. (1980). Protocols for public key cryptosystems. *IEEE Symposium on Security and Privacy, 122,* 122–134.

Mihaljević, M., Mihaljević, M., & Stančić, H. (2015). *Arhivistički rječnik. Englesko-hrvatski, hrvatsko-engleski* [Archival science dictionary. English-Croatian, Croatian-English]. Zagreb: FF Press. Retrieved from https://infoz.ffzg.hr/Stancic/Arhivisticki-rjecnik/

Stančić, H. (2018a). *Model for preservation of trustworthiness of the digitally signed, timestamped and/or sealed digital records (TRUSTER Preservation Model) (EU31).* InterPARES Trust. Retrieved from https://interparestrust.org/assets/public/dissemination/TRUSTERPreservationModel(EU31)-Finalreportv_1_3.pdf

Stančić, H. (2018b). *Model for preservation of trustworthiness of the digitally signed, timestamped and/or sealed digital records (TRUSTER Preservation Model) (EU31) – Blockchain bibliography.* InterPARES Trust. Retrieved from https://interparestrust.org/assets/public/dissemination/TRUSTERPreservationModel(EU31)-Blockchainbibliographyv.1_.0_.pdf

Stančić, H. (2018c). *Model for preservation of trustworthiness of the digitally signed, timestamped and/or sealed digital records (TRUSTER Preservation Model) (EU31) – Case Study 1 – digitally signed retirement fund records.* InterPARES Trust. Retrieved from https://interparestrust.org/assets/public/dissemination/TRUSTERPreservationModel(EU31)-CaseStudy1v1_2.pdf

Stančić, H. (2018d). *Model for preservation of trustworthiness of the digitally signed, timestamped and/or sealed digital records (TRUSTER Preservation Model) (EU31) – Case Study 2 – digitally signed e-tax records.* InterPARES Trust. Retrieved from https://interparestrust.org/assets/public/dissemination/TRUSTERPreservationModel(EU31)-CaseStudy2v1_2.pdf

Stengård, M., Almgren, H., & Stančić, H. (2018). *Model for preservation of trustworthiness of the digitally signed, timestamped and/or sealed digital records (TRUSTER Preservation Model) (EU31) – Case Study 3 – digitally signed medical records, procurement and supplier contracts, official political decisions and minutes of meetings.* InterPARES Trust. Retrieved from https://interparestrust.org/assets/public/dissemination/TRUSTERPreservationModel(EU31)-CaseStudy3v1_3.pdf

Thibodeau, K. (2002). Overview of technological approaches to digital preservation and challenges in coming years. In *The state of digital preservation: An international perspective* (pp. 4–31). Washington, DC: Council on Library and Information Resources (CLIR). Retrieved from https://www.clir.org/pubs/reports/pub107/pub107.pdf

22 Conclusion to Part III

Part III of the book investigated records in the networked environment by first deliberating on the appraisal procedures of websites at their different levels – at the level of a website, but also at the section level. Analysis using the example of the English website of the Ministry of Foreign Affairs, Government of Israel, showed that the appraisal process in general should follow the same principles as for conventional and digital records, but that additional aspects should be considered such as the users, i.e. their interests and behaviour, while using the website contents, as well as characteristics and content of records that constitute a section. Although an appraisal formula was proposed, its testing showed that it still cannot be relied upon as the sole method for appraising archival material from a website. However, it proved helpful in better understanding of the website's complexity and its dynamics. On the other hand, investigation of the metadata accompanying the process of website appraisal concluded that a granular approach was not used, and that the metadata from the level of the website was also used at the level of sections. Therefore, a more granular approach is recommended.

Taking a broader view, investigation of metadata elements used to describe digital cultural heritage objects offered online by the chosen MLA institutions in Turkey showed the difference in their usage at national and local levels. Institutions at the local level work with more financial constraints and have difficulties following the accepted national and international metadata standards, implementation of unique identifiers, controlled vocabularies, and sufficient description of digital cultural heritage objects. It is recommended that the systems used for making the digital objects available should be based on the models specifically developed and standardized for the digital environment, i.e. the models enabling their integration and interoperability.

Having integration and interoperability in mind, but also process efficiency, next the focus was put on still underdeveloped practices of ingest, storage, and preservation of digital print masters. Research into the practices, policies, and legal regulations guiding legal deposit of conventionally published materials, offline e-publications, online publications, and web content in the countries geographically belonging to the European Union showed a scarcity of good examples of digital print masters deposits. The recommendations to make digital print masters part of the standard legal deposit, or to create a system whereby the publishers could deposit them on a voluntary basis, are given. However, what can be considered as publication from the legal point of view – only the published edition, or its digital print master, as well – should be resolved first. The analysis showed that there are examples of contracts being made between publishers and depository institutions to guarantee that only the digital print masters used to print publications are deposited. Although this approach means that individual contracts should be made with publishers, instead of legally regulating the process, this seems to be a good transitional solution, which is in many ways more efficient than scanning the printed materials that were prepared digitally. That way, not only cooperation based on cost sharing and mutual benefit could be established, but also the ingest process could be automated, facilitating storage and preservation.

However, preservation of some archival materials may not be straightforward and without challenges. Good examples of this are digitally signed records – the signing certificates they rely upon have rather short validity periods. Investigation of possibilities to preserve the validity of digital signatures after the certificates' expiration showed that blockchain can be used. The TrustChain solution has shown as promising. By registering the validity of digital signatures in the blockchain, without storing the records themselves on the chain, the records with expired certificates can be used later as if their signatures are still valid. The already existing recordkeeping and archival systems could easily be upgraded with the proposed solution. This is an example of how new, disruptive technologies can be incorporated into document and records management, and archival processes.

Conclusion

Hrvoje Stančić

The book *Trust and Records in an Open Digital Environment* examines the interrelationship and interplay of state, citizens, and digital records' documentary form in the context of open government initiatives, open access aspirations, and requirements for long term preservation of trusted digital resources in the networked environment.

It began by examining the role of records managers and archivists in an open government environment and claiming that the challenges of maintaining trusted digital records having evidentiary value should not be theirs alone, but those of an interdisciplinary team of professionals. However, if records professionals are to stand up to the task of preserving interconnected networked records, their gaps in skills and knowledge identified will need to be filled. The obstacles – technical, managerial, and process related but also societal, including employees' resistance to change – will have to be taken into account when planning important ICT developments. These challenges might partially be solved by creating a homogeneous regulatory framework to rely upon because the current, fragmented legislation related to cloud offerings of recordkeeping and archiving solutions does not make a favourable environment for long term preservation of trusted records. Challenges can also be solved by implementing information governance principles, tools, processes, and systems, which can help in achieving data and information quality, i.e. in transforming them into assets. This can significantly improve the efficiency of public administration services. Their quality is, the research studies show, influenced by the maturity of records management systems – the more mature use of the system, the better the e-service design. However, interoperability is a different thing – it requires finding a common ground between different e-services at the national level, but also internationally. The research shows a multitude of possible benefits if inter-organisational cooperation is established in the development of e-services. This is shown by taking the example of digital archiving as an infrastructural e-government investment in an e-service whereby storage cost efficiency was achieved. If e-services are developed that implement *digital by default* and *trust by design* principles, they will not only enable public administrations not to ask citizens for information they already have, but also enable trusted transborder data exchange between the EU member states, and possibly worldwide. The suggested federated approach to e-services development, storage, and preservation will inevitably rely on cloud solutions. However, the research detected significant issues of trust not only in the continuity and sustainability of cloud services and their long term economic viability, but also in meeting records management and long term preservation requirements. For example, if a cloud service provider (CSP) converts records to a new file format or migrates them to a new medium, who is the owner of the conversion or migration metadata, which are important for confirming authenticity of the preserved records? It should be the institutions contracting with the cloud service and trusting it with their records, not the CSP. Understanding the risks and benefits of using cloud solutions for records management and archiving brings us a step closer to trusting them. Understanding and using costing models in the decision-making process of choosing CSPs can help records professionals to choose the appropriate ones. The developed checklists, which can be found in the appendices of this book, can guide records professionals along the way.

Entrusting records to the cloud, being transparent, and opening them to the public brings along new challenges. In the data-driven economy, it is challenging to find a fine balance between openness and privacy, transparency and anonymisation, technological developments and community concerns, and participatory governance and data activism advocating refusal of personal data sharing – just to name a few. The UK *care.data* case study shows how a poorly managed functional transparency of one governmental e-service can easily disrupt public trust in the government in general, despite the obvious benefits. However, the argument that citizens should be able to control their data on a more granular level surfaced another idea – that of incentivizing personal data. Although seemingly interesting at first – to be able to charge someone for using one's personal data – the idea has its counter argument. If the data is anonymized, should a person still be allowed to incentivize it? In that case, does it still belong to the person? Of course, there is no universal answer to that question, and the idea can be challenged from different standpoints in different situations, but the trend has emerged, and records professionals should be part of the interdisciplinary team addressing it. In any case, the data and the records based on it should be preserved as authentic. Therefore, the research also addressed users' perception of authenticity of born-digital materials, i.e. in which situations they consider the materials to be "the real thing." Being part of electronic records management systems (ERMS), those systems also play a key role in the provision of authentic records. It is argued that a heuristic evaluation method can be used to successfully conduct ERMS usability tests, thus directly improving the procurement processes and indirectly users' experience with the system, and consequently with the records and their notion of authenticity. All this shows the breadth and depth of knowledge and skills the records professionals need to acquire. In the hybrid, analogue, and digital – networked and interconnected – environment, it is a mix of traditional and digital skills education that records professionals need if they are to manage trusted and yet open digital environments. However, citizens in general should also be made aware of the foundational archival principles and concepts so that they can critically view the data, information, documents, and records being presented to them in digital form.

Metadata plays an important role in the confirmation or assessment of authenticity. It is also a basis for appraisal procedures of websites – a networked and interconnected type of records. The research shows that the appraisal process of websites can benefit from a more granular and innovative approach – one combining traditional principles applied to conventional and digital records with analytics of the users' behaviour while using content of different website sections. Metadata is also important in the context of the description of digital cultural heritage objects enabling their interoperability and interconnection. The research also focused on a specific type of digital objects to be preserved – digital print masters. Instead of preparing publications digitally, printing them, and depositing paper copies with the legal deposit institutions, which will in turn digitize them, a more straightforward approach is proposed – automated ingest and storage of digital print masters – a process that is more efficient and can ensure the quality control and provision of storage and retrieval metadata. A key to establishing it would be cooperation with the publishers and development and implementation of policies, practices, standards, and legal regulations addressing the status of digital print masters as equal to publications and regulating digital content archiving and preservation. It was shown that such regulations are still largely missing in the EU countries.

The book closes by proposing a model of blockchain-supported long term preservation of digitally signed records. The example of digitally signed records was chosen because their signing certificates expire before the end of the retention period. The TrustChain model for signing certificates' validity information preservation shows that, by using blockchain and distributed ledger technologies, the digitally signed records may be used as if the signatures are still valid even after their validity has expired. This shows how digital preservation systems can seamlessly integrate the so called "disruptive technologies" and benefit in the process.

Although often viewed as a traditional, paper-oriented profession, this book brings results of cutting-edge international, interdisciplinary research in the field of archival science oriented towards digital, networked, interconnected, and cloud-based records. In addition to offering guidance to archival and other ICT professionals in relation to the current challenges around creating, managing, accessing, storing, and preserving trustworthy digital records, this book also identifies new challenges, showcases the use of new, disruptive technologies, and offers visionary solutions to the future problems. It analyzes current policies, procedures, regulations, standards, legislation, and user perspectives, and proposes new approaches, strategies, and models, all the time addressing issues of trustworthiness and trust in digital records at the interconnected focus areas of state, citizens, and digital records' documentary form, thus providing a synthesised European perspective on the topic of trust and records in an open digital environment.

Appendix 1

Checklist for the assessment of implemented governmental e-services

This Checklist is designed to offer guidance to records managers and archivists in businesses, government agencies, or other organisations to assess implemented governmental e-services in the context of trusting e-services and the data they are holding and preserving. It is the result of the Inter-PARES Trust project's study *Comparative Analysis of Implemented Governmental e-Services* (EU09) (Stančić et al., 2015).

The set of questions in the checklist is considered as sufficient to provide enough information on an e-service in order for the users to consider the e-service as responsible, reliable, accurate, secure, transparent, and trustworthy, as well as that it considers privacy issues, duties to remember (i.e. digital preservation), and the right to be forgotten (i.e. safe deletion). The research team believes that the developed checklist can on the one hand provide guidance for the users, and on the other hand function as guidelines for the e-service providers on what information about the e-service they should put online.

The checklist consists of 52 questions divided into six categories as follows:

1   basic service information (11 questions)
2   users (7 questions)
3   business optimization (4 questions)
4   technological solutions (14 questions)
5   storage and long term content availability (10 questions)
6   system operation transparency (6 questions).

The key question, by which it should be determined whether to proceed with the analysis of an e-service or not, is Question 5 – determination of the level of informatisation. In order to proceed, the e-service needs to be at maturity level 2 or higher. If it is lower, it is not considered an e-service. The maturity ranking used for the assessment is as follows:

Maturity level	Level	Description
0	No information available	Information is not available online, or the service provider does not have a webpage.
1	Information	Only information about the service is available online (e.g. description of a procedure).
2	One-way interaction	Downloadable forms are available online. Empty forms can be filled in using computer or can be printed.
3	Two-way interaction	Forms can be filled in online for which authentication is needed. By submitting an online form, a service is initiated.
4	Transaction	A complete service is available online – fillable online forms, authentication, payment, delivery, or other types of complete services.
5	Iteration	Iterative services (e.g. obligatory statistical reporting) which are automatically initiated and create automatic reports on a service being completed.

Checklist for the assessment of implemented governmental e-services				
Question	Y[1]	N	?[2]	Answer / additional info[3]
1 Basic service information				
1	Service URL				
2	Is it clear to which category the service belongs?[4]			
3	Is it clear what category/type of institution is authorized for the e-service?			
4	Is the start date of the service development/implementation available?			
5	What is the level of informatisation of the e-service?	[Do not proceed] 0 1		[Proceed] 2 3 4 5
6	Is the service connected with any other governmental services and, if yes, which?			
7	Is there a difference between official and actual development of the e-service?			

Question		Y[1]	N	?[2]	Answer / additional info[3]
8	Are there limitations to the service's work schedule (e.g. does it work 24/7 or is not available in certain periods)? If yes, what are they?				
9	Short description of the service.				
10	A screenshot of the service.				
11	Does the service do what it is described as doing?				
2 Users					
12	Is using the service mandatory for a certain category of users? If yes, for which category of users is it mandatory?				
13	Are there different groups of users?				
14	How many users are there per user group?				
15	What percentage of users use the service electronically (there might be users who obtain the service in a non-electronic, traditional way)?				
16	Which age groups are prevalent in using the service?				
17	Is the service adapted for users with disabilities?				
18	What is the users' satisfaction (are there any indicators available)?				
3 Business optimization					
19	Are there positive financial indicators for the e-service (for the institution responsible for the service and for users)?				
20	Has there been a decrease in time required to process users' applications (are there any indicators available)?				
21	How did the service affect the organisation of work processes in the responsible organisation in terms of the required number of workers?				
22	What are the plans for upgrading and expanding the service in the future?				

(*Continued*)

(Continued)

Question		Y[1]	N	?[2]	Answer / additional info[3]
4 Technological solutions					
23	What type of authentication is used?				
24	Is the communication between the server and client station encrypted (SSL, or some other protocol)?				
25	Does the service use eID? If yes, which one (list all if more than one eID is used)?				
26	Does the electronic signature use digital certificates?				
27	If yes, which format of electronic signatures is used?				
28	In what way do the users fill in and send data (downloadable forms, send by e-mail, online, etc.)?				
29	Do the users send attachments with the filled-in data? If yes, in what way?				
30	Do the users have predetermined types of document formats while sending out data? If yes, which ones?				
31	Is the service implemented through open-source, or commercial technologies? Which technologies are being used?				
32	What type of application is used on the client side?				
33	Through which channel(s) is the service available (computer, mobile, etc.)?				
34	Is the service hosted within the responsible institution?				
35	If the responsible institution is hosting the service, does it have the required certificates?				
36	If the service or any of its parts is hosted outside the responsible institution, does it use the cloud?				
5 Storage and long term content availability					
37	What is the retention period for the data in the system?				
38	Is the retention period defined by a law/regulation or some other act? If yes, which one(s)?				

Question		Y[1]	N	?[2]	Answer / additional info[3]
39	Is the data deleted after the retention period expires?				
40	What is/are the preferred long term preservation format(s)?				
41	Does the service use a method of materialisation of data (conversion from digital to analogue format, e.g. printing, microfilming, etc.)?				
42	Does the service comply with any of the long term preservation standards? If yes, which one(s)?				
43	Does the service offer use of an electronic archive as an additional service? Are there *electronic document safe* services?				
44	Is the data received through the service stored within the responsible institution's information system?				
45	Does the responsible institution possess the required certificates that guarantee security of the stored data?				
46	If the data is at least partially stored outside the responsible institution, e.g. in the cloud, is the cloud/data centre located within the same country/jurisdiction as the responsible institution?				
6 System operation transparency					
47	Is there a defined service use policy?				
48	Are there any proclaimed technological measures guaranteeing the users that their data is only used for the defined purpose(s)?				
49	Are the employees required to sign a non-disclosure agreement?				
50	Can users access and view their data through the service?				
51	Can users correct or update any of their data within the service? If yes, can the request for correction be sent electronically?				
52	Can users monitor status of their application?				

Notes

1 The questions which are not simple "Yes/No" questions, i.e. require an elaborated answer, have the "Y/N/?" fields shaded.
2 The "?" column indicates a situation where no information is available, or the question is not applicable to your situation.
3 The "Answer / additional info" column can be used in situations where either a question is not a "Yes/No" type of question or a simple "Yes/No" answer can be supplemented with useful information, e.g. the web address of a central e-government portal, or a link where additional information on the matter in question can be found.
4 According to the categorisation defined as the "representative basket of 20 services" (European Commission. [2010]. *Digitizing Public Services in Europe: Putting ambition in action. 9th Benchmark Measurement.* Retrieved from https://ec.europa.eu/newsroom/dae/document.cfm?doc_id=1926), or any other appropriate categorisation.

Reference

Stančić, H., Brzica, H., Adžaga, I., Garić, A., Poljičak Sušec, M., Presečki, K., Stanković, A. (2015). *Comparative analysis of implemented governmental e-services* (EU09). InterPARES Trust. Retrieved from https://interparestrust.org/assets/public/dissemination/EU09_20160727_ComparativeAnalysisImplementedGovernmentaleServices_Final Report.pdf

Appendix 2

Recommendations for planning and designing e-services between public administrations

The purpose of these recommendations is to align the requirements for security and trust in e-services provided by public administrations with the requirements put before external providers of similar services. These recommendations are grouped into four sections

1   e-service planning
2   e-service regulation
3   e-service design and provision
4   presumption of authenticity.

E-service planning

1   **distinctiveness**: identify characteristics, organisational and technological context of the administrations, potential users of the service, and how they will use the platform that provides the e-service
2   **intermediation function**: assess the usefulness and potential of the intermediation platform to interconnect all the e-services for the public administrations and to facilitate integration with their own systems
3   **holistic approach**: enter description of functions and basic requirements of e-services into a single inter-administrative catalogue of e-services used by all public administrations in order to simplify identification of an e-service, its provider, and the operating conditions.

E-service regulation

4   **general policies**: the key elements for trust, such as requirements of security, confidentiality, data protection, and preservation of authenticity, should be included in general policies
5   **regulatory granularity**: if a single policy does not cover the entire institution, all e-service platforms, or each e-service, it is necessary to regulate all levels in order to build a complete trusted environment – from general policies to operational policies

6   **statements of responsibility**: if certain information cannot be included in a policy because it could cause a breach in the system security, the institution should publish a statement of responsibility regarding its information security policy

7   **terms and conditions (SLA)**: requirements and conditions of provision of each e-service and management of possible incidents that may arise, including its cancellation, have to be defined clearly and be available for public administrations as users

8   **regulation of procedures**: the agreement regulating access of a public administration to an e-service must be defined by a specific procedure which should also regulate user (de)authorisation.

E-service design and provision

9   **file transfer orientation**: communication of e-services between public administrations should be based on direct file transfer through shared repositories and not on sending records as in the paper documents framework

10   **user control**: access to an e-service must be specific for each person, while the public administration, as a user, should be able to easily supervise all authorised persons through the users' registry module

11   **levels of access**: in case several persons of a public administration have access to the same e-service, it is necessary to foresee the possibility of establishing different levels of access according to the degree of confidentiality of the data and different roles of the authorised persons.

Presumption of authenticity

12   **records creation**: the *Benchmark Requirements Supporting the Presumption of Authenticity of Electronic Records (Requirements Set A)* of the first InterPARES project (Authenticity Task Force, 2002, pp. 4–7) should be used to assess the point of creation and capture authentic digital records in any e-service

13   **authentic copies**: the e-services using an inter-administrative approach in records or data consultation, or verification, always must provide authentic copies or evidence of what has been consulted with enough guarantees of authenticity and trust

14   **traceability**: all actions carried out by users must be properly registered as audit trails and they must be available to the public administration's authorised users

15   **open integration**: integration of e-services into the management systems of public administrations facilitates control of their records and reinforces automation to prevent manual ingest of records between systems. Thus, e-services integration by design is recommended.

Reference

Authenticity Task Force. (2002). Requirements for Assessing and Maintaining the Authenticity of Electronic Records (Appendix 2). In L. Duranti (Ed.), *The Long-term Preservation of Authentic Electronic Records: Findings of the InterPARES Project*. Retrieved from http://www.interpares.org/book/interpares_book_k_app02.pdf

Appendix 3
Checklist for single sign-on systems

This checklist is designed to offer guidance to records managers and archivists in businesses, government agencies or other organisations to assess single sign-on (SSO) systems, as well as by SSO developers in order to ensure that they have provided sufficient information on the system they are developing in order to detect the possibilities of exchanging identification and authentication credentials. It is the result of the InterPARES Trust project's study *Analysis of the interoperability possibilities of implemented governmental e-services (EU15)* (Stančić et al., 2015).

The checklist is based on the assessment form used in the study, which investigated the differences in the level of development of e-services with a focus on aspects important for their implementation as *trusted* e-services. The research team believes that this checklist provides sufficient information to assess the possibilities for trusted transborder exchange of identification and authentication credentials.

The set of questions in the checklist is considered as sufficient to establish the minimum amount of information necessary to support users' trust in an IaaS provider and position the provider as a trusted cloud service provider. The research team believes that the developed checklist can on the one hand provide guidance for users, and on the other hand function as guidelines for cloud service providers on what information about a service they should put online.

The checklist consists of 19 questions divided into five categories as follows

1   legal framework and strategies (1 question)
2   portals (1 question)
3   single sign-on (SSO) (11 questions)
4   trust mechanisms – technical details (5 questions)
5   future plans (1 question).

Single sign-on systems checklist				
Question	Y	N	?[1]	Answer / additional info[2]
1 Legal framework and strategies				
1	Is there a national IT strategy concerning e-government?				
2 Portals				
2	Is there a central e-government portal?				
3 Single sign-on (SSO)				
3	Is there an SSO system in place?				
4	Is the system implemented after <relevant year>?				
5	How are users authenticated?				
	Username/password				
	e-Certificate				
	eID card				
	e-Signature				
	m-token/mobile ID				
	PIN				
	Single-use code				
	Smart card				
	Token				
	Other				[Add method]
6	Is there a physical aspect involved in e-identification (token, smart card, SIM card, etc.)?				
7	Are there one or more levels of access depending on different users' credentials?				
8	Is there a central identity data governing body? (central directory/register?)				
9	What is the source of users' identity for obtaining user authentication?				
	Social security number (SSN)				
	Driver's licence				
	ID				
	Passport				
	Other				[Add source]
10	Are there different terms of use for domestic and foreign users?				

(Continued)

(Continued)

Question		Y	N	?[1]	Answer / additional info[2]
11	Which services are connected via SSO?				
	Income taxes: declaration, notification of assessment				
	Job search services by labour offices				
	Social security benefits				
	Personal documents: passport and driver's licence				
	Car registration (new, used, imported cars)				
	Application for building permission				
	Declaration to the police (e.g. in case of theft)				
	Public libraries (availability of catalogues, search tools)				
	Certificates (birth and marriage): request and delivery				
	Enrolment in higher education/university				
	Announcement of moving (change of address)				
	Health-related services (interactive advice on the availability of services in different hospitals; appointments for hospitals)				
	Other				[Add service]
12	Is there a possibility of log-on to a connected service without using SSO, i.e. by accessing their website directly and using their log-on service (different credentials than SSO credentials)?				
13	Is it possible to obtain an e-document from one e-service and send it to another e-service via safe transfer methods (safe document transfer)?				
4 Trust mechanisms – technical details					
14	Does the system have single sign-off implemented, i.e. when user logs off from one service, does the system automatically log off the user from all services (s)he accessed during that session?				
15	Are there any federated authentication standards supported and used (e.g. SAML)?				

Question		Y	N	?[1]	Answer / additional info[2]
16	Does the system require digital signatures? If yes – which type(s) – standard or advanced, XMLDSig, XAdES etc.?				
17	Is it possible to achieve protocol interoperability (LDAP)?				
18	Is the SSO conformant with the CEF eID building block?				
5 Future plans					
19	Are there any plans in place for future identity federation?				

Notes

1 The "?" column indicates a situation where either no information is available or the question is not applicable to your situation.
2 The "Answer / additional info" column can be used in situations where either a question is not a "Yes/No" type of question or a simple "Yes/No" answer can be supplemented with useful information.

Reference

Stančić, H., Ivanjko, T., Bonić, N., Garić, A., Lončarić, K., Lovasić, A., . . . Stanković, A. (2015). *Analysis of the interoperability possibilities of implemented governmental e-services* (EU15). InterPARES Trust. Retrieved from https://interparestrust. org/assets/public/dissemination/EU15_20160727_InteroperabilityGovEServices_ FinalReport.pdf

Appendix 4
Checklist for ensuring trust in storage using IaaS

This checklist is designed to offer guidance to records managers and archivists in businesses, government agencies, or other organisations to assess the security and ongoing trustworthiness (i.e. authenticity, reliability, and accuracy) of their data when stored in an Infrastructure-as-a-Service (IaaS) platform. It is the result of the InterPARES Trust project's study *Ensuring Trust in Storage in Infrastructure-as-a-Service (EU08)* (Stančić, Buršić, & Al-Hariri, 2015).

The set of questions in the checklist is considered as sufficient to establish the minimum amount of information necessary to support clients' trust in an IaaS provider and position the provider as a trusted cloud service provider (CSP). The checklist can on the one hand provide guidance for clients, and on the other function as guidelines for CSPs on what information about a service they should put online.

The checklist consists of 36 questions divided into ten categories as follows

1 general information (4 questions)
2 governance (4 questions)
3 compliance (4 questions)
4 trust (5 questions)
5 architecture (6 questions)
6 identity and Access Management (1 question)
7 software Isolation (2 questions)
8 data Protection (5 questions)
9 availability (2 questions)
10 incident Response (3 questions).

IaaS checklist				
Question	Y[1]	N	?[2]	Answer / additional info[3]
1 General information				
1 Which components are used in IaaS?				
2 What types of services are offered in IaaS?				
3 What technologies are being used?				
4 What implications do the used technologies have on security and privacy of the system?				
2 Governance				
5 Is it possible for a client to monitor security of the computing environment and data security? How?				
6 What kind of security assures a client that their data is not mixed with another's?				
7 What kind of security assures a client that no data is shared with employees?				
8 What audit mechanisms and tools are used to determine how data is stored, protected, and used to validate services and to verify policy enforcement?				
3 Compliance				
9 Does the service comply with other countries' laws, regulations, standards, and specifications for clients outside the country of service?				
10 How is the service secured against unauthorized access, use, disclosure, disruption, modification, or destruction of data?				
11 What technical and physical safeguards does the service assure?				
12 Does the service use subcontractors for any part of the used technology or offered service?				
4 Trust				
13 Is the service secured from denial of service (DoS) attack?				
14 Does the service secure ownership rights over data?				
15 Does the service have any certificate relevant to the service?				

(*Continued*)

(Continued)

Question		Y[1]	N	?[2]	Answer / additional info[3]
16	What kind of risk management does the organisation provide?				
17	What kind of physical and logical security is assured for the virtual servers and applications?				
5 Architecture					
18	How is a hypervisor or virtual machine monitor secured?				
19	How does the service secure virtual machine images from attacks looking for proprietary code and data?				
20	Does the service use an image management process to govern the creation, storage, and use of virtual machine images or containers?				
21	How is the service secured from attacks on the client side?				
22	How is the service secured from attacks on the server side?				
23	Does the service use encrypted network exchange?				
6 Identity and access management					
24	How does the service protect ancillary data? • details about the clients' accounts • data about client-related activity • data collected to meter and charge for consumption of resources • logs and audit trails, and other similar metadata that is generated and accumulated within the environment • data of an organization's initiative (e.g. the activity level or projected growth of a startup company) • metadata collected by the provider				
7 Software isolation					
25	How does the service prevent man-in-the-middle attacks?				
26	Is the service secured from attacks on the server that target passwords?				
8 Data protection					
27	What kind of encryption does the service use to secure data stored in IaaS?				

Question		Y[1]	N	?[2]	Answer / additional info[3]
28	Has the service conducted deliberate attacks to test the system's protection?				
29	What procedures are used for data sanitisation upon termination of service; i.e. how does the service ensure that the data is not recoverable after deletion or hardware decommission?				
30	Where, geographically, is the data stored?				
31	Where, geographically, is data backup stored?				
9 Availability					
32	In a situation of a lawful raid, how is the service availability assured to the clients not being lawfully raided?				
33	Is there a policy regarding client data availability in case of a bankruptcy or other facility loss, and how is it defined?				
10 Incident response					
34	Is there an incident response plan, and how is it defined?				
35	Does the service keep track of the data about the scope of an incident, and can the assets affected be determined?				
36	Does the service keep a forensic copy of the incident data for legal proceedings or as needed by the client, or does the service give incident data to the client?				

Notes

1 The questions which are not simple "Yes/No" questions, i.e. require an elaborated answer, have the "Y/N/?" fields shaded.
2 The "?" column indicates a situation where either no information is available or the question is not applicable to your situation.
3 The "Answer / additional info" column can be used in situations where either a question is not a "Yes/No" type of question or a simple "Yes/No" answer can be supplemented with useful information.

Reference

Stančić, H., Buršić, E., & Al-Hariri, A. (2015). *Ensuring trust in storage in Infra structure-as-a-Service (IaaS)* (EU08). InterPARES Trust. Retrieved from https://inter parestrust.org/assets/public/dissemination/EU08_20160727_EnsuringTrustStorage IaaS_FinalReport_Final.pdf

Appendix 5
Metadata elements relevant for retention and disposition of websites

Schenkolewski-Kroll and Tractinsky (2017, pp. 13–17) developed the following table showing metadata elements relevant for retention and disposition of websites. The table has four content columns: the name of the metadata element, description of the element, source showing the originating standard, and similar or identical metadata fields already existing on the Israeli government's Ministry of Foreign Affairs website, which was used as the example in the research (see Chapter 18).

No.	Metadata element	Description	Source	Original metadata of Ministry of Foreign Affairs website
1	Web platform	Include specific software applications and where available intended browser applications and versions. Every time the platform is changed, it must be noted.	DoD (C2.T5.8.), AUS (Format 19, 19.3. Creating Application Name, 19.4. Creating Application Version), COP (A2.3.2)	
2	Web platform date	Date of web platform installation. When a new web platform is installed, it is necessary to document the date of the new installation.	New	
3	Website name	Title of the website from the main entry page.	DoD (C2.T5.9.)	
4	Website uniform resource locator	Include the filename of the starting page of the transferred content, i.e. the address of the section.	DoD (C2.T5.10.)	
5	Content management system	Application used to manage files on the web.	DoD (C2.T5.25.)	
6	Web content structure change	Change in the web content structure. The change may include change in contents between the sections, closing a section, and transferring the section from place to place on the file tree.	New	
7	Modified	Date on which the section was changed – changes in the section, such as addition or deletion of records. Date on which the resource was changed.	Canada (WCMS)	Scheduling end date

(*Continued*)

(Continued)

No.	Metadata element	Description	Source	Original metadata of Ministry of Foreign Affairs website
8	Creator	Creator of section.	Canada (RMR [Agent], DCM), UK (2.7), COP (A2.2.4), AUS (Agent)	
9	Covering dates	The dates of the oldest and most recent items in a collection, series, or folder.	ICA MAT (125)	GovXEventDate
10	Chronological date	Date of creation of the file in a digital system Chronological date (and possibly time) of compilation and capture (ICA MAT).	COP (A2.2.2), ICA MAT (96)	
11	Title	Title of the section. Name of the section.	Canada (WMCS), UK (2.24), AUS (3 NAME)	Name of folder
12	Issued	Date of formal issuance of the section.	Canada (WMCS), UK (2.8)	Scheduling start date
13	Description	A free-text description of the section.	UK (2.9), AUS (5)	GovXContentSection
14	Registration identifier	A unique identifier for the section.	Canada (RMR), UK (2.13), COP (A2.2.2), AUS (2)	
15	Aggregation	The section's level or position in a hierarchy. Each of the entity's classes identified in ISO 23081–1:2006 (i.e. record, agent, mandate, business, records management business) exist at different layers of aggregation. For example, within the entity "agent," an	Canada (RMR), COP (A2.2.3), UK (2.3)	

No.	Metadata element	Description	Source	Original metadata of Ministry of Foreign Affairs website
		individual, a work unit, a department, division, branch, or the organization as a whole, can be described. Within the entity class "record," an item, a folder, a file, a series, etc., can be described. Each of these layers is referred to as an aggregation.		
16	Classification system	Information on classification of the entity according to a business or functional classification plan.	Canada (RMR), COP (A2.2.4)	
17	Integrity	Information that indicates that the entity and its metadata remained in their entirety from the moment of their creation.	Canada (RMR), AUS (22)	
18	Link to file outside the system	Information on links to files outside the system.	New	GovX Description Img (link to a picture document) GovX Main Title (link to a film file)
19	Disposition authority (also disposal authority)	A formal instrument that defines the retention periods and consequent disposition actions authorized for classes of records described in the authority.	ICA M2 (148, 154), MoReq 2010 (Mandate, M14.4.51), DoD (C2. T1.5.)	
20	Disposition action	The action to be taken when a disposition date occurs (e.g. interim transfer, accession, or destroy) (DoD).	ICA M2 (152), DoD (C2.T1.4.), MoReq 2010 (M14.4.18)	

(Continued)

(Continued)

No.	Metadata element	Description	Source	Original metadata of Ministry of Foreign Affairs website
21	Disposition trigger	The point from which the disposition action is calculated. This can be a date on which action is completed or a date on which an event occurs (ICA).	MoReq 2010 (M14.4.94), ICA RKR (85)	
22	Retention period	The length of time after the disposition trigger that a record must be maintained and accessible. At the expiration of the retention period, a record may be subject to a disposition action (ICA).	ICA M2 (153), DoD (C2.2.2.7.), MoReq 2010 (M14.4.90)	
23	Disposition action date	The fixed date on which the records in a file become due for final disposition (DoD).	MoReq 2010, DoD	
24	Review	A process in which the retention schedule is changed. In Israel, the retention process is changed when the new retention schedules are entered into the Archives Law.	ICA M2 (165)	

Referenced standards (sources)

AUS. (2015). *Australian Government recordkeeping metadata standard (AGRkMS).* National Archives of Australia. Retrieved from www.naa.gov.au/sites/default/files/2019-09/AGRkMS-Version-2.2-June-2015_tcm16-93990_1.pdf

Canada (RMR). (2010). *Standard on metadata. Appendix B: Recordkeeping metadata requirements.* Retrieved from www.tbs-sct.gc.ca/pol/doc-eng.aspx?id=18909

Canada (WCMS). (2010). *Standard on metadata. Appendix D: Web content management system (WCMS) metadata requirements.* Retrieved from www.tbs-sct.gc.ca/pol/doc-eng.aspx?id=18909

COP. (2009). *InterPARES 2 project chain of preservation (COP) model metadata.* The InterPARES 3 Project. Retrieved from www.interpares.org/ip2/display_file.cfm?doc=ip2_cop-model_metadata_v1.0.pdf

DoD. (2007). *Electronic records management software applications design criteria standard* (DoD 5015.02-STD). Retrieved from www.esd.whs.mil/Portals/54/Documents/DD/issuances/dodm/501502std.pdf

ICA M2. (2008). *Principles and functional requirements for records in electronic office environments – Module 2: Guidelines and functional requirements for electronic records management systems.* Retrieved from www.naa.gov.au/sites/default/files/2019-09/Module%202%20-%20%20ICA-Guidelines-principles%20and%20Functional%20Requirements_tcm16-95419.pdf

ICA MAT. (2013). *Multilingual archival terminology.* Retrieved from www.ciscra.org/mat/

ICA RKR. (2013). *Principles and functional requirements for records in electronic oOffice environments – Recordkeeping requirements for multiple functions supported by one business system.* Retrieved from www.ica.org/sites/default/files/11.%20Recordkeeping%20Requirements%20for%20Multiple%20Functions%20supported%20by%20one%20Business%20System.pdf

ISO 23081–1:2006. (2006). *Information and documentation – Records management processes – Metadata for records – Part 1: Principles.* Retrieved from www.iso.org/standard/40832.html

MoReq (2010). *Model requirements for records systems (MoReq). Core services and plug-in modules.* Volume 1. DLM Forum. Retrieved from www.moreq.info/

UK. (2006, 29 August). *e-Government metadata standard.* Cabinet Office, e-Government Unit. Version 3.1. Retrieved from www.nationalarchives.gov.uk/documents/information-management/egms-metadata-standard.pdf

Reference

Schenkolewski-Kroll, S., & Tractinsky, A. (2017). *Archival appraisal, retention schedules and metadata in Web sites – The case study of the Ministry of Foreign Affairs, Israel* (EU36 Final report). InterPARES Trust. Retrieved from https://interparestrust.org/assets/public/dissemination/EU036_20171120_AppraisalWebsites_Final Report.pdf

Index

Note: Page numbers in **bold** indicate tables.

Printed in the United States
By Bookmasters